County Compa

C000319276

Somerset
Jack Rayfield

Cadogan Publications Ltd
Holding Company: Metal Bulletin PLC London

Contents

Editors: Paula Levey
         Leone Turner
Assistant Editor: Kate Raison
Illustrations by Patricia Hare
Series design by Information Design
Workshop
Cartography: Line and Line

© Cadogan Publications 1985
All rights reserved

ISBN 0 947754 09 1

First published 1985 by Cadogan
Publications Ltd
Holding Company: Metal Bulletin PLC
16 Lower Marsh, London SE1 7RJ

Typeset in Great Britain by
Photocomp Limited
Printed in Great Britain by
Purnell & Sons Ltd.,
Paulton, Bristol

How to use this guide

places of interest and other important features such as caravan parks.

Complete Guide

The first section of the book describes all the major towns and villages of interest in Somerset. They are included, along with outstanding attractions, in alphabetical order. After each name there is a map reference locating the place on one of the detailed maps. Places of interest to be found in the various towns and villages are described in this section but all details of their opening times, charges, facilities and other information can be found in the Leisure Directory. All places of interest in **bold** have a listing in the Leisure Directory under the relevant section. For example: **Poundisford Park** (Historic Homes) This indicates that the details for Poundisford Park can be found in the Historic Homes section of the Leisure Directory. **Clark's Shoe Museum** indicates that details for this museum can be found under the Museums section of the Leisure Directory.

Maps

Four detailed maps of Somerset on which are located all major

Town Directory

The major towns are listed here with the facilities and places of interest to be found in and nearby those towns. All details about the places to visit can be found in the Leisure Directory. For example: **Museum:** Burrows Toy Museum This indicates that details for the Burrows Toy Museum (under Bath in the Town Directory) can be found in the Museums section of the Leisure Directory.

Town Maps of some major towns can also be found in this section with places of interest located.

Leisure A-Z

This section lists activities and places to visit, giving all important details. A full list of the topics included can be found on the Contents list at the front of this book. All entries are in alphabetical order. Where relevant, a map reference is given immediately after the name of the place of interest, locating it on one of the detailed maps.

The telephone number of the place is then given, followed by the location and all other details.

Symbols

- 🚐 caravan park
- ♪ angling
- ⛳ golf course
- ℹ tourist information centre
- 🅿 Parking
- ✕ licensed restaurant
- ☕ snacks
- ♿ access for disabled visitors
- 🛍 shop
- 🎪 picnic site
- 🏊 swimming pool
- ♀ bar
- ⚓ sailing
- U riding
- 🏕 campsite
- PO post office
- ▼ place of interest

DofE Standard Opening Times

The following opening hours apply to all buildings and other historic monuments which are managed by the Department of the Environment. Some buildings are open for further periods in the summer and these extra opening hours are listed with the entry in the Leisure Directory.

March–April & October:
weekdays 9.30–17.30
Sundays 14.00–17.30
May–September:
weekdays 9.30–19.00
Sundays 14.00–19.00
November–February:
weekdays 9.30–16.00
Sundays 14.00–16.00

All DofE buildings and monuments are closed on December 24–26 and January 1. Some of them also close for the lunch hour which is normally 13.00–14.00.

Complete Guide

Ashcott Map 2 Bb

Ashcott has been described as a 'misty miasma of the
moors. . . where peat and not pasture occupies the mind
and aids the incomes'.

The villages and hamlets were given peat allotments
for fuel and even today there are those who use the
chocolate coloured blocks which can be seen alongside the
narrow undulating lanes, which have signs that proclaim
that they are liable to subsidence – a warning to be
ignored at the fast driver's peril. For the most part the
use of peat today is horticultural and the labourer's
shovel has been replaced by large mechanical diggers,
much of the work and the workings being administered by
a major consortium which deals in chemicals.

Nevertheless the sign 'Peat for Sale' is everywhere
and nowhere else will it be so cheap. Ashcott, on a ridge of
the old Poldens rising out of the flat soggy moors has
long been one of the main centres of the peat industry
with one or two neat village shops, a post office and a
rather imposing hostelry where food and drink are
of the best beside the abandoned railway track. The nearby
village of Shapwick is also on the northern edge of the
Poldens as one descends to the peat beds. Shapwick
House, now a hotel, is early 17th century with
18th century alterations and additions. The local church
has a fine timbered roof.

Axbridge Map 2 Ba

Strawberries and more strawberries – at least during the
appropriate season. As one approaches the town which
nestles under the Shute Shelve of the Mendips a plethora of
plastic sheeting, looking like chalk stripes etched into the
hillside, shields and cossets the rosy berries that ripen
beneath. Pinks and carnations are sometimes on sale by the
roadside with other items of garden produce that are
cultivated opposite the lakelike reservoir which is separated
from the hillside by a bypass that was once a railway.

In the 11th century Axbridge had its own Mint and a market brought pedlars from afar to serve the needs of the Mendip settlers and farmers, later it also had its own Mayor and Corporation – which finally disappeared in 1886. The borough records are still held in the town which was once in the hands of two Lords of the Manor, one William Longsword and the Bishop of Bath and Wells. Two fairs were granted to them, one by Henry III on St Barnabas' Day and the other by Edward I on St Bartholomew's Day. Trade was in Mendip wool.

In the town, dominating the cluster of buildings that surround the sloping square that is part road, part car park, is the imposing 15th century church of St John, in Somerset perpendicular. It has a splendid west porch and the nave roof holds Jacobean plaster work in a series of geometric shapes.

There is a fine jettied and timber framed merchant's house known as **King John's Hunting Lodge** (Museums).

King John's Hunting Lodge, Axbridge

B

Banwell Map 4 Ab

Banwell was named after a millpond said to have healing
properties, but as if in response to the ancient adage
'physician, heal thyself', it has disappeared! What we
have left in this busy outskirt to the seaside resort
of Weston-Super-Mare is Banwell Court, otherwise known
as the Abbey, (1443-65), with the original chapel still
standing at the end of the south front. The building,
built by Bishop Bekynton of Wells is now privately
owned as is the Victorian folly three quarters of a mile to
the south east. Complete with battlements, a gatehouse
and turrets, its warlike defences are a sham, concealing a
comfortable home.

Banwell's splendid church is one of the finest in the
region with a tower over 100 feet high. A fine gallery
stands over the porch, the south doorway is
beautifully carved and includes an engraving of a mason's
compass and square. The 15th century Flemish stained
glass was brought from Belgium in 1855.

West of the village are the Bone Caves of Banwell Hill,
discovered in the early years of the last century. So
many remains of prehistoric mammals have been excavated
from these caves that they have been accepted as one
of the greatest finds in Western Europe.

Barrington Map 2 Bc

The manor house known as **Barrington Court** (Historic
Homes) stands apart from the village in its own extensive
grounds. Dating from about 1570 it replaced an earlier
building which had been the home of the Daubeneys, an
ancient Breton family, since 1225. In 1552 the property was
mortgaged by William Clifton, a London merchant.
Restoration was probably completed by his son.

The Court is an 'E' shaped building, comprising a
central block of Ham stone with two long wings, the
impressive third floor forming one long gallery. A stable
block was added in 1674 by William Strode, but from the

mid 18th century a succession of irresponsible tenant
farmers turned the building into something of a ruin and it
was in danger of being demolished and rebuilt in America.

When it was acquired by the National Trust restoration
was carried out by the lessee Col. Abraham Lyle, a member
of the sugar family. The gardens were laid out by Gertrude
Jekyll while the farmhouses and additional buildings which
make up the estate today were designed by architects
Forbes and Tate.

Outside the grounds the village has some attractive
golden Ham-stone houses, some of them thatched. The
village school is in the shape of a barn and the church,
standing above the remains of the village green, has an
octagonal tower.

A mile to the south east Shepton Beauchamp is a
sizeable village appearing from the distance to lie in the
centre of open fields, for all round is fertile farming
country. The Ham-stone and lias church has a fan vault
which carries the 'bat's wing' motif of the Daubeneys.

Bath Map 4 Bb

Opinions differ as to the best way to approach 'this jewel
in Britain's crown' but, if you arrive as a stranger to this
city that has just about everything, then make your way to
the Abbey Churchyard – its very heart.

More appropriately it should be thought of as a
courtyard, a meeting place, for the famed **Roman Baths
and Pump Rooms** (Roman Sites) lie on one side, at right
angles to **Bath Abbey** (Church Buildings), while on the
north side there is one of the most delightful Tourist
Information centres in Europe.

Bath – Aquae Sulis – was known to the Roman
Legionaries long before the Regency and Beau Nash. Both
have left ample evidence of their life styles, for, in the
Pump Room, coffee and Bath Buns can be taken beneath
the statue of Beau Nash while the great Roman Bath
steams beside the windows and the **Roman Baths
Museum**, reflecting the coming of the Romans and the

B

civilisation they left behind, lies beneath.

Outside, Regency Bath is all around: in the **Guildhall** (Other Historic Buildings), with its 18th-century Banqueting Room in Adam style with paintings by Sir William Hoare and Sir Joshua Reynolds, in the **Assembly Rooms**, in the wide pavements of Milsom Street, in the narrow alleys, with their tiny shops and in the oldest house in Bath – Sally Lunn's. One of the most elegant sights of Bath is the famous honey coloured Royal Crescent which looks south towards the city over Royal Victoria Park, where thirty terraced houses unite beneath a single curved cornice supported by 114 Ionic columns. East of the Crescent Brock Street leads into another triumph of architecture, the Circus, 318 feet across, in three sections, each composed of houses in Tuscan, Ionic and Corinthian tiers.

As you journey through the streets, alleys, squares and circuses, let the eye travel upward to the plaques that commemorate the famous: Beau Nash, John Wood,

Bath Abbey

10

Sir Isaac Pitman, Richard Sheridan, William Pitt, Gainsborough and Josiah Wedgwood are in good company for there are a hundred others.

South from the Abbey Churchyard lies busy Stall Street and Southgate, modern Bath, largely rebuilt with its complex of paved and covered pedestrian precincts and fashionable shops. The city's transport – rail and bus – are centred here cheek by jowl with multi-storey car park. Nearby another successful conversion lies in the engine sheds and station that once housed the Somerset & Dorset Railway terminus, preserved with modern appendages. One now strolls down Platform One to enter one of the nation's major provision merchants.

There are many museums. The **Museum of Costume**, in the Assembly Rooms, houses a collection from Shakespeare to Dior and Yves St Laurent. The **Carriage Museum** contains over forty carriages from past centuries. The **Camden Works Museum** shows Bath at work, the **Victoria Art Gallery** boasts not only a fine collection of paintings, prints and drawings but also ceramics, glass, watches and local history material. The name of **Burrows Toy Museum** indicates the content as does the **Geology Museum**. The **Holburne of Menstrie Museum**, housed in a Palladian building at the end of Great Pulteney Street, contains a fine collection of works of art including Flemish, Dutch and Italian old masters and works by Gainsborough and Stubbs. The **American Museum** at Claverton Manor is a unique recreation of American History set in a delightful 1820 manor house; the Bath **Postal Museum** and the **Museum of Bookbinding** are both absorbing, the former being the finest of its kind in the country while the recently opened **Royal Photographic Society's National Centre of Photography** (Museums) transferred from London, has constantly changing exhibits of apparatus and photographs.

But open air Bath should be sought. There is much on offer and, as might be expected of a city which has so often been the winner of the Annual Britain in Bloom contest, the city is always bedecked with flowers.

As well as the lanes with their floral hangings and

baskets there are many city parks. The Botanical Gardens in Royal Victoria Park contain 5,000 varieties of plants. The Sidney Gardens rise from the end of Great Pulteney Street to descend towards the Kennet and Avon Canal. Across the famed Pulteney Bridge over the Avon lies Henrietta Park, intimate and sweet scented, while on the bank of the river Parade Gardens, with brass bands and refreshments is an oasis amidst the Bath stone of the city centre.

The city possesses one of Britain's most historic theatres the Theatre Royal. Recently restored at a cost of over two million pounds, most of which was raised within the city, it is now one of the country's finest Regency theatres, attracting National Theatre productions as well as the leading touring companies. The **Bath Festival** (Events) which involves almost all the historic buildings in the city takes place annually between the last week in May and the second week in June. The city also has three cinemas: The Gemini, The Little and, appropriately, The Beau Nash.

Outside the city lies **Beckford's Tower** (Museums), built in 1827 for an eccentric millionaire. The staircase has 156 steps and the top commands remarkable views and has a small museum.

In Bath there are churches of many denominations: ten Church of England, two Roman Catholic and 13 Free Churches but only one building has spanned the centuries since the decline of the city after the Roman occupation – Bath Abbey. In AD973 Edgar was crowned here in a ceremony which formed the basis of that used today. The Victorians added pinnacles and buttresses to a stubbier building and Sir Gilbert Scott guided the installation of the beautiful stone fan vaulting which had been designed for it by the master mason William Vertue. Today the superb West Front stands sentinel over the Churchyard.

The Brendon Hills Map 1 Bb

Between the mass of Exmoor and the ridge of the Quantocks, and with the Bristol Channel a few miles to the north, lies an area that has a sparse population, no industry – and an arresting beauty. In the Brendon Hills there are a few scattered farms and a hamlet and inn at Raleigh's Cross but the villages are found at the edge of the hillsides.

The Romans are believed to have opened the iron workings and German miners were there in the 17th century, but the real story of the Brendon Mines started in 1852 when two Welsh miners from Ebbw Vale formed the Brendon Hills Iron Company to feed the furnaces across the Bristol Channel. By 1857 a railway line had been opened from Combe Row, at the foot of the Brendons to the port at Watchet. By 1877, over 52,000 tons of iron ore were going down the precipitous slope on the railways which ran from each mine that fed the line. But soon after political changes and the end of certain wars brought decline. The Cornish miners drifted away and only a few locals remained in hope. The railway finally closed, to open for a brief two years in 1907. The first World War saw the track go for scrap.

The mining community never numbered more than 700. Some lodged in farms, many more in Luxborough almost on top of the Brendons with its superb views and 14th century church. Others lived in Gupworthy and Brendon Hill village. Brendon Top abounds with relics of the mining; the ruined cable house, derelict shafts and the last sad remnants of miners cottages. Treborough too, was in the heart of iron ore country at one time. On Treborough Common is a bronze age barrow and right in the heart of the Brendons a church and a farm appear to constitute all that there is of Withiel Florey – where grass grows in the middle of some roads and the sudden gradients are alarming.

Red sandstone makes its appearance in the Brendons, a marked change from the characteristics of most of Somerset which relied in the main on the greys of lias or the golden glow of Ham or Bath stone. The Court of 1599 in Nettlecombe is of red sandstone, as is the neighbouring church of 15th century origin which possesses the oldest

dated plate in England. Monksilver, in the foothills, also
has a red sandstone church with a wagon roof. Hard by is
Combe Sydenham (Historic Homes), home of Sir Francis
Drake's wife Elizabeth Sydenham. The Manor goes back in
part to medieval days. Expansion, demolition, rebuilding,
further neglect, sum up the history of the hall until its
rescue by present owners who are gradually restoring the
house, garden and grounds, the mill, fishponds and British
Birds of Prey Centre.

On the stone flags in the Great Hall is a 100lb cannonball, known locally as Drake's cannonball. Legend has it
that although Drake wooed her before going to sea,
Elizabeth Sydenham was at the church door when the ball
hurtled through the air to fall between the would-be bride
and stranger groom. Drake sailed into Plymouth on the
next tide.

Set in agricultural country Stogumber is a village of
diverse houses and cottages dominated by a large church of
14th century origin with a stone pulpit. Elworthy Barrows,
an iron age camp, towers 1,300 feet above the village of
Elworthy with its small low church and 13th century tower.

In the village of Tolland an avenue of Hazels leads to
Gaulden Manor (Historic Homes), home of the
Turbervilles. Above it, rising high from the Brendon Hills
is Willett Hill while Brompton Ralph, situated on the
eastern hillside, has a church with a great perpendicular
tower and a rood screen which had been broken up and lost.
When it was recovered no funds were available to effect
its restoration and it is said that a wealthy American
arrived to trace his ancestors. He found them here – and
paid for the restoration and installation of the old screen.
Which is as happy a note as any on which to pass on
from the Brendon Hills, the 'green hills of Somerset'.

Brent Knoll   Map 2 Ba

Climb, if you can, to the Iron Age fort at the top of this
well rounded hill, a landmark above the Somerset
fenlands where the main road from Weston-Super-Mare

forms a triangle with that from Bristol. (One should use the A38 since it is impossible to leave the motorway until the Burnham exit.)

From the summit there is a splendid view across the moors, Glastonbury Tor and Crooks Peak, the Welsh coast, the Bristol Channel and the hills of Mendip. There are public footpaths leading up from East Brent village and from Brent Knoll village itself where the church is famous for carved bench ends which include a fox dressed as an abbot, presumably a slur on one of the Abbots of Glastonbury who lived locally. Swine and monkeys are also featured and to add to the macabre display the grotesque tower gargoyles make one wonder if some Quasimodo-like creature once rang the bells.

The Iron Age fort on the summit of the Knoll at 457 feet is remarkably preserved and the mound reverted to its island status for a brief period in 1607 when the plains below became flooded.

Interesting bench ends, 17th century plaster ceiling and a graceful spire distinguish the church at East Brent where 15th century glass can be found.

Bridgwater Map 2 Ab

In a county owing much to Bath stone, Ham stone and lias, Bridgwater at first sight seems as alien as a coal mine in the Swiss Alps with its rows and rows of red brick terraced houses, muddy water and the cellophane and other works out on the Bristol road and elsewhere. For all that, it is a town with a considerable history, and was once a major port. Though the River Parrett, on which it stands, continues as a tidal force for many miles, the Bridgwater Bridge precluded the passage of vessels over a certain size – in fact it has been said that Bridgwater merchants controlled the county's trade. The bridge, originally a medieval three-arched structure, gave way to a Coalbrookdale bridge in 1779 and then to a second iron bridge in 1795.

Little evidence of the port's trade survives today save the Water Gate and stone walling on the West Quay, which is

B

surrounded by some good 18th century houses. Castle Street, just off the Quay has been called the most perfect Georgian Street in Somerset, designed for the Duke of Chandos in 1721, the last house being finished in 1730.

The most imposing building is the church of St Mary, part of the centre of the modern town that clusters round the Corn Exchange and Market Hall with its substantial dome. The church is 14th century, famed for its Jacobean screen, benches and wood carving. There are also a number of interesting monuments and an altar picture attributed to Murillo. The low tower of the church has a tall graceful spire and was once used by Monmouth to train his spyglass on the royal army at nearby Westonzoyland, for the town was the Duke's headquarters before the ill-fated Battle of Sedgemoor, the last to be fought on English soil.

St Mary's Street, facing the churchyard, has some good 18th century houses as does Friern Street, once the site of a Franciscan Friary, founded around 1245, but now nowhere to be seen. An old model of the town shows the castle built by William Briwere who died in 1226. It must have dominated the town on the high ground that is now King Square. A well known building society has offices in the square today – a peep into their foyer is rewarding for there is a magnificent mural of dimensional tiling depicting the history of the town, central to which is the figure of Robert Blake.

Cromwell's admiral, Blake, was one of the great sons of Bridgwater and his statue stands on the pavement in the middle of Cornhill. The gardens, by the banks of the river and the **Admiral Blake Museum** in Blake Street both bear his name, the latter occupying the building that was, indeed, the Admiral's birthplace. The town's newest bridge, bypassing the main shopping centre, is also named after him. He was educated at Somerset's own Oxford College of Wadham; in 1640 he became the town's member for Parliament and Taunton's defender in the Civil War. His great sea service took place against the Netherlands and Spain.

Bridgwater Fair (Events), is an annual event which lasts

for four days. It is held in St Matthew's Field, and
overflows into wide West Street, normally the gateway,
through Durleigh, to the Quantocks. At Durleigh there is a
small but picturesque reservoir, which looks almost like a
natural lake. Overlooking it, at West Bower, is the Manor
House, a wonderful old building thought to have been built
by a local lawyer, which looks like a backdrop for a
musical comedy. The nearby church has one of the oldest
bells in Somerset. Enmore nestles among the Quantock
foothills, its church of St Michael still contains
Norman work in the archways. Set in delightful parkland,
Enmore Castle has areas which survive from its
1779 original.

Spaxton, among the hills, bears evidence of the county's
woollen trade in the church bench ends.

Barford Park (Historic Homes) is a Queen Anne house
with an 18th century hall. The dining and music rooms
are highlighted by contemporary furniture, porcelain
and silver.

About 5 miles north of Bridgwater begins the **Bridgwater
Bay National Nature Reserve**, a large area of mud flats
and salt marshes which supports a wide variety of birds,
including white-fronted geese.

Bristol   Map 4 Bb

By a charter of 1373 it was to be a 'county by itself and
called the County of Bristol forever' – today it is the very
heart of the new County of Avon exerting a considerable
influence on north Somerset, serving many of those
outlying districts that were Somerset or Gloucestershire
before the new county boundaries were established by Act
of Parliament in 1974. If Bath is the tourist centre of the
South West then Bristol is now firmly established as the
regional capital. Although it is well inland, the River Avon's
flow into the Bristol Channel has provided the city with a
gateway to the world, and the city's thousand years of
history are linked irrevocably with the sea. Many
seafarer's inns line the wharves and banks from Pill, where

B

the Pilots came aboard, right up to the old City Docks in the centre of the city.

Over the Avon Gorge Isambard Kingdom Brunel's Suspension Bridge looks down upon the engineer's **S.S. Great Britain** (Unusual Outings), which was recovered from the Falkland Islands to stand on permanent exhibition in the dock where it was built. A short distance away in the city centre Brunel's statue, cast in bronze, stares disapprovingly at the motorised traffic which flows unceasingly beneath his gaze. It is possible that his spirit takes some comfort from the proximity of Temple Meads Station which was built in 1839 to his design when he was engineer to the Great Western Railway which had its origins in the city, linking the docks with the rest of the country.

Other links with the sea include the **Cabot Tower** (Other Historic Buildings), standing high on Brandon Hill commemorating John Cabot's journey in 1497 when he set sail to discover Newfoundland. It is well worth the few pence required to pass through the turnstiles to climb the 180 odd steps in order to enjoy a breathtaking view. On the wharfside below, the Watershed, once a series of warehouses, now houses one of the newest concepts in Bristol. The building is an entertainment complex which includes exhibition halls, projection rooms, restaurant and a waterside esplanade with shops. Possibly the most noteworthy of all the exhibitions held is the **World Wine Fair** (Events), which every summer brings vintners from all over the world. The **Wine Museum** in Denmark Street is a permanent feature of the city's various standing exhibitions.

Rich collections local and world wide are to be found in the City Museum and Art Gallery in Queen's Road. Ancient history, the natural sciences, fine and applied arts mix with Bristol ships, Egyptology, Chinese Glass and the Bristol School of Artists.

The **Industrial Museum** is also housed by the City Dock while the nearby **Arnolfini Centre** (Art Galleries) presents contemporary visual arts, video, music and film.

The Frome flows under the city centre. Once ships

moored alongside to discharge their pipes of port and butts of sherry into the city's cellars. For a time the ship's masts gave way to the tramway. Today a vast landscaped road island splits Bristol in half with its famous Hippodrome casting a neon glow over the flower beds towards Corn Street and the business and banking centre, off which lie fascinating alleys, lanes, arcades and market halls fortunately untouched by the repeated night raids of the 1939-45 war. In front of Bristol's Exchange are four of the 'nails' used for cash transactions in days gone by, giving rise to the expression 'pay on the nail'. Antique markets are held on weekdays in the Exchange.

Merchants once lived in historic King Street, so called in celebration of the Restoration, in fact many of the half-timbered buildings date from that period though their Elizabethan or Jacobean looks belie it. Today the street is still famed for some of the best restaurants in the city as well as the lovely Theatre Royal, which originally opened in 1766, making it the oldest active theatre in the country, with a theatrical tradition that is now continued by the Bristol 'Old Vic'.

By the great College Green stands St Mark's Church, the Lord Mayor's Chapel. Civically owned, it was bought by the Corporation in 1541 to become the official place of worship for the Mayor and corporation. Its dark interior, full of heraldry, holds monuments and escutcheons, many of them proof of the city's ventures abroad over the centuries.

One of the city's great benefactors was Sir Edward Colston who made so much of his money in the slave trade. His name crops up in the name of streets and almshouses but particularly in the pseudo-gothic facade of Colston Hall, which was twice burnt out. But in its second rebuilding in 1945 it gained remarkable accoustics making it a venue for concerts ranging from symphony orchestras to modern groups. Adjacent to Colston Hall are the Christmas Steps, fascinating, steep, but hardly seasonal with a collection of bookshops, a violin maker, girlie magazine emporium, clothes and foreign stamps. At the top of the climb stands

B

the chapel of the Three Kings of Cologne, named after the statues of the Magi in Cologne cathedral.

Dating from 1760, St Nicholas Church, in Georgian style, replaced a medieval one. It is now one of Bristol's many archives, for, turned into a museum, it houses church silver, water colours of Bristol's churches and an immense religious triptych by Hogarth. There is even a brass rubbing centre.

Today, largely as a result of the blitz, Bristol is becoming a skyscraper city of office blocks, insurance companies and building societies predominating. But there are some attractive reminders of the past even within the new and controversial Broadmead shopping centre. The Arcade of 1824 is full of small shops selling anything from sheet music to shoes and screwdrivers. Nearby is **John Wesley's New Room** (Church Buildings), the world's first Methodist Church. The Merchant Taylor's Almshouses have been restored in green and white to house a leading bank.

There are many parks and open spaces – no fewer than 264 according to the calculations of the City Council. Ecclesiastically, despite losses in the blitz, there are some fine churches particularly St Mary Redcliffe with its lierne vaulting, ornate paintwork and gilding, and tombs of Bristol's merchants and seafarers, including Admiral Sir William Penn, the father of the founder of Pennsylvania. **Bristol Cathedral** (Church Buildings) was founded in 1140 as St Augustine's Abbey. Its architectural features encompass Norman, Early English, Decorated and Perpendicular. Attached to the Cathedral is the Cathedral School. Both stand on College Green as does the Municipal Library, at right angles to the curved façade of the Council House with its striking gilt unicorns, in contemporary style.

Even more contemporary is Clifton Cathedral, opened in 1973 and built in just over three years. It contains many fine works of art, the splendid coloured windows of Henry Haig and concrete murals depicting the fourteen stations of the Cross. The building is often used for concerts and recitals.

Leading to Clifton is the steep hill of Park Street which

like Queen's Road, offers a mix of department stores, booksellers, small shops and restaurants as well as the imposing 215 foot tower of Bristol University, which exists through the generosity of various members of the Wills tobacco family.

The outlying village of Clifton was brought within the boundaries of Bristol in 1835, when most of the area was in the hands of the Merchant Venturers. Some of the Victorian opulence has departed with so many of the old lofty terraced houses split up into flats. Fortunately developers have been resisted and in 1972 the area was designated a conservation area. The many small boutiques, craft shops, antique dealers and traditional traders make the narrow shopping streets of Clifton a pleasant change from the modern chain stores that are massed across the city in Broadmead. In Clifton, a mixture of styles define the Royal West of England Academy of Dramatic Art. Built in 1857 it is one of the survivors of the Blitz which gutted so much of the city during the last war.

On the northern edge of Clifton, split by the road which sweeps away from the city via the Clifton Suspension Bridge, lie The Downs, with an Iron Age Camp and an old windmill. The latter is now an observatory and contains a camera obscura. On these Downs the citizens of Bristol and their guests can stroll, play games, take in the Flower Show, look across the Avon Gorge which drops away at the edge, or just sit in their cars with an ice cream. They can also visit the nearby **Bristol Zoo** with its collection of animals and beautifully arranged flower gardens.

The city is the headquarters of the West Region of BBC Television and Radio as well as Radio Bristol, all in Whiteladies Road, another important shopping centre. Radio West is situated down on the City Dock and on the Bath Road the HTV complex serves a wide area stretching from Dorset to Wales and Swindon. All the stations are served by transmitters situated high up on the Mendips.

The A 38 road was once a nightmare! With the coming of the road bridge over the Avon near Avonmouth the motorways have siphoned off the West Country bound

B

traffic from London, the Midlands and the North. It is now possible to slip out of the city centre through the former spa at Hotwells, over the Plimsoll Bridge at the Cumberland Basin and on to Lulsgate and Bristol Airport.

Isambard Kingdom Brunel's masterpiece, The Clifton Suspension Bridge, stands as solidly as the rocks from which it springs. It spans 1,350 feet across the river and hangs 250 feet above it. The classical gateway of nearby Leigh Court leads into Stockleigh State Forest and there are some fine walks in Leigh Woods towards the Avon's banks.

To the north of the city, encircled by its development and ultimately sealed in by the thrust of the M5 motorway and the open space of Filton Airfield, lies a cluster of interesting villages and attractions. Nearest to the motorway (exit 17) is Henbury, once an Iron Age hillfort and Roman stronghold. In its churchyard there is a notable tomb to a negro. The epitaph, 'I who was born a pagan and a slave, now sweetly sleeps a Christian in my grave', is a reminder of Bristol's slave trading days.

Clifton Suspension Bridge, Bristol

West of the churchyard lies the Blaise Castle estate, consisting of a splendid house built in 1796 for a Quaker baker, a sham castle tucked away on a wooded hill, and Blaise Hamlet, a group of estate houses designed by John Nash and built to house the servants on the estate. A fascinating stage set, as improbable as Selworthy (q.v.), the entire estate was purchased by Bristol Corporation in 1926. The main house is now an intriguing folk museum.

Sweeping away to the south west the old hunting ground of Kingsweston Down leads to Kingsweston House, a ponderous pile surprisingly designed by Vanbrugh who has included such a proliferation of single chimneys as to give the effect of a central castellation.

The little river Trym is sluggish in the vicinity of Westbury on Trym. White-washed cottages, pot plants and rural back lanes contrast with the skyscrapers of the city of Bristol that lies just over the hill.

Once an ecclesiastical centre, home of a monastic family, by the 15th century a Bishop of Worcester had established a college. A gate tower, angle turrets, some foundations and a few buildings survived the fire set by Prince Rupert in 1643 in an attempt to prevent Parliament using it against the Royalists. In the ancient parish lies Redland, a development of the 18th century with the notable Redland Court and Redland Chapel. The chapel has some fine woodcarving and stands in a delightful green.

Bruton   Map 3 Bb

Although Bruton is a sizeable place, housing a public school and two other educational establishments, its main street is narrow and one way. If you overshoot your required stopping point carry on to the end of the street and cross the River Brue, whose valley cuts the town in two, and then turn back.

It is worth leaving the car to explore the 14th century parish church of St Mary, with its two towers, one over

B

100 feet high. Internally there is a magnificent roof, but what first attracts is the chancel, rebuilt in 1743 with all its original decor preserved intact. Then make your way round Bruton on foot for it is the only proper way to explore the delights of a once prosperous, medieval town, which since its wool and silk industry has long since departed, has taken its conservation as a residential and educational town seriously.

The Abbey Dovecote still stands, near a railway line, but the Augustinian priory which became an Abbey in 1511 is long gone, only the one mysterious isolated wall remains between the road and a headmaster's house. The school, Kings, goes back to the last years before the Reformation.

In the main street stands Sexey's Hospital of 1658, with its monastic heraldry and nearby is the Abbey Court House. Interestingly – and surprisingly – among the quaint, privately owned shops stands a sophisticated art gallery, known by connoisseurs all over the world.

The Pack Horse Bridge, Bruton

B

Brympton D'Evercy Map 3 Ac

One of the nation's lesser known but most delightful stately homes has been restored with loving care by the present day incumbent Charles Clive-Ponsonby-Fane who returned to the house of his ancestors a few years ago.

The estate consists of Manor House, Chantry or Dower House and church, all in the local Ham stone, set in formal gardens by a small lake. The Sydenham family came to the house in 1434, but it has almost disappeared and it is the additions of the 16th and 17th century which enhance the estate today. Sold by the Sydenhams in 1722, Brympton was bought by Francis Fane, brother of the Earl of Westmorland. The Fanes and their descendants have lived in the house ever since except for a few years when it was a private school. It has the longest straight staircase in England.

The parish church of St Andrew is the only reminder of the former village. Its top heavy bellcot tower and carved and painted beam suggest a rood loft.

Burnham-on-Sea Map 2 Aa

Miles of sand with the Mendips and the Quantocks in sight have turned what was once a fishing village into a small Victorian resort. In the distance, across Bridgwater Bay, you can see the atomic station at Hinkley Point.

The Trinity House lighthouse built in 1832 is a graceful building with its slender white tower and its flanking keepers' cottages. Another, on wooden piers, stands sentinel at the water's edge. In the sands are traces of a slipway with embedded railway lines where the tracks of the Somerset Central railway line of 1858 were hauled up and down between the station and the boat for Wales.

The historic centre of the old village is marked by a 14th century church with a leaning tower that is visible proof of the parable – for Burnham is built on sand. The carvings in the church came from the royal palace at Whitehall and are by Grinling Gibbons.

B

Nearby Berrow and Brean are camp and caravan country. Their respective churches are feminine by name: St Mary's and St Bridget's, both 13th century.

Burrington Map 4 Ab

Although a stroll through this tidy village in summer reveals little lanes that are bright with flower bedecked gardens, most visitors are drawn to its sheltered Combe. Burrington Combe quite literally splits the Mendips as surely as Cheddar Gorge. The two are not dissimilar save that Burrington's gorge is less violent.

There are many caves, and some of them were occupied in pre-historic times. Among the better known are Goatchurch Cavern and Aveline's Hole, where skeletal remains have been found. To one of these caves, in the early eighteenth century, came a curate from neighbouring Blagdon who rejoiced in the name of Augustus Toplady. Sheltering in a cleft in the gorge during

Brympton D'Evercy

a thunderstorm he is said to have penned the popular hymn 'Rock of Ages'.

Above the gorge an enormous earthwork, Dolebury Camp, dates from the Iron Age. The church, in Burrington itself, is full of interesting monuments and fragments of 15th century stained glass while the main fabric is of the same period.

Butleigh   Map 3 Ab

Sadly many of the great elms that led from the village to the Glastonbury Moors have fallen to the ravages of Dutch elm disease and the fireplace. Butleigh is a typical Somerset village with well built farms and cottages, although its heart has been sullied by a modern development on one of its meadows.

Away from the bricks and boxes the splendid little St Leonard's church lies in a beautiful setting and boasts some early 14th century work and monuments to the seafaring Hood family, one of whom is commemorated some distance away by the high column on a ridge in the Polden Hills.

Butleigh Court, lined with graceful cedars, was built in Tudor style in 1845, but was allowed to fall into disrepair until conversion took place recently. In the High Street there is a cottage dated 1673 and in nearby Butleigh Wootton, which means nothing less complicated than 'wood town' there is an 18th century house with a splendid iron verandah.

Much of the woodland above Butleigh is in private hands, except the narrow walk to the Hood Monument. A little further west, over the crossroads by Marshall's Elm, a farm on the Somerton-Street road, lies a youth hostel designed to resemble a Swiss mountain chalet. From this road a look to the north at night will reveal the twinkling lights of Street – below it, to the south the Polden Ridge drops sharply to Butleigh Moor, a flat area interrupted by the hills above Compton Dundon and High Ham.

C

Camerton   Map 4 Bb

Situated on the little river Cam, the village is marked by
a conical hill which is so uniform in shape that one instantly
assumes it to be artificial. It is, for this was once a colliery
village and the landmark is no more than a vast slag heap
now landscaped with grass and trees. Further evidence
exists in the name of 'The Jolly Collier'. Central to its
forecourt is an enormous fibreglass model of a miner, a copy
of a bronze made for the National Coal Board in 1951 for
use at the Festival of Britain.

The Camerton Colliery closed in 1950 and the local
railway line which linked it with other collieries soon
suffered the same fate, to be given a temporary reprieve a
year or two later while a film crew used it to make *The
Titfield Thunderbolt*.

In literature, of course, Camerton became celebrated
through the writing of John Skinner, a local rector in the
early 19th century who bequeathed his diaries to the British
Museum. He had an intense interest in local antiquities and
recorded much about his life and times in the area. He
presided throughout the district but especially at St Peter's,
in Camerton itself, where the lords of the Manor were the
Carew family from 1584-1750. Their house adjoined the
church but by 1835 it had been replaced by Camerton
Court, which lies in such a hollow that the church itself is
almost out of sight. There are Carew tombs within, but the
most ancient remains in Camerton are the Bronze Age
barrows and the remains of a Saxon cemetery.

Castle Cary   Map 3 Ab

To the newcomer Cary can be a little confusing for its
friendly streets are on the narrow side and there is a one way
system. It is best to go to the bottom of the town and use the
car park and walk down the long main street with the
delightful independent 'family' shops radiating from a large
Market Hall, built in 1855. The Hall is a mix of classical
styles with columns and Jacobean windows. Stand in the
parlour of the historic George Inn and admire the view.

There is little wonder that the 'Cary' folk have all but deleted the 'Castle' from their vernacular, for the edifice of the Percevals which withstood two sieges during the civil war, subsequently fell into ruin and the only traces are the remains of the keep foundations, now no more than an earthwork among the bracken.

Behind the Market Hall up a steepish incline stands an unlikely Georgian Post Office, looking like a private residence which it probably once was. In front of it, on Bailey Hill, stands the Round House, much photographed as one of the best examples of a lock-up in the entire country. It was built in 1779 at a cost of £23 and one wonders how many miscreants have slept off the effects of 'scrumpy' under its pagoda-like roof.

Centred on a large agricultural area British Rail have found it profitable to stop a couple of Inter City trains at the tidy railway station, in the morning and evening. With London but 1½ hours away by this route there are many who take the 'awayday' and one or two even commute.

Castle Cary Lock-Up

C

Typical of this neat little town is the unusual pond at the bottom of the hill – evidence of the rise of the River Cary. Unusual in that the war memorial stands in the middle of it; typical of Castle Cary inasmuch as it is kept clean.

Looking serenely down on the whole scene is the high spire constructed in 15th century style of the church which was largely rebuilt in 1865. Inside is a fine 15th century pulpit in solid oak. But even the spire of the church can be looked down upon by the cattle who graze on the sheer hill which protects Castle Cary from the east wind.

Chard   Map 2 Bc

Little remains of the ancient Saxon origins of the town through which the Great West Road sweeps from London to Bath, because in 1577 the town was almost completely gutted by fire.

It lies in a gentle hollow of the Blackdowns not far from Windwhistle Hill and the wildlife park of Cricket St Thomas. The pleasant wide Fore Street which sweeps up again to lead us out into Devonshire has samples of almost every kind of building style from the classical Tuscan columns of the Town Hall and Market to Victorian bay windows and thatched roofs. Opposite the Town Hall 'The George' is also resplendent with classical columns, while westward, on the north side of Fore Street the attractive Manor Court is really a collection of some of the town's oldest buildings, dating from approximately 1580. Today a number of small businesses are neatly housed within a building reputed to have connection with the notorious Judge Jeffreys.

Less harshly thought of than the Judge was Chard's own John Stringfellow, inventor of the aeroplane. In 1844 he made a model aircraft of some size which flew for some 120 feet before it crashed; its drawback being a loss of motive power, for the combustion engine was not available to Stringfellow and he used – steam! Although John ran 'out of puff' his invention has a proud place in the Victoria and Albert Museum in London. His house still stands, with a commemorative plaque, in the High Street.

Chard can claim another first in Miss Margaret Bondfield, who was born in Chard and became the first woman ever to become a Cabinet Minister as Minister of Labour in the Labour Government of 1929-31.

Chard had a thriving woollen industry for over 600 years, but in the 19th century what we would now call diversification started and over the years light industry has come to the fore in the shape of glove making, pencils, twine, brushes, lace making and dairy products.

The one building to survive the disastrous low and perpendicular fire is the church, tucked away in Old Town. a surviving arch from Norman times may be found in the chancel wall. Back in the main street the Choughs Hotel and Godworthy House, which houses the **Chard Museum** are both of the late 16th century.

Cheddar Map 2 Ba

The 'Grand Canyon' of the Mendips wanders for almost two miles from the top of the hills, above Cheddar.

The village gave its name to a cheese which is now manufactured in Ireland, New Zealand, Canada and elsewhere. A small quantity is still produced locally and in such outlying Mendip villages as Chewton and Redhill.

The Medieval Market Cross survives as does the school building in which Hannah More started her philanthropic work among the local population in 1789. It is known today as Hannah More's Cottage. There are fascinating street names: The Barrows, Tweentown, Dag Hole, Round Oak Road and Tuttors Hill.

St Andrew's church is the result of rebuilding in the 14th century with the addition of tower, chancel and aisle windows. The church contains the tomb of Sir Thomas Cheddar, whose father was a rich Bristol merchant whose ancestors came from Cheddar. It stands among the few remaining farm houses and cottages but despite some degree of modern 'urban type' sprawl, or indeed perhaps because of it, there are some very good shops in an area

C

which was once a resting place for royal hunting parties, for the Saxon kings had a palace here. The remains of a medieval chapel from the palace stand in the grounds of the Kings of Wessex schools.

Nevertheless it is to Cheddar Gorge that all and sundry turn their attention; so much so that there is tarmac in every nook and cranny in the canyon – the better to park the car and coach. The Gorge is impressive with its highest point rising almost 500 feet sheer from a road which was once a river bed. The stream has long since gone to earth and hollowed out the caves, with their stalagmites and stalactites which have been formed over aeons of time. Here are shades of copper green and manganese pink; hues of darkened lead contrasting with white limestone. **Cheddar Caves** (Unusual Outings) are near the gorge bottom on the east side.

The two main caves, Cox's and Gough's, contain fine stalagmites and stalactites and the bones of prehistoric men

Cheddar Gorge

who once inhabited the caves are now displayed, along with their artefacts, in **Cheddar Caves Museum**.

A climb up the 322 steps of Jacob's Ladder affords some splendid views over the Gorge while below Walton Hamlet is Cheddar's latest venture, an indoor shopping precinct which contains a cluster of shops surrounding indoor water and flower gardens.

Chew Magna   Map 4 Bb

The fact that it is now a village for commuters from Bristol does not detract from its setting, and the view across it to the Chew Valley lake from the A38 over the Mendips is breathtaking from dawn till dusk.

The main street of this village is Georgian in character, with a high railed pavement raised above the main street with shops and banks on one side and one or two good pubs on the other. At its extremity a small village green is bounded by an unusual church house (c. 1510) with a gabled entrance carrying the arms of the St Loe family. The church itself is Norman but with so many additions that it comes over as a 15th century building. The tomb of Sir John St Loe is impressive as is that of Sir John de Hauteville. Other memorials commemorate the Strachey family, the occupiers of Sutton Court after the St Loe family. At the church's end, through an unusual stile, stands Chew Court, once the medieval home of some of the Bishops of Bath and Wells. It has a fine gate house and 17th-century windows.

Chew Magna produced cloth, stockings, edge tools and a substance called ruddle which was used to mark sheep. There is a fine medieval bridge with three pointed arches over the River Chew. Only the elderly know of the hamlet Moreton, and if asked will smile knowingly and point to the centre of the **Chew Valley Lake** (Picnic Site) which was completed in the mid fifties. The remains of a medieval site, a mill and a Roman villa all disappeared with the flooding of the great valley, but not before many of the valuable

C

discoveries had been conveyed to the Bristol Museum. Besides supplying the city of Bristol and its environs with water the lake has a secondary function as a good picnic area with facilities for bird watching and boating as well as the opportunity to catch fish of some quality.

Chew Stoke, standing at the head of the lake, was famous for the Bilbie family who, from their foundry, sent bells all over Somerset, bells that can be heard today, although some were cast as long ago as the 1700's.

Chipping Sodbury   Map 4 Ba

Hatters Lane and Horse Street, Bowling Hill and Clayton Fold – the very names attract to this early planned speculation of the 12th century, engineered by a developer with the apposite name of William the Fat, son of Stephen FitzOdo! The market was established in 1228 by Henry III when he granted a charter for the market and fairs but the town's prosperity did not materialise until the 18th century when, after it had become a centre for the manufacture of cloth, a number of Georgian houses were added. Today the main street is wide and lined with interesting mullioned and gabled 16th to 18th century houses mixed up with some Victorian Gothic, the whole in a melange of lias stone and Pennant sandstone.

The church of St John the Baptist is 13th century but much was added in the 15th. There is an extraordinary concentration of inns: the George, the Royal Oak, the Beaufort Hunt, the Portcullis (where the Beaufort Hunt actually meets). In the middle of the High Street stands a clock tower on a wide paved area which was used, at one time, for market stalls. Chipping means market, incidentally. There is also an old Grammar School now converted into a library in the High Street. The 15th century Tudor Hall stands in Hatters Lane.

An old coaching inn stands in the village of Old Sodbury, an area in which there are some splendid views of the beginnings of Cotswold Country. A mile to the north lies Little Sodbury where there is the impressive walled camp of

34

an Iron Age fort. It can be approached by a footpath from the A46 and in the entrance a stone marks the parish boundary between Little and Old Sodbury.

The church of St Adeline in Little Sodbury was built in 1859. On sale there is a pamphlet telling the story of William Tyndale who served as chaplain to the Walshe family between 1521 and 1523 during which time he resolved to write the first English language version of the Bible by translating it directly from the Greek and Hebrew text. For his pains he was burned at the stake in 1535.

Three miles north east of Chipping Sodbury stands the small manor house of **Horton Court** (Historic Homes). It was once owned by William Knight, who was appointed prebendary of Horton, protonotary of the Holy See and, in 1572, Henry VIII's envoy in the unsuccessful divorce negotiations. Around the doorway of the manor each of these advances is recorded: the arms granted on the prebendaryship, the protonotary's hat and carved renaissance columns for the return from Rome!

Churchill Map 4 Ab

Any one driving down the A38 would be forgiven for thinking that the great wartime leader had either been born here, died here, or at the very least planned some of his war campaigns here, for names such as 'The Sir Winston', and the 'Churchill Arms' proliferate to such an extent that at any moment one expects to come across 'The Victory Cafe' with the appropriate sign.

In fact the family connection is tenuous and has nothing to do with the image. Certainly there is a Churchill Court a mile or so away near to the church on the hill from which the village name was derived; but the original owner was a certain Robert Jenkyns who died in 1572, and is said to be the ancestor of Sarah Jennings, wife of the first Duke of Marlborough. A cousin of the Duke, Sir John Churchill bought the court and one historian asserts that he probably did so because the village bore his

C

surname. The church is perpendicular in style and has many interesting tombs and effigies including those of Sir John and his wife and their many children. The village itself, bisected by an A38 that is considerably quieter since the coming of the Motorway, is interesting enough and was once the home of the miners who worked the nearby hills for calomine. If the 'church on the hill' is really noteworthy it is because it marks the end of the Mendips, for those hills disappear here into the urban landscape of the environs of Bristol.

A hill fort, Dolebury Camp, which can be reached by a short climb from the road at Churchill Rocks, is part of Dolebury Warren, a rabbit breeding ground on Mendip. The camp itself is immense with impressive ramparts and spectacular views.

Clevedon   Map 4 Ab

A short sea front gives a wide outlook on the Bristol channel across to the Welsh Coast. The dignified and spacious Victorian stone houses are quite enchanting, especially as little attempt has been made to exploit amusement arcades and the like. The scenery inspired Coleridge whose cottage can be seen in Old Church Road. Tennyson, Southey, Lamb and Thackeray were also visitors.

Old St Andrew's church with its Norman tower stands where the coast road ends and a footpath begins to climb the headland. Overlooking Clevedon Pill is an Iron age earthwork (Wains Hill Camp) and below on the coast is the famous pier with its severed causeway.

On the town's outskirts, at East Clevedon, is **Clevedon Court** (Historic Homes), an outstanding Manor House in the keeping of the National Trust. It dates back to the 12th century with a fine garden and chapel that was added in the 14th century. The house was once fortified and still possesses a portcullis. The Old Kitchen has been dated back to the 13th century. Through the centuries there have been many changes of ownership since the house was built

by St John de Clevedon. The Wake family of
Northamptonshire lived there until the mid 17th century
and made many additions including the sham tower on the
hill above.

A Bristol merchant family, the Eltons, bought the house
and surrounding estates in 1709 and it was that family that
was responsible for the growth of Clevedon. The Rev. Sir
Abraham Elton enclosed much of the common land and
made it available for building while a successor, Sir Arthur
Hallam Elton, built the cottage hospital and lending library
and also had much to do with the running of the famous
pier. A local product, the colourful pottery known as Elton
Ware, was the invention of Sir Edmund Elton. There is a
late Norman church which is rich in carvings and
memorials to the Eltons and the Hallams.

Congresbury Map 4 Ab

Avon and Somerset combine to confuse with a selection of
Hewishes or Huishes not to mention the Cadburys. Here at
Congresbury the latter name occurs twice, once at the Iron
Age camp called Cadbury Hill Camp (which should not be
confused with the one near Tickenham village nor the
South Cadbury earthworks) and again at Cadbury House
beneath.

The church of St Andrew is imposing with both tower
and spire. There are 13th century features and a Norman
font with cable carving, but local legend says that the
original church was erected by one St Congar who planted
his stick to provide shade whereupon it grew. All of which,
to one writer at least, sounds like a little bit of one
upmanship directed at Glastonbury. The Vicarage is
part 15th, part 19th century – without doubt one of
England's finest medieval parsonages, its origins reaching
back to the days of Bishop Beckington.
NB. The Bishop's name occurs in various records with a
number of versions of its spelling, the most common,
and the one I prefer, is Bekynton.

The village has grown over the last 30 years and

C

vast new housing estates sit on its outskirts. The basic development is earlier, however, for the village was always on an important road junction on the Bristol – Weston-super-Mare road. No doubt as a result of all the turnpike traffic there seems to be a large number of old inns: the 'Ship and Castle', 'Plough', 'Old Inn', and the 'White Hart'; all within a stone's throw of one another. The 'Old Inn' is 17th century and there is said to have been a brewing house on the site even before that.

A village cross of gracious proportions and tracery stands opposite the 'Ship and Castle', by the Bristol road. Within the bounds of the churchyard – by its hedge, in fact, stands a large pink granite monument to Charles Hardwick, citizen of the parish who, in 1830, was responsible for turning the tables on a highwayman and handing him over to the law.

Crewkerne Map 2 Bc

Somerset is renowned for its carnivals and fairs and it was in the 1270s that Crewkerne's St Bartholomew's Fair was established. To this day, once a year the centre of the town, the main square and side streets are taken over by the full fun of the fair – and pity the motorist on the A30 who runs straight through the jollifications.

Close to the county of Dorset the town was once a Royal estate and there was a Mint back in the 10th century. By the 16th century the town had grown and become a post stage with several inns and hostelries. As the town expanded it became involved in a variety of trades concerned with cloth and sail making. Today it has many small industrial plants involved in engineering, printing and other trades. It is also the base for a firm of auctioneers and estate agents who have become renowned nationwide for their expertise in antiques.

The Market Hall is Victorian and set in the old fashioned square opposite a coaching inn. In East Street Merefield House with its classical pillars and wrought iron gates was built before Waterloo; Abbey House is largely Victorian like many of the houses in Market Street although there are some Georgian frontages. In Hermitage Street stands the Unitarian Chapel, built in 1733 with windows of that date. Chubb's Almshouses, well restored, still stand in West Street. Davis's Almshouses were built in 1707 and are picturesque.

Set high above the town, overlooking a graceful green valley, stands St Bartholomew's church with its twin turrets and central tower reminiscent of Bath Abbey. Indicative of the long history of successful trade within the town it has wide and lofty windows, a fan vaulted oak ceiling and a medieval roof supported by stone angels.

North of the church the old Grammar School of 1636 once had Thomas Masterman Hardy among its pupils while the new Grammar School on the Yeovil Road was built in Tudor style in 1872.

Following that same road brings one to Windwhistle Hill beneath which lies the village of Cricket St Thomas, best known for a **Wildlife Park** (Unusual Outings) in the grounds of Cricket House, the former home of Sir Alexander Hood, the celebrated Admiral, later to become Viscount Bridport. For a time the house was owned by chocolate manufacturer F.J. Fry. There is a tiny church in the grounds with large monuments to Viscount Bridport and to Nelson's nephew and heir. The facade of the house is known to millions today as the stately home from the TV series *To The Manor Born*.

On the other side of the main A30 hilly lanes lead to Cricket Malherbie where the Court was built for Admiral Pitt on the site of an old Tudor house. A little 19th century church stands opposite.

South of Crewkerne is **Clapton Court Gardens**, one of Somerset's most beautiful gardens with rare and unusual trees and shrubs in formal and woodland settings.

Curry Rivel   Map 2 Bb

Baskets of all kinds are made here and displayed on the

D

forecourt of the premises on the main road through the village. The osiers or withies, the weaver's materials, are grown a few paces away on the flat moors which fall away beyond Curry Rivel's church. Nearby is the home and studio of one of the country's foremost water colour artists, E.R. Sturgeon, and some of his work can be seen in the local gallery.

On the slopes of a park on the road towards Taunton stands the Burton Pynsent Monument, erected in 1765 to Sir William Pynsent by William Pitt in return for the gift of the property which had been a token of his services to the nation. The monument was designed by Capability Brown and is built of the local blue lias faced with Portland stone, and topped with an urn. A dangerous edifice at the moment of writing, but the present owner is engaged in securing its restoration. Very little remains of the large Elizabethan mansion; a modern dwelling and a farm now occupy the site.

Away towards the village of Drayton stands **Midelney Manor** (Historic Homes) which dates back to a charter of 693 when King Ine granted the little island above the marsh lands to the Benedictine monks. The house was built by two Trevilian brothers in the 16th century, and it is still lived in by their descendants. The sturdy partition wall inside was not breached until 1921.

The house possesses some Louis XV and Georgian furniture and its decorations include sheriff's banners, paintings, portraits and an interesting model of the house in silver which is, in fact, a city freeman's presentation casket. The garden is enchanting, and there is a falcon's mews to be seen which dates from the early 18th century.

Dodington   Map 2 Ab

Failure to obtain planning permission to extend certain 'fun fair' types of attraction to the once famous coach exhibition has resulted in the last owners – the Codrington family – selling off the entire estate. At the moment the

Bristol Tourist Office can only tell me that it closed, quote 'off the circuit'. The last guide book published (Michelin) omits it entirely. Certainly there are chains across the gate and it is not possible to enter.

Dundry Map 4 Ab

Stand at the top of the lane outside the churchyard after the sun has set and all before you is magic. The village of Dundry may be an outpost of Mendip but it has a wonderful view of Bristol. Its myriad lights twinkle like stars with the illuminated Clifton Suspension Bridge as their focal point.

Bristol also looks pretty good from the same spot during the day, for there cannot be a finer view of the populated part of the Avon valley. Conversely the church tower is a landmark for every road that leads into Bristol, it was built for that purpose as a beacon for sailors by the Merchant Venturers in 1484 – the rest of the church followed in 1861. The churchyard contains a dole table in the form of a stone block. It was used to dispense charity.

Dunster Map 1 Ba

Sinister or serene – the ambient look of **Dunster Castle** (Castles) can be either, according to the light afforded by the prevailing weather. I first saw it in a thunderstorm against grey clouds rising from Exmoor – it looked distinctly Draculian. On the other hand County Historian Dr. Robert Dunning has described it as 'almost fairy tale' and who would disagree with that. The castle looks down upon a wide High Street with a **Yarn Market** (Other Historic Buildings) at its far end – cover up the postcards and other tourist essentials, lay a quantity of straw upon the highway and you have the perfect medieval scene.

In fact, at the height of the season the place is chock-a-block with tourists and it is essential to leave one's vehicle outside the town where an enterprising council has provided a large car park below Conegar Hill. Few bother

D

provided a large car park below Conegar Hill. Few bother to climb up that particular hill to the 1765 folly though it is easy enough to reach. Most walk the short distance into the village, passing, or otherwise, the 16th century Luttrell Arms with its fine hall and solid oak. It is at this end that the Yarn Market stands. Octagonal and dormered it was rebuilt in the 17th century to dominate the High Street, a street in which many of the little shops nestling within their 17th or 18th century houses devote themselves to tourism, with local crafts well to the fore. The Molly Hardwick Doll Collection in the Memorial Hall is worth a visit. There are over 700 dolls, and some date back over two centuries.

Church Street, as its name implies, has a number of buildings relating to a priory which was founded in 1090. They include a priest's house and an early medieval pigeon house which boasts 500 nesting holes set in its four foot thick stone wall. The **Old Dovecote** (Other Historic Buildings) stands near the end wall of a priory garden behind St George's church. The church, rebuilt by the local monks, contains some splendid examples of

Yarn Market, Dunster

local carving and a 54 foot screen which crosses the nave
and aisles, dividing the interior in half – it was made
after a dispute in 1357.

There are tombs to the Luttrells of course, for Dunster
Castle has stood on its site commanding the plains of the
Avill valley for nearly a thousand years, although during
that time it has seen many changes. The present version is
largely 19th century but during its stand it has only known
two families (or three, if you count the National Trust).
The first owner, William de Mohun, accompanied the
Conqueror and built the original fortifications. By the end
of the 14th century the Luttrell family had purchased the
site and much else but it was not until the advent of George
Fownes Luttrell during the 19th century that the
present building took shape.

The gatehouse is 15th century. Inside the body of the
castle there are two main halls, the inner chamber being
part of the old Great Hall. Everywhere evidence of the
Luttrell years is to be found in portraits and coats of arms,
but by far the most outstanding monument to the family is
the grand staircase carved with leaves and flowers in
solid elm that is inches thick.

The castle water mill can be reached either from within
the castle grounds or through Mill Lane, off West Street.
It has been there since Domesday, but was abandoned at
the turn of this century although brought back into
use during the last war. Now in the hands of tenants
its final restoration was completed in 1980.

Dunster is the true gateway to Exmoor, the route
which, once the village is passed, follows the lovely Avill
valley. Gallox Bridge lies opposite the curiously named
Grabbist Hill, and leads back into Dunster Deer Park. The
hills around Dunster Castle carry weird and wonderful
names: Bat's Hill, Black Ball and Vinegar Hill.

Dyrham   Map 4 Bb

The manorial village rests beneath its church and the walled
grounds of the great manor house. Some 200 people

live here in the 17th-18th century stone houses built near the site of a battle between Saxons and Britons in 577.

Dyrham means 'enclosure for deer' and the park is kept stocked. The formal gardens include parterres, fountains and cascades and it is not unusual to see the odd pheasant. Looking down to the house, so magnificent in its Cotswold setting, it is difficult to conceive that three kings were killed here.

The house we see today is the combination of expertise of two great architects: Talman, a deputy to Christopher Wren and a Huguenot, and Samuel Hauduroy. Together they built the edifice for William Blathwayt, a diplomat, in the reign of William III. He spent much of his time abroad, but married the heiress to the older property which stood on the site.

Today Dyrham is administered by the National Trust and an internal tour will reveal all that remains of the original Tudor house in the Great Hall – and much else besides!

East Coker

It was of East Coker that T.S. Eliot once wrote: 'In my beginning is my end. Now the light falls. . . '. As if answering one of his own summons if not one from his ancestors the poet's ashes were laid to rest in the village church. It is a pretty village with tree lined lanes, Ham stone houses and cottages. The imposing Coker Court stands close to the church which is externally mainly 15th century while the stone gabled Helyar almshouses were founded in 1640.

Navigator and explorer William Dampier, one of the first Englishmen to cast eyes on Australia, was born in the village in 1651 and he is suitably commemorated in the church.

Near at hand, on the busy A30, the original great route to Exeter and the west, stands West Coker at the base of a high Ham stone cutting known as Packhorse Lane.

Stores, post office and church are clustered together north west of the centre while on the main road a hotel, motel and the delightful Castle Inn are equally welcoming. Once again Ham stone predominates as it does in nearby North Coker which lies along rich sandstone cuttings.

Exmoor Map 1 Ab

Brown Willy may be in Cornwall, the Malverns in Worcestershire and the Black Mountains in Wales but all are visible from many points on the high, wide plateau topped by Dunkery Beacon, that is Exmoor.

If Dunkery dominates on the high rock line above the heather, then the wooded combes below hide and shelter the remote villages which are to be found within the National Park, most of which have names associated with the streams that cascade down the hills. The two principle rivers are the Exe and the Barle, the former flowing through wooded valleys until its confluence with the Barle just below Dulverton. The Barle is more beautiful with Simonsbath a centre for exploration where the river is young. Roads meet here and there is accommodation in hotel, guest house and farm. The village church, slate hung against the wild weather, dates from 1865. Nearby Cow Castle is a small but impressive earthwork dating from around 500BC.

Withypool, high, wild, entered in Domesday as Widepolla, stands astride the Barle, bridged at this point. The weatherbeaten parish church is set among pleasant cottages and houses. Up over the majestic common a road turns steeply for Lanacre Bridge, a sturdy and imposing structure with granite piers bracing themselves against a possible torrent. Further down the Barle from Withypool, but not on the main road, lies one of Exmoor's mysteries, Tarr Steps, reputedly the oldest river bridge in England. Tracks lead to it from the car parks which are a short distance away, ensuring that the seventeen spans made up from solid stone slabs lie in a sylvan setting.

E

The slabs are each about seven foot in length and four foot
wide; they, in turn, are protected from the river's force
by sloping stones set against them from the depth of
the river bed.

The steep road up from Withypool leads on to the lonely
village of Hawkridge and then on through increasingly leafy
slopes into the splendid tourist base of Dulverton, where,
beside the river in an elegant setting lies Exmoor House,
built in 1858 as a workhouse and now the administrative
headquarters and centre of Exmoor National Park. At the
top of Fore Street stands the church of All Saints, largely
rebuilt in 1852 but still possessing its 13th century tower.
Most of the buildings in the town are 19th century, and
mainly of local stone. A son of Dulverton, scarcely
remembered today, is Sir George Williams, born on
Ashway Farm in 1821. He was the founder of the YMCA.

East of Dulverton lies the valley of the little river
Haddeo, or what is left of it because most of it is submerged

Tarr Steps, Exmoor

beneath the 892 million gallons of water stored in the
Wimbleball Reservoir, a magnificent project, recently
completed by the water authority. The banks have been
beautifully landscaped and the waters stocked with
thousands of trout. Nearby Exton, with its two bridges over
the Exe, will lead back over the moor, first to Winsford,
with its inn, mill, pack horse bridge, 13th century church
and a megalithic monument known as the Caractacus Stone.
Officially listed as 'an inscribed stone of the Dark Ages',
the legends and theories about the origins of the
seven hundredweight mass are legion, but no one, as yet,
has uncovered its archaeological secrets.

The next and last village on the Exe before we reach the
open moor is Exford, clustering round the sturdy river
bridge. A lush village green is faced on the north side by a
village store and post office and there are several small
hotels and guest houses, for it is a centre for tourism as well
as hunting. The Devon and Somerset Kennels are based in
the village and much of the local employment is based upon
the needs of horse and hound. The Youth Hostel occupies
Exe Mead, an estate bought by the Somerset County
Council in 1964. With loose boxes and paddocks it is
completely equipped for the 'adventure holidays' that are
sought by many members.

Under the shelter of Dunkery, Wheddon Cross owes its
importance to a junction of roads. An inn, shop and some
cottages stand where the road from Dunster up the pretty
Avill valley turns off for Dunkery Gate. Nearby
Cutcombe has a 13th century church and Timberscombe,
just out of Dunster, lies amidst tree lined lanes. The
Horner Water plunges down from Dunkery Beacon to
Horner, a small collection of cottages, by a single
span packhorse bridge. Luccombe has an old church
with a splendidly carved screen and the remains of
an ancient cross.

Set in a valley off the Porlock/Lynmouth Road lies Oare,
made famous by Lorna Doone. The church has been
carefully restored, as well it might, for the fictional shooting
of the heroine of R.D. Blackmore's novel, by Carver

F

Doone, has attracted more pilgrims over the years than J.R.'s ever will to Dallas. It is a perfect setting, 15th century with high box pews and a chalice of 1573. Outside rushes Oare Water hurrying from Robbers Bridge to join Badgeworthy Water while all around the high hills close in with the purple of heather in one season and the white flecks of sheep's wool in another.

Farleigh Hungerford   Map 3 Ba

The picturesque ruins of **Farleigh Castle** (Historic Homes) are situated overlooking the valley of the River Frome where the river enters Avon by the Wiltshire border. A manor house belonging to the Montfort family had stood on the site since the reign of William Rufus. It passed to the family of a colleague of Sir Thomas Hungerford who purchased it in 1369. By 1383 when he had become the Speaker of the House of Commons, he had probably completed the rectangular building with its circular towers, fortifications and gatehouse.

After his death in 1397 Sir Thomas was buried in the nearby church of St Leonard. He was succeeded by his son Walter, also to become a Speaker of the House of Commons, High Treasurer under Henry VI and a baron. Walter extended the castle southwards creating the present entrance with square gatehouse with drawbridge. The little church thus became an integral part of the Castle and Sir Walter built a larger one for the villagers on the estate. It was consecrated in 1443 and a portrait of Sir Thomas in a nave window can be recognised by the Hungerford sickle. Restoration took place in 1830, by which time the castle itself was said to have been in a parlous state, having been garrisoned by the Royalists in 1644.

Nearby Farleigh House has a chapel and a lodge remodelled from an older house in the 19th century.

At Rode, 2½ miles away, are the **Tropical Bird Gardens** (Bird Parks) a 17 acre park and wooded flower garden which provides a setting for over 170 species including strutting pheasants, flamingoes and free-flying macaws.

F

Frenchay Map 4 Bb

Originally Fromeshaw, after the river from which it derived
its original name, Frenchay has its oldest part at the far side
of its common by the tiny bridge over the river. Although a
suburb of Bristol, Frenchay still retains all of the
characteristics of village life, to the chagrin of the native and
the delight of the commuter. Georgian houses surround the
common on which the great W.G. Grace once played
cricket. The Manor House is by one of Bath's great
creators, the elder Wood, who designed it for a Quaker
linen merchant. Other Quaker connections appear –
Frenchay Grove was the home of J.S. Fry the chocolate
manufacturer, and William Penn, who founded
Pennsylvania, is associated with the Quaker Meeting House
which was first erected in 1673 and rebuilt in 1807. Cedar
Hall, just south of the Meeting House, was the home of a
leading Quaker Banker.

Nearby, Frenchay Park is now part of the hospital
complex for which the area has become noted. There are
pleasant walks along the banks of the river and in the
grounds of Oldbury Court, an estate which was bought by
Bristol Corporation in 1937 and laid out as a park. Many of
the walks lead back to the river which once provided power
for a number of corn mills. All that remains today are a
number of weirs and the odd sounding Snuff Mills Park.

Frome Map 3 Ba

Once upon a time there was a popular ballad which referred
to a 'quaint little old fashioned town' and continued with
a rhymed reference which declared that the streets 'run
uphill and down'. This is that town and they still do but the
authorities are not too old fashioned to recognise the
need for a bit of by-passing here and there!

Steep stone steps approach the church from one direction
while the little streets seem to fall away everywhere with
houses and shops on all sorts of levels. Those streets
bear intriguing descriptive names: Stony Street, Back

F

Lane, Angel Lane, Behind Town, Wine Street and many more including the unbelievable Twattle Alley. Almost as unbelievable are the number of pubs. After my legs had given out I counted at least 42 within a square half mile on a map of 1978.

Track and stream attracted early mankind. The town was finally settled when Aldhelm raised the church of St John the Baptist in about 685; it has work dating from between the late 12th century and the 15th, and again from the 19th centuries. By the 14th century the wool trade had become the base upon which the by now prosperous town rested. It was a prosperity that was to increase until well into the 19th century. With its collapse the enterprising citizens turned to pastures new and other industries were developed. It is true to say that the industrious citizens of Frome are still 'hard at it' and one of the most interesting examples is the printing firm of Butler and Tanner, responsible for some of the nation's finely printed books including *Who's Who*.

Cheap Street, Frome

As you would expect of such an industrious town there is an abundance of substantial houses, 17th to 19th century in origin, not to mention seven other churches and chapels in addition to the parish church. The town was noted for its temples of Protestant Nonconformity and Rook Lane Congregational Church, set back from the top of Bath Street, is claimed to be England's finest with its triangular pediment and massive Tuscan pillars.

Some of Frome's quaint little streets have already been lost to progress but there are enough left to intrigue and recall the past. Most noteworthy is Cheap Street. Running east of the market place, cobbled and pedestrianised, it has a fast flowing conduit down its centre and boasts an overhanging upper storey to a 16th century building. Where it meets King Street stands the Court House with its peculiar shell shaped doorway.

One of the most striking features of the Market Place is the plain Georgian frontage of the George Hotel. Next to it the Frome branch of the National Westminster Bank was originally the premises of Stuckey, the banking family that enhanced so many of the county's banking establishments as well as controlling much of the county's trading arrangements. At the end of the Market Place a graceful Regency bridge with one single arch spanning the main channel allows the river which bears the name of the town to pass on its interesting course to Bristol where modern requirements and technology have sent it underground.

Those self same modern requirements are in evidence in the new housing estates at the east end of the town where a theatre called 'The Merlin' can be found.

The Somerset County Historian once said that 'Frome has had a bad press in the past'. Be that as it may the only ups and downs that matter today lie in those quaint little streets that lead you down and then send you scurrying back up again. Catherine Hill with its little shops and the cobbled Gentle Street are sheer delight. There are countless others so Frome is not the place for the tourist with a car. Park it – and keep walking and you will find that

G

the only reason that Frome doesn't make good press is because the natives want to keep it all to themselves.

Frome's most noteworthy beauty spot is Vallis Vale, which runs towards Hapsford Mill in deep wooded valleys. A little further afield stands the delightful unspoiled village of Mells, much of the surroundings being preserved, anachronistically, by a famous quarrying company which has been making considerable inroads into the rocky countryside. John Horner was a tenant of Glastonbury Abbey at Mells. The Horner family was to acquire much of the Mells property – the 'plum' that was the origin of the famous nursery rhyme. The successors still remain in the village, their home lying next to the churchyard with its small lane at the splendid late Gothic church's gate leading off the one main street of the village with its inviting inn.

The church tower somehow seems to suit the small village, despite its magnificence and height, over 100 foot. Inside the church there is an equestrian statue by Sir Alfred Munnings. Nearby Mells Park, altered and rebuilt by Lutyens in this century, is now owned by that local quarrying firm who have done much to maintain it. Passing through this delightful spot in the Wadbury Valley it is hard to believe that it was once industrious and made edge tools, scythes, spades and shovels to name but a few items.

Glastonbury Map 3 Ab

Glastonbury is one of the most identifiable spots in the whole of Great Britain. Standing slightly to the east of the town, Glastonbury Tor dominates the landscape. The climb to the summit is steep and the ruined tower of St Michael is all that is left of the 13th century church which once stood on the site. The breathtaking view takes in 360 degrees over the whole Vale of Avalon and the red brick town below, where the 15th century tower of the parish church of St John soars upwards to meet the eye. It too, can be seen for miles around and within its walls are some fine Italian paintings, 15th century stained glass and linenfold panelling.

G

Glastonbury abounds in legends. Legends of Arthur and Guinevere, Joseph of Arimathea and the Holy Grail – the cup of the Last Supper. The Glastonbury thorn grows on Wearyall Hill, originally by-passed by the Romans on their way west. The thorn is reputed to have sprung from Joseph's staff but, alas, the original was felled by a zealous Puritan and the replacement has, for many years, been surrounded by a protective iron guard rail. A larger tree stands just off the busy High Street in St John's churchyard, and yet another thorn tree stands in the grounds of Glastonbury Abbey.

With so many legends it is no wonder that Glastonbury is a principal focus of pilgrimage in the West County, a tourist attraction made doubly amenable by the presence of Wells just a few miles away.

St Dunstan, who came from nearby Baltonsborough, was a member of the Benedictine monastery here, the richest in England with the possible exception of Westminster, and it is **Glastonbury Abbey** (Church Buildings) with fragments of ruined arches, transepts and chapel that remains to attract the traveller. Three English kings, Edmund, Edgar, and Edmund Ironside were buried here and by the time the Normans came the Abbots of Glastonbury owned an eighth of the county. During the Dissolution its very stones were quarried, many of them being used to pave the road to Wells.

Only the Abbot's Kitchen remained complete, to be used by weavers in the 16th century and later as a Quaker Meeting House. The entire site was purchased by the Church of England early this century when much of the original layout was restored. The well tended lawns make a pleasant oasis from the busy town that surrounds them and the Abbot's Kitchen houses an exhibition depicting the Abbey's history.

Just off the Abbey estate, in Bere Lane, the Abbey Barn of 14th century origin has been lovingly restored in recent years by the County Council. It is now open to the general public as the **Somerset Rural Life Museum**.

In the town's High Street the pre-Reformation inn, the

G

George and Pilgrim once dispensed the hospitality of the
Abbey to the traveller. Now known as The George it is still
a thriving hostelry, one of many in the town. A few paces
brings us to the **Tribunal** or Court House, now a small
museum specialising in finds from the lake-villages. Round
the corner, past the early Victorian market cross lies the
town hall with its simple Georgian façade of 1818. Further
on another Georgian building was erected as the pump
house for Glastonbury's short lived Spa which took its water
from the **Chalice Well** (Archaeological Sites) at the foot of
the Tor.

The industry for which Glastonbury is best known, other
than the many small crafts and artistic endeavours, is the
tanning of sheepskin. Morlands of Glastonbury took
the name of the town round the world. Starting with
primitive slippers and fur lined boots the business
progressed with 'bomber' jackets and flying boots during
the war and afterwards introduced the top coats for both
men and women that were to be seen on race tracks and

Abbots Kitchen, Abbey Ruins, Glastonbury

farms throughout the land for years thereafter. Competing
with the neighbouring Bailey's tannery for many
years Morlands sadly became a victim of recessionary
times and was recently taken over by its neighbour.

Great Badminton Map 4 Ba

A fine collection of late 18th and 19th century houses,
including cottages ornés with rustic verandahs and diamond
window panes surround a charming village green and its
active sports club.

The Park is famed for its annual Horse Trials but
Badminton House, not open to the public, is scarcely
visible, guarded by trees, hedges and ornate lodges of
Cotswold stone. The estate, bought originally from the
Botelet family in 1608, has remained in the hands of the
Somerset family ever since, the Dukedom of Beaufort being
created in 1699. Originally the house consisted of one
central block with wings on each side until further wings
linked to pavilions were added, designed by William Kent,
who was responsible for other buildings in the park
including Worcester Lodge, later altered by Capability
Brown. The church of St Michael, dominated by Beaufort
memorials, is attached to the house.

Little Badminton, with its village green and small church
lies one mile to the north.

High Ham Map 2 Bb

At first sight, unprepossessing, with what appears to be a
builder's yard adjoining its pub, High Ham improves
past the modern houses at its northern entrance above the
steep rise from Sedgemoor.

A Tudor farmhouse first catches the eye, and then the old
vicarage and cottages that nestle round a village green
which is a picture when the 'candles' blossom on the horse
chestnut trees. In medieval times a whole ridge of hills
hereabouts were dotted with windmills. Only Stembridge

H

Mill in High Ham now remains in a state of perfect preservation thanks to the National Trust who recently renewed its sails and carried out other renovation. Early 19th century in origin the mill was in full use until 1910. A little further west along the ridge, Turn Hill is a magnificent spot from which to view much of Sedgemoor across to Bridgwater through to the nuclear station at Hinkley Point.

The tower of High Ham church dates back to both the 14th and 15th centuries. There is some fine Somerset tracery and the superb nave roof stands off arched braces springing from supporting angels. A mile or so away Low Ham's church comes as a complete surprise, standing, not in a churchyard, but smack in the middle of a field with the odd farmbuilding around it. Not even a path leads to the door, just a track. The Roman's once had a fine villa here – the remains of the bath houses and a wonderful mosaic floor have been removed to the Castle Museum in Taunton.

Hinton St George   Map 2 Bc

Hinton St George is off the beaten track (try the road from Crewkerne leading back to the A303 at Lopen Head). It has a very broad main street that is a perfect blend of Tudor, Jacobean and Georgian.

The church, tall and pinnacled, has a 15th century tower with gargoyles, so appropriate to a village which celebrates 'Punkie Night' on the last Thursday in October, when children make lanterns with hideous faces out of turnips, mangolds and pumpkins symbolising the wives of Hinton searching for their menfolk at Chiselborough Fair.

The estate on the west side of the village is headed by Hinton House, home of the Poulett family for over 500 years until 1968 when the 8th Earl Poulett sold everything. The park was the temporary home for many regiments during the last war. Czechoslovakians, Irish, and English were billeted and finally, Americans, who, apparently did things in great style, leaving behind a

I

considerable number of almost permanent buildings.

Today Hinton House is a series of self-contained dwellings, the stables alone constituting some of the finest examples of conversion.

Nearby Merriot, astride the Crewkerne road, has a fertile soil which has led to the development of market gardening and, in consequence, a nationally known garden centre and supplier. Once sailcloth was made from the flax which was successfully grown on that same soil. The village has its own shops, post office, pubs and a tithe barn which is put to good use for village functions. In the lower part of the village are some wonderful old houses.

Horton Map 4 Ba

One of the main jewels of the 'Cotswold fringe' is the village of Horton with the National Trust in occupation in the restored Horton Court, a 16th century manor house.

The manor house, church, and farm have been described by historian Dr. Robert Dunning as a truly English group. The hall is a survivor from Norman times although alterations have been made through the years. Certainly the timbered roof is 14th century but subsequently the hall was split into two floors with successive uses as a Catholic chapel and a school until the late 19th century when reconversion back to a hall took place.

The house is of much later date, built by a Bishop of Bath and Wells, William Knight, in 1521. His arms surmount the main entrance door. Next to the manor stands the church of St James, restored in 1865 but retaining some 14th and 16th century detail.

Ilchester Map 3 Ab

Once Ilchester was an important Roman station on the Fosse Way, now its inhabitants are the officers from the outlying Royal Naval Air Station of Yeovilton. The swish of togas and the clatter of standards have been replaced by the whirr of the helicopter and the whine of the jet engine. Fortunately the town is now by-passed and with the elimination of the frequent road jams rests in peace. It is possible today to stand on the heavy 12th century bridge to watch the River Yeo danger to life and limb.

The Town Hall is being restored and once possessed the oldest staff of office in England, the Mace, dating from the 13th century, which is now in the County Museum, Taunton.

Opinions differ as to the number of churches that have been built in Ilchester over the centuries. In 1724 it was reputed to have 16. The latest research makes clear that there were at least six parish churches, a friary, a hospital (later a nunnery) and a chapel. At all events there is but one survivor, the 13th-century St Mary Major just off the Yeovil Road with an octagonal tower whose style appears to have been repeated in such nearby villages as South Petherton and Barrington.

The other church linked with the village stands, in fact, in the parish of Northover, a stone's throw across the River Yeo. Standing on a low hill site, a red light on the tower serves as a guide – and a warning, to all those pilots making a night landing.

A number of Roman remains have been found in the Northover area as well as the ruins of a medieval barn. A few paces back over the river bridge brings one to the main village centre with its wealth of small shops, garages, hotels and restaurants and the inevitable antique shop – all one would need today whether traveller or resident, but a far cry from the 4th century walled town which by the 10th had its own mint and was to withstand a siege in the 11th.

A market town, indeed at one time the County town, it was visited periodically by the Sheriff and circuit judges, a factor which gave rise to the county jail in 1166 and the establishment of a midsummer fair by 1183. By the end of the 13th century Ilchester was sending two representatives to Parliament; a franchise which ceased in 1361, returned again in 1621, and was lost altogether with the passage of the Reform Bill, but not before the town could number among the members it has returned to Parliament one Richard Brinsley Sheridan, in 1807.

The riverside gaol which had gained so much notoriety over the years was finally closed in 1843 and today only parts of the laundry and bakehouse survive, the rest of the site now lies under a private garden. Royal manor, county town, centre of dairy farming land, Parliamentary seat. Ilchester has been all of these throughout the centuries. Consistently it has been a centre for transport. The Fosse Way, created by the Romans which made it a staging post; the River Ivel (or Yeo) which once brought barges up from Bridgwater and Langport to unload; the busy A303, for the last half century bringing London to the west country, and now, as time has removed the motorist to his by-pass, the Naval Air Station, all provide the modern link with its destiny.

Ilminster   Map 2 Bc

Queen Victoria slept here! The plaque on the 18th century frontage of the George Hotel proclaims the fact though to tell the truth she was really Princess Victoria when she and her mother lodged in the town.

The town was prosperous in the 18th century, trading in gloving and weaving. Today modern industry is still providing a fair share of wealth, for dairy products are made on the outskirts of the town as well as the important invention 'Minsterstone', which although associated with fireplaces, is a reconstituted stone which graces the façade of many an important modern building throughout the United Kingdom, all of it produced, moulded and carved on what was once a few acres of farmland west of the town.

The Minster – St Mary's parish church – on the River Isle (elsewhere translated to *ILE* as in the outlying villages of Ile Brewers and Ile Abbots) is believed to have been founded by King Ine in the 7th century. A lofty tower, beautifully carved parapet, rich tracery, pinnacles and other appendages all point to considerable affluence in the middle ages. To the north of the churchyard is the attractive area known as Court Barton with some 18th century houses of quality and even some thatch. The Chantry, formerly a school, is a Georgian house with some windows and a doorway from the 15th century. It lies in the north west corner of the churchyard.

The town centre, while not by-passed, has, thankfully, two through roads and wisely the transport authorities have restricted main road traffic to one of them – a necessary evil at busy times when enormous tankers and lorries are slowly struggling up the hill past the town's largest hotel. The ruse does, however, preserve the pretty market centre of local shops around the open sided Market Hall built in 1813. Eastwards of the centre runs the hill known as Lovers Lane.

A mile from the town, down a rustic approach road, lies Dillington House. The house is largely 19th century with a 17th century wing; it was home to the Speke family, and for a time home to Lord North after the park had been created in the 18th century. The house was much smaller then and was enlarged and remodelled in the 19th century, later becoming the home of the Vaughan-Lee family whose further extensive additions included the fine stables, an orangery and an arboretum. The stables have now been turned into a theatre complex, with bars and other facilities close at hand including a modern exhibition hall. The whole house is now a splendid Adult Education Centre run by Somerset County Council.

Further eastwards lies Seavington, in reality two separate villages each with its own church: St Mary's and St Michael's. Seavington St Mary is well known to motorists on the A303 for the hospitable Volunteer Inn and for the nearby complex of thatched cottages and farmhouse which some genius has turned into the combination of accommodation and first class restaurant known as The Pheasant.

Iron Acton   Map 4 Ba

A linear village – an early example of ribbon development
if you like but, for all that, the home of the Poyntz
family through the centuries. The ornate churchyard cross
is probably a memorial to one of the members of the
family, carrying shields and coats of arms. The family
home, Iron Acton Court, approached through an
equally elaborate archway, lies to the north of the village.
Built in the 16th century it is alleged that Sir Walter
Raleigh once walked in the gardens and had water thrown
over him while puffing on his new fangled pipe!

The Lamb Inn is of interest with its ancient bar. The
main street, narrow, but intriguing, leads to a
church which has been built on a raised site with a
striking tower and a lofty nave. Inside are more tombs
dedicated to members of the Poyntz family.

Keynsham   Map 4 Bb

The dominant sight at this once small settlement, situated
where the little river Chew gains the Avon, is the enormous
red brick chocolate factory which Cadbury took over
from the Quaker family, Fry.

In medieval times the town was a single street with a
market place at one end and an abbey at the other. In 1945 a
population of 7,000 was recorded – today it is some 25,000
and many new shops and supermarkets have been added.
The area has become less frenetic since the coming of the
by-pass in 1966 which siphoned off the main road traffic
from the Bath-Bristol road.

Keynsham Abbey has had a chequered history. It was
founded in about 1167, became a quarry after the
Dissolution and a mansion was built on the site. Today – if
anything remains – it is merely rubble lying under Abbey
Park. The parish church, however, has something more
positive to offer. There is a 13th century chancel with
lancet windows and a Gothic tower, built after a
thunderstorm had wrecked the original in 1632. There are a

L

number of interesting monuments within – some dating from Elizabethan times – and two fine screens.

The nearby village of Queen Charlton surrounds a small green which still has the shaft of an old cross standing on a stepped base. An 18th century manor house stands opposite a Norman arch which may have come from the church whose central tower and masonry are also Norman.

Langport   Map 2 Bb

The 15th century arch beneath the Hanging Chapel forms as imposing an entrance to any town you will find today. Through its single aperture (pedestrians beware!) the narrow road widens to accommodate the houses of the wealthy merchants of yesteryear, for here was 19th century opulence.

The church of All Saints has one of those soaring towers so typical of Somerset. It dates from the 15th century although it still retains a stone relief from the Norman church on the site. From the church and nearby convent the

The Hanging Chapel, Langport

L

hill sweeps steeply to meet Cheapside and Bow Street which were the main shopping areas until the building of a modern precinct and car park. Looking down the length of Bow Street the premises on either side seem to lean back slightly into the moors behind. At its far end the town terminates abruptly as the road crosses the River Parrett, the waterway which initially brought wealth to the town when it was navigable. Coal, lime, salt, fish and even woad came to the port. It was the river which gave inspiration and birth to the merchanting and banking enterprise of the Stuckeys and the Bagehots which dictated so much of Somerset's economy.

The Langport Arms Hotel is situated appropriately between the two banks but sadly its porch suffers from the occasional battle with one of the massive vehicles which attempt the narrow street.

Huish Episcopi, half a mile to the east, has a church partly of blue lias and partly Ham stone. To the south lies Muchelney, with the remains of the Benedictine **Muchelney Abbey** (Church Buildings) and a surviving Priest's House. Immediately adjoining is the parish church, noteworthy for its brilliantly painted wagon roof.

Long Ashton Map 4 Ab

The population of Long Ashton on the Bristol fringe has more than doubled in the last two decades. What it has gained in people and houses it has lost in traffic for the main road from the city which once led to Weston-super-Mare has been replaced with a by-pass. The old buildings which once lined the turnpike still remain and there is a shopping centre of adequate proportions. The town was originally an estate village belonging to **Ashton Court** (Historic Homes), home of the Smyth family through four centuries. The Court's parkland was purchased by Bristol City Council in 1959 thus preserving an open space for posterity. The Court itself has a frontage of over 300 feet – wide by any standard. The oldest part of the house is Elizabethan with later additions and there is a turreted gatehouse.

Nearby Long Ashton Observatory is a 20th century folly – thatched roof, dome and all! Of more importance to mankind today is the Long Ashton Research Station, a part of Bristol University. It is dedicated to agricultural research mainly concerned with fruit growing and preservation. Between Long Ashton and Clifton are Abbotsleigh Woods, with some of the finest walks in Avon.

The late medieval All Saints church has an altar stone of uncertain antiquity. Monuments to the Smyth family abound and there is a good screen, the family having been gracious benefactors. Also to be noted is the colourful tomb of Sir Richard Choke, one time Chief Justice of the Common Pleas. The buildings around the church include a 15th century barn and, in contrast, a Georgian farmhouse. At the top of Church Lane stands the appropriately named 'Angel Inn'. According to the records, it was given to the village as a Church House, conditional on the prayers of the villagers being dedicated to Sir Richard 'for ever more'. The wily souls must have had other ideas and grasped an opportunity for 'The Angel' has been their local pub for a couple of centuries!

Marshfield Map 4 Bb

Marshfield lies about two miles from Avon's eastern extremity, protesting as do many other villages, that it belongs to Gloucestershire. The village, clinging to a church that has some Norman fabric left, added what is now its High Street around 1260. Owing its prosperity to Cotswold wool, it soon became a borough and ultimately the fourth most prosperous town in Gloucestershire. A Toll House still stands opposite the Crispe Alms-houses at the west end, while to the east the small triangle that forms the Market lies cheek by jowl with the 17th century Manor House which has an 18th century façade.

Marshfield once stood on a main road and in consequence was noted for its inns, which, like so many of the buildings in the village, are 18th century. On Boxing Day each

year the Marshfield Mummers perform in the High Street.
Their play depicts the inevitable conflict between Good and
Evil with the local worthies who participate clad in
costumes made from strips of newspaper.

Martock   Map 2 Bc

Situated a little north of the busy A 303 on the plain
between the River Parrett and the River Yeo, Martock has a
curious charm of its own even if the long narrow main
street from the old, disused station to the market cross
contains too many parked cars for comfort.

There are many fine Ham-stone buildings. A particularly
beautiful example is the archway leading to the church. And
what a church! Large, kept by people who take a pride in
it – and its surroundings. Even the long rear walk through
the churchyard to the open fields beyond is well tended with
tall smart conifers keeping sentinel. Inside the roof, with
angel heads and tracery, is yet another of those glories
of Somerset. It was built around 1500 although parts of the
church date from about the 12th century.

Opposite the church stands the Treasurer's House, so
called because the rectory of Martock was once held by the
Treasurers of Wells Cathedral. Dating from the 13th
century it contains a medieval hall and wing with a kitchen
that was a later addition. To the west of the churchyard
are the remains of Martock's main manor house with its
moat. The present Manor House stands to the north and
was built in 1679. The Town Hall is Georgian. Outside
its portals stands the market cross looking very much like
a Roman remnant. Not so long ago it bit the dust after
an argument with a French lorry but it was swiftly restored
in the interest of L'Entente Cordiale!

Martock appears to straggle but the Ham-stone
dwellings, be they 18th century houses or mere cottages,
are solidly built. In the 'suburb' of Bower Hinton there is a
splendid 17th century house known as The Hollies, now
used as a restaurant. At the extreme northern end of
Martock the old station yards house local industry including

M

a famous maker of portable wooden sheds that have been erected all over England as garages, stables or (as they started life) chicken runs.

Nearby Ash is known for the Bell Inn to which musicians travel from all over the country for its justly famed jazz sessions. The village consists of cottages, some modern dwellings and a church built between 1840 and 1887 with a tower added as a memorial to those who fell in the 1914-1918 War.

To the north the village of Long Sutton has an important church built in about 1490 in typical Somerset style – a wagon roof in the chancel, angel supports in the nave. The Manor House is 17th century and the unusual corner site on the main road is dignified by the Friend's Meeting House. The early Tudor Court House contains the curiously named Spigurnel Hall which has a collar beamed roof and once even boasted a minstrel's gallery. About a mile away the delightful little hamlet of Knowle possesses a group of houses, cottages and farms, many of them thatched, as well as a water wheel set amidst orchards.

Allerford, Minehead

Minehead   Map 1 Ba

A hillside village clings to the slopes and clusters round its
church with seafarer's cottages and a harbour below.
To the east lies a marshy area which is now a holiday camp.
Link the two to a considerable town – this is modern
Minehead, a popular holiday resort and retirement area.

Minehead became an important port in the 15th century
trading with Ireland in stock and wool. It was the Welsh,
however, who provided the name *mynydd* or hill on which
St Michael's church stands. The church, beautifully
decorated and maintained, dates mainly from the 15th and
16th centuries, its high tower, standing 900 feet
from the sea, a landmark for sailors. Bathing began in
the 18th century; the railway came from Watchet in 1874
and, although it disappeared under the 'Beeching axe' in
1971 it reopened in 1976 as the **West Somerset
Railway** (Railways), the longest privately owned railway
in the country. Although the Gaiety Theatre is but a
memory the modern seafront and Blenheim Gardens still
exude the charm of yesteryear when Pavlova graced the
stage of the Queen's Hall.

Westwards, towards Greenaleigh Point, are the remains
of Burgundy Chapel. Bratton Court, one mile west of
Minehead, is a 15th century manor house. To the east,
Carhampton possesses a very fine rood screen in its
red sandstone church.

Montacute   Map 3 Ac

A real village inn, the King's Arms, resplendant in an ivy
'cosy', nestles beneath St Catherine's Church with its fine
15th century tower, Norman chancel and the monuments to
the Phelips family who owned much of the village.
Sir Edward Phelips – a successful lawyer, Speaker of the
House of Commons (1604) and Master of the Rolls (1611) –
built the main attraction, **Montacute House** (Historic
Homes). It was not until 1931 that the family sold the

M

House to the Society for the Preservation of Ancient Buildings who have been succeeded by the National Trust.

An almost entirely Ham-stone village surrounds the main square, 'The Borough', in which, appropriately, lies the Phelips Arms close by the public entrance to Montacute House. The late 16th century mansion is perfection, both in its setting and internally. Here can be found splendid plasterwork, paintings, tapestries, heraldry, panelling and period furniture. The paved, terraced gardens have a calm dignity and the well trimmed yew trees and low walls frame the well proportioned lawns. Statues on the terrace peer out over this setting with obvious satisfaction.

Two miles away is Tintinhull, a small suburban village with an early 13th century church, St Margaret's, which has much 15th century work. **Tintinhull House** (Gardens) (NT) is a jewel in a village cluster that includes nearby Tintinhull Court, a largely Jacobean residence though it still contains some 16th century features; and the Dower House, late 17th century. All are in that same warm Ham stone.

Montacute House

Norton St. Philip   Map 3 Ba

In the Middle Ages the village was an important collecting point for Mendip wool. Today's tourist comes to view, and no doubt photograph, the picturesque George Inn which dates from the 15th century and is a most interesting hostelry. The stone built walls of the ground floor support two storeys, half-timbered, which overhang. The roof above is of stone slate; underneath it, there was room to accommodate guests, several to a bed in earlier times. An elaborate central archway leads to the rear while the façade is completed by an external staircase and gallery. The Duke of Monmouth made his headquarters here during the battle on 27 June 1685.

The ubiquitous Samuel Pepy's called at the inn in 1668 and remarked 'dined well, 10s'. The Carthusian monks of Hinton built the inn in the 13th century to use as a monks' hostel until completion of the Priory at nearby Hinton Charterhouse. The inn was subsequently used as a guest house, for the Priory farmed sheep and needed to entertain merchants coming to the August cloth market. At that time of year the upper floors of the George would be crammed with stock and samples from the Priory.

Inside, harnesses, copper warming pans and various other objects hang from high beams. The lead musket ball lodged in one of the oak beams is said to have been fired in 1685 by a bounty hunter who was after the Duke of Monmouth.

Interest in the George Inn can detract from the church lying at the foot of the hill which can be reached by a stroll over the fields behind the hostelry. The tower, in Somerset perpendicular, was given by a rich merchant of Norton, and while most of the building is 15th century the south doorway seems to go back to the thirteenth. Stone from the Priory at Hinton may well have been incorporated in the church fabric.

Opposite the church the school building of 1827 has some interesting pinnacles while a little to the west a 17th century house has an outhouse with oval windows.

N

Nunney Map 3 Ba

The Nunney Brook, used in cloth making days as a
'pavement place to wash wool', runs beside the solid
looking, though hollow **Nunney Castle** built by
St John de la Mare who crenellated it in 1373. Though it
ceased to be a residence after the Civil War it still stands
with its four drum towers dominating the village. North
west of the castle Manor Farm is early eighteenth century
with a graceful façade. The church of All Saints, almost
entirely rebuilt in the nineteenth century, still has a
thirteenth century chancel but the fifteenth-century wagon
roof disappeared in the 1950's because of death
watch beetle.

There are a number of dated houses ranging from 1693
to 1744. A good inn, village stores and post office complete a
quaint village that, of recent years, has had its fair share
of new houses.

Nunney Castle

Pensford Map 4 Bb

On the little River Chew – a river that became so large in 1968 that it swept away the road bridge while, ironically, leaving untouched the massive railway viaduct which had not carried a passenger since 1959.

From this viaduct the walker can look down on the village of Pensford below with its coaching inn, a medieval bridge that was brought into use when the floods overtook the new road bridge (now rebuilt), the interesting Bridge House and the church of St Thomas à Becket which is surrounded, moat like, by a split in the Chew. Here exhibitions and various meetings are held for the church has not been used as such since the flood which caused so much chaos within the small village which lies on the main road into Bristol from the south. That flood level reaching many of the bedroom windows is marked on the corner of the main road and Church Street. It is still a talking point with the older villagers, although many of today's occupants are commuters from the Bristol area. Also standing is the 18th century lock-up, a fine example of its kind.

Once the industry was mining and the Miner's Institute still stands although the prosperous origins of the village go back to the water power that enabled its early settlers to set up their looms.

A Mendip village at heart, its best known son is neither peer nor landowner but a musician known to all and sundry as Acker Bilk.

Pilton Map 3 Ab

This attractive village has a vineyard attached to a chateau which seems more French than many seen in France. This manor was one of the summer houses of the Abbots of Glastonbury and has a turret which still shows traces of medieval work. Sixteenth century mullions prevail at the rear although much of the façade is Georgian. A square dovecote, vaulted cellar and arches belonging to a cloister

P

are further evidence of a Glastonbury presence. **Pilton Manor Vineyard** was founded by an Abbot who saw the advantages of the protective slopes of the Pennard Ridge. Today it is well stocked with Muller-Thurgau vines.

An imposing church stands close to the manor house. The magnificent Somerset tower was begun in the 13th century and finished in the 15th. There is a glorious 15th century timbered roof with painted angels whose wings spread over the beams. A hundred pieces of oak panel the chancel and the fine windows contain some original glass.

Across the A361, away from precipitous Pilton, as one historian has described it, lies another vineyard of local renown – **North Wootton Vineyard**. The village of North Wootton with its small 15th century church and rustic bridge may be off the beaten track but a local hostelry, the Crossways, has a reputation for good, inexpensive pub food which has spread far and wide.

Pilton Manor Vineyard

P

Porlock   Map 1 Aa

The view across Porlock Bay from a spot near Porlock's
somewhat notorious hill is probably one of the most
photographed scenes in the south of England after Gold Hill
in Shaftesbury. Both the ascent and descent of the hill are
dangerous (in places the gradients are 1 in 4) as you would
expect of a rise of 1,350 feet in under 3 miles.

Porlock lost the top of the shingled spire of its church
during a thunderstorm in the 17th century. St Dubricius
is its delightful name dedicated to the Celtic saint, also
known as St Dyfrig, and it dates back to the 13th century.
Inside is a monument to Sir John Harington, knighted on
the field of Agincourt by Henry V, and an Easter Sepulchre.

Sheltering under Exmoor's northern slope, Porlock
enjoys an equable climate and unashamedly caters for its
tourists. The Ship Inn, useful shops, and groups of
cottages, blend well with the remains of the 15th century
Manor House called Doverhay, which now serves as the
information centre during the summer months. The
Saxon name of the village meant 'enclosure by the harbour'
though the latter is now difficult to trace. The cluster of
small cottages and hotel beside a patch of shingle about a
mile away distinguish themselves by the name of Porlock
Weir, a later development. It is difficult to imagine that
imports of salt, limestone, fish and cloth were once
landed at this tranquil spot, much less transported away
over the rising ground.

From Porlock Weir a toll road leads towards Culbone,
where, in a wooded valley, stands possibly the smallest
parish church in England, only 35 feet long, with a tiny
slated spire that looks like the missing tip from
St Dubricius back in Porlock.

Priddy   Map 3 Aa

Hurdles for Mendip sheep stand, stacked, on the village
green. With a thatch on top they look like a medieval
peasant's dwelling or primitive hut. Stone walls take the
place of hedges around this, the highest village in Somerset,

P

indeed, one of the highest in England. To the north of the village lies the **Priddy Nine Barrows** (Archaeological Sites), four large earthwork rings which are a complete mystery. Past the old lead mines en route for the Miners Arms is Priddy Pool, set among the pine trees. No indigenous miner will be found in the hostelry, however, for today it is an epicurean restaurant of no little acclaim with Mendip snails a feature of the menu.

The village church has a 13th century tower and 14th century windows. Beyond its weather worn bulk, through a winding combe, lies one of the most enchanting caves in the Mendips, Swildons Hole. But pot holers beware, this is strictly one for the professionals.

One of the many attractions which enhance this remote dip in the Mendip plateau is the annual **Sheep Fair** (Events), held in August. Hundreds come to participate and many will take the opportunity to wander off and take in the view from Deer Leap. One of the best in the county, it takes in Exmoor, the coast, most of south and east Somerset right round to the Wiltshire border and beyond – given a clear day!

Pucklechurch   Map 4 Bb

Translated as Purcelas' church, it was owned by Glastonbury Abbey from AD 950 until the reign of King John and was then taken over, in exchange by the Bishops of Bath and Wells until the Crown stepped in and forcibly acquired it in the 16th century.

In the 18th century Pucklechurch produced coal, black marble (now only seen on old gravestones) and felt hats, and despite being in the Bristol 'fringe' retains an independent village aura. Around the 13th century church of St Thomas there are clusters of grey stone cottages and 17th century houses connected with the Dennis family who lived in the Grey House and who were responsible for the building of Syston Court, a 16th century mansion now divided into separate dwellings, in the village of Syston to the south west.

Q

The Quantocks Map 2 Ab

The Quantocks take their name from the Celts who saw
them as a circle, or rim, of hills. Today they are
designated as an area of outstanding natural beauty
associated with Wordsworth and Coleridge. Softer, more
intimate and secretive than Exmoor, they still remain
ideal walking country with breathtaking views across to
Taunton Deane and out over the Bristol Channel to Wales.

The red deer are still at home here, cheek by jowl with
the sheep, cattle and horses that graze among the fern
brakes and the beeches that line the prehistoric ridgeway.

North of Taunton is Kingston St Mary. The village gave
its name to a cider apple. North of the Elizabethan
Manor House and the exquisitely pinnacled church tower
the land climbs steeply away. Eastwards is Thurloxton,
with its medieval church, restored in 1868. Goathurst has a
sandstone church tower of 14th century origin and
Halswell House, built in 1689, with its temples and grottos
is one of the most important houses of its age in the country.

A little to the west of Goathurst, at Broomfield, lies
Ruborough Camp, above the Traveller's Rest Inn. Here
amidst heather and bracken is a well preserved Iron Age
earthwork, while in the broken hill country of Bagborough
the views extend in all directions. The church here is
15th century and is set in the parkland of Bagborough
House, itself late Georgian with a colonaded front.
Triscombe House, about a mile away, is also late Georgian,
remodelled this century by Sir Ernest Newton. Above is
the Triscombe Stone, a local landmark on the way to
Will's Neck, the highest point in the Quantocks.

There is a beautiful Jacobean manor house at
Cothelstone, on the southern side of the hills. A small
village, there are several old cottages with preserved
Elizabethan plasterwork although the folly tower on
Cothelstone Beacon is now a ruin.

Alfoxden Park (now a hotel) sits in one of the most
delightful of the Quantock glens on the outskirts of the
village of Holford where Wordsworth lived. Old cottages

S

mix with new in a village that was once on the busy
Minehead Road, now bypassed, as is Nether Stowey with
its restored church. Stowey Court, nearby, goes back to the
14th century, possessing an 18th century gazebo,
visible from the road. Good cottages abound, notably
Coleridge Cottage (Historic Homes) (now a National Trust
Property) where S. T. Coleridge wrote *The Ancient
Mariner* and the first part of *Christabel*. There is a peculiar
wooden clock tower built in 1897 to commemorate
Queen Victoria's Diamond Jubilee. High above the village
almost 1,000 feet up lies another Iron Age earth work,
Danesborough Camp.

Further into the hills among the pines is Over Stowey.
Coleridge frequently walked over the hill to Bicknoller with
its views towards the Brendons and the Blackdown Hills.
Bicknoller's church not only has a fine rood screen
but the bench ends are carved with a wealth of detail. The
inn which refreshed the poet and his friends still
dispenses good hospitality.

Crowcombe is also famed for the bench ends in its
14th century church with its fine font and beautiful screen.
South west of the church, Church House has an early
Tudor doorway and Jacobean windows while Crowcombe
Court, begun in 1725, is one of the loveliest houses in
Somerset. A mile to the west is Halsway Manor which,
although almost entirely a rebuild of the 19th century,
appears old, embattled and pinnacled in a delightful setting.

Almost on the coast, West Quantoxhead, known
locally as St Audries, has a Victorian Tudor-style mansion
which is now a school with an attendant modern church.
Its neighbour, East Quantoxhead, is at the end of a
lane that winds down almost to the waters edge and stops
by the village pond, farm, church and Court House, home
of the Luttrell family for the last 600 years.

Saltford   Map 4 Bb

Situated in the Avon valley between Keynsham and Bath,
in urbanised commuter land Saltford still has the nucleus

of an old village, but really comes into its own for those who love boats. An old brass mill by the weir is now part of the boat yard used by many of the craft that sail the Avon and hereabouts. In the area known as the Shallows there are pleasant riverside walks with an inevitable Jolly Sailor Inn.

Isambard Kingdom Brunel's former Great Western Railway tunnels run beneath the village – indeed Tunnel House in the High Street is an apt description for the trains still pass underneath on their way between Bath and Bristol.

A manor house situated next to the village church is said to be one of the oldest inhabited buildings in Britain. Although the front is 17th century, its origins are Norman in common with the church. A large carved lion crouches on a roof ridge, seemingly guarding the treasures – which include a large wall painting, circa 1200, and some magnificent ceiling beams.

Sedgemoor   Map 2 Bb

The last battle on English soil was fought in this beautiful water flatland in the field of Chedzoy and Westonzoyland. The Bussex Rhine, tactical ally to the winning side during the Monmouth Rebellion, has long since been filled in, but from higher ground one can still gaze down on the King's Sedgemoor Drain (cut in the 1790s) and the many other rhines or drains. Nearest to the scene of the battle which is marked by a stone at the end of a track lies the village of Westonzoyland. The church, with its magnificent 100 foot tower has a sad history for in it were imprisoned many of Monmouth's soldiers after his battle was lost. The church records contain an account of that battle fought on July 6th, 1685, from which we learn that the prisoners numbered about 500 while some 300 were killed on the spot. Two men were paid to clean up and it is recorded that frankincense and saltpetre were used to fumigate.

The Sedgemoor area was shared in the Middle Ages

S

largely between the monks of Glastonbury, Wells, Muchelney and Athelney. Known as the Somerset levels much of the area was almost submerged until drainage was started in the Middle Ages.

To the south, the Isle of Athelney rises from the willow covered country adjacent to the banks of the Tone. Osiers grow, so basket weavers flourish beside the main road to Taunton. Focal point of the Isle is the cottage lined village of Athelney. Above the village of Burrowbridge lies the aptly named Burrow Mump, surmounted by the ruined St Michael's Church. Its successor was built below in the early 19th century and Burrow Mump itself, now administered by the National Trust, stands as a memorial to the men of Somerset who did not return from the first World War.

Inevitably the local hostelry is blessed with the name of King Alfred. Supposedly he had a fort nearby and the persistent legend of the burning of the cakes during his altercation with the Danes is still perpetuated – and why not? The monument commemorating the occasion is a modest granite stone which was erected in 1801. It stands high in a field surrounded by railings to protect it from modern invaders, proud of the waters which occasionally return to remind us and all who dwell among the withy beds and cattle grazing country that this was once the sea.

A little to the south in a fertile belt of pasture stands the village of Stoke St Gregory. A good 13th and 15th century church has some Jacobean carving and a pre-Reformation pulpit. Elsewhere there is an interesting farm, Tudor, with its own moat.

Selworthy   Map 1 Ba

Photographs of this lovely village appear on table mats, calendars, picture postcards and magazine covers. A few thatched cottages surround a pretty green beneath a wooded hillside that protects it from the sea. You can see the Exmoor hills and Dunkery Beacon from the green.

Making further use of the theatrical setting the
16th century church stands like the icing on the Selworthy
cake – completely white. In keeping with its appearance the
wagon roof within is one of Somerset's finest, richly
decorated with shields and angels. A stone tithe barn,
the remains of a 16th century cross and a dovecot
complete a picture which can be left behind by ascending
the path beside the church to Selworthy Beacon, itself
rising 1,013 feet above the sea.

In the same area the pack horse bridge, high arched over
a forge, is Allerford's claim to fame. Less well known,
but, if anything, more exciting, is Bossington, lying at the
foot of the great coastal hill below Hurlstone Point with its
walnut trees, curious stone pillars and high reaching
chimneys (to raise the level of log fire smoke above cottage
level). A small stream makes its way to the sea, smoothing
over the beach whose rounded rocks now grace many of
the cottage walls and porches in this unique area which is
now cared for by the National Trust.

Shepton Mallet Map 3 Aa

Architecturally the redeeming features of this town upon
the Fosse Way are the fine Market Cross and one of
the best of the wool churches. Industrially its present day
claim to fame must lie in the invention of 'Babycham' by the
cider making Showering family. Standing high on the
modern factory with its storage tanks and empty crates
is the enormous chamois – or, at least, a stylised
version of the creature which adorns beer mats and bottles
all over the country.

Lying close to the very edge of the Mendips, the town's
foundation was based on the wool which, by the
14th century, had brought a considerable prosperity. It was
a prosperity that was to last until the silk manufacturers
replaced the woollen weaving in the early 19th century
and it is quite co-incidental that the World Sheep
Shearing Competition is held annually on the nearby site of
the once peripatetic Royal Bath and West Show. So much

S

for Shepton, the sheeptown. As to the Malet in the title, the Malet family are recorded as having held Shepton in the 12th century from the Abbey of Glastonbury. By the 15th century the town was in the hands of the Duchy of Cornwall.

The landmark which must guide any traveller from the north today must be the great mid 19th century viaduct which all but towers over the town with its 27 rock faced arches striding over the main road and the Showering Gardens. Once it carried the Somerset and Dorset railway, linking the Midlands, via Bath, with Bournemouth. The railway was known locally as the 'Slow and Dirty' until it came under the threat of the Beeching Axe, when the conservationists saw fit to give it the more up market soubriquet of 'Serene and Delightful'!

Below the viaduct, as the valley rises steeply into the town, the church of 11th century origin contains an enormous waggon roof with 36 angel supporters and over 300 carved oak panels, no two of which are alike. This, proof of the prosperity brought by wool, is accompanied by a pulpit cut from one solid piece of stone, presumed to have come from the nearby quarries at Doulting in the Mendips. Both roof and pulpit are of the 15th century. The church is rather hidden from the centre of the town where, by courtesy of a member of the Showering family, a new shop development, flats, and a large entertainment complex have been built at the end of a new courtyard or precinct. In the precinct are some of the preserved remains of the medieval shambles or market stalls as well as the Market Cross, a delicate edifice built in 1500 and endowed by Walter and Agnes Buklond. An inscription beseeches us to pray for their souls.

On Cornhill stands the sinister looking entrance to Shepton Mallet's famous gaol, for some time an Army 'glasshouse'. Its forbidding walls look out over little streets with curious names like The Batch and Cat's Ash, leading into Pike Lane and Zion Hill. In nearby Lower Lane stands The Crown Hotel of 1800 while in Draycott, beside the Sheppey or Doulting Water, to give the town's brook and original source of power its real name, stand Monmouth House, Sales House with its Tuscan Collonade, and the Old Silk Mill built in 1800.

Above them all rests the imposing looking building known to this day as the Anglo-Bavarian Brewery which in its heyday produced lager beer – today it operates as trading estate offices.

Nowadays all liquid refreshment comes from the opposite end of the town. Garston Street, where one Francis Showering was listed as a beer seller, leads to Kilver Street – the growth of a family business has been the transformation of a considerable part of Shepton Mallet.

Which is, more or less, where we came in.

Two miles south of Shepton Mallet is the 65 acre showground, permanent home since 1965 of the agriculturally based Royal Bath and West and Southern Counties Society which was originally founded in the city of Bath in 1777. The **annual show**, which lasts four days, often under Royal Patronage, takes a year to mount and brings farmers and pleasure seekers from all over the south west of England as well as stall holders and fair ground operators from all over the country.

Croscombe, west of Shepton and further up the river valley has a church of Doulting Stone with a spire instead of the usual Somerset tower. The rood screen, bench ends and pulpit are all superb examples of the Jacobean wood carver's art.

North is **Oakhill Manor** a 19th century tudor-style house standing 700 feet above sea-level. Visitors ride the ¾m though the grounds to the house in an open carriage steam train.

Somerton   Map 3 Ab

'Ancient capital of Wessex' they claim here, in this village of many inns, small select shops and surprisingly, a very large and busy bookseller. The largest inn, once the Ilchester Arms, now the Red Lion, still boasts that it is

S

'licensed to let post horses'. It also sports the arms of
Fox-Strangeways.

An appropriate market place has a battlemented
17th century market cross facing a square. It is surrounded
by the old Town Hall, Georgian houses and the
occasional Ham-stone mullioned window are set in among
the blue lias stone and crowned by the churchyard and
church on the north side.

St Michael's Church, a mixture of several building ages,
has a fine 15th century roof although the church dates from
the early 13th century. It is a building full of riches.

Broad Street, wide and dignified, is tree lined like a
French boulevard. Notable buildings in the vicinity
include the Old Parsonage with its 17th century façade and
oriel window, Somerton Court, a large house with a
fine porch and mullioned windows dating from 1641, while
the Hext Almshouses of 1626 have unusual windows set
in deep niches, where the aging inhabitants sometimes sit,
to enjoy life and wish good morning to the passer by.

Somerton Cross

At nearby Compton Dundon, Dundon Beacon rises to almost 300 feet from the moors. On its summit there is an iron age camp with stone walls, some of which are 10 feet high. Across Compton village with its charming old houses of local stone lies Dundon's early 14th century church with its fragments of medieval glass.

Four miles to the south of Somerton, Lyte's Cary was the home of the Lyte family for over 500 years after the building of the first dwelling on the site by William de Lyte, a law officer to Edward 1st. Two 16th century oriels carved from Ham stone rest beneath swan and gryphon finialled gables. Many of the Lytes were botanists and the most famous of them all, Henry, created the present garden and published the work known as Lyte's Herbal in 1578. Copies of some of the pages are on view in the Oriel Room.

The house fell into decay during the 18th century to be rescued by Sir Walter Jenner, son of the famous physician, in 1907. He restored the house and grounds laying out the forecourt in Elizabethan fashion, the yew alley being a distinctive feature. The building is in the care of the National Trust.

South Cadbury Map 3 Ab

The great fort of **Cadbury Castle** (Archaeological Sites) towers over the village. Some would have it that this was King Arthur's Camelot and excavations have been made to seek evidence. The Iron Age earthwork is situated at the top of a mile long stony track, the banks of which are a mass of primroses during the spring months. Turn back from time to time and gaze at the unfolding panorama of the village and countryside below – then, upon arrival, gaze at the total view all around from the height of the great fort, the area of which must be all of fifteen acres.

Succeeding ages have used the site since Neolithic times. The finds include pottery and weapons from the Dark Ages, although it was the Iron Age Briton who first palisaded the great ramparts and created the defending

S

ditches before the Roman conquest. Certainly this is one of
the most important archaeological sites in the country.
The village below is not without interest either. At the
base of the lane leading to the hill fort lies Castle Farm, with
mullioned windows, bearing the date 1687. Other pleasant
houses in stone complement the hill, including the
18th century Rectory, older than the outer fabric of a
church that was largely rebuilt in 1835.

Across the nearby A303, a modern road of which the
Romans would have approved, lies North Cadbury with a
church that looks as if it had grown out of the neighbouring
Cadbury Court. The Court is Elizabethan and possesses
some fine heraldic stained glass from 1580 while the
added stables date from 1715. The date given on some of
the bench ends in the church is 1538, however, and a
close look at the rich dark wood will reveal a cat and mouse,
dragons, a windmill, and even a man leading a horse.
Away from all the manorial finery, past some good stone
houses lies the village inn with the unusual name
of 'Catash'.

Stanton Drew Map 4 Bb

The little village of Stanton Drew, with its handful of
inhabitants and solid 18th and 19th century houses
standing where roads cross in the village, has a greater
claim to fame than its little church or the intriguing
thatched toll house.

It is the site of one of the most important prehistoric
remains in England, the famous **Stanton Drew Circles**
(Archaeological Sites). The three circles beside the
River Chew date from the Bronze Age and are made up
from three kinds of stone, each being approximately
six feet in height. The stones were brought from the
nearby Harptrees and Dundry, high above Bristol.

Legend has it that the stones should not be counted or
drawn lest harm immediately befall the perpetrator. Clearly
the legend originated long before the invention of
photography otherwise you would not be reading these

words. The 27 stones stand in a field adjacent to a farm, the largest circle being some 350 feet in diameter. They rank as the finest Stone Age monument in Wessex.

Stoneaston   Map 4 Bc

Just off the A37 road from Wells to Bristol the little village of Stoneaston has little to commend it save the fine English country house in Stoneaston Park.

Listed as a Grade 1 Palladian mansion it contains some of the most exceptional architectural and decorative features of the period to be found in the west country. More extraordinary is the fact that a few years ago the property was condemned to demolition, lead had been stripped from sections of the roof, and considerable effort and money was needed to effect restoration.

The house, as seen today, was started in 1739 for the Hippisley family, one of the larger Somerset landowners. The restoration was started by William Rees-Mogg during his tenure of the Editor's chair at The Times. Since his departure the renewed efforts of the Smedly family have transformed the building to almost all its former glory so that it presents a rare glimpse into the 'Upstairs, Downstairs' world of the 18th century. Although the building functions as a first class hotel today, visitors and guests are invited to view 'Downstairs' – the early kitchens, a fine linen room, servants hall, billiard room and wine cellars – all in use again.

Stratton on the Fosse   Map 3 Aa

The church of St Vigar was extensively rebuilt in several stages in the 18th century. Its most unusual feature, an organ that was built for George IV and came from Brighton Pavilion, was sold to the U.S.A. some years ago. The Benedictine monks of Douai who, after leaving England and Wales during the Reformation were forced to

S

return from Douai University after suppression during the French Revolution, had settled at Stratton on the Roman Fosse Way by 1814, buying the 17th century mansion of Mount Pleasant.

Since then the monastic and school buildings have proliferated. The great Abbey church, larger than Truro's cathedral, was built between 1870 and 1938 in a neo-Gothic style with a tower which rises a full 166 feet and is somehow akin to the Somerset perpendicular tradition even if the French influence seems to assert itself internally with its rib vaulting, colourful windows, statuary and paintings. The seven chapels contain collected works of art of diverse origin. The Adoration of the Magi, a 16th century triptych, hangs in Holy Angels chapel and is Flemish. A statue of the Madonna (Spanish) and a copy of the statue of the Notre Dame de For from Dinant, Belgium, are to be found in the St Placid Chapel. Equally interesting paintings and pieces are to be found in the St Sebastian, Sacred Heart, Our Lady and St Benedict chapels.

The community is about 50 strong today with over 500 boys present during term. The church is open to the public and can be approached by a small lane.

Street Map 3 Ab

At first glance a trip up the High Street may suggest that the town is a little off balance for it seems to retain more than a normal quota of shoe shops – shops selling quality shoes, mass produced shoes, 'seconds', and even rejects – the footwear emporia judiciously spaced between the normal requirements of any village that has developed into a sizeable town. The growth of footwear and the town is entirely due to the presence over the last hundred and fifty years of one Quaker family, the Clarks, whose first factory and Friends Meeting House stand almost side by side.

The factory was started in 1829 after the successes when one Cyrus Clark joined his brother James to produce sheepskin rugs and slippers. It was a venture that was to ensure the family's fortune and philanthropy and the wellbeing of the many employees who have also prospered. The factory stands today, one of many, and it is distinguished by a clock tower at the factory gate. It was erected in 1897 and now houses the **Street Shoe Museum** which traces the development of the shoe from the Roman sandal to the present day. There is a large bronze statue by Sir Henry Moore on the front lawn in front of the factory.

Opposite the entrance stands a temperance hotel, built in 1894, the same year as the Crispin Hall.

The town was a settlement in Roman times, indeed the Romans gave the name of it to the track which ran to the east of the town where the Parish church now stands. Now known as Holy Trinity, it is a 13th century building once dedicated to St Gildas, a figure from Welsh monastic circles.

Near to the church is the modern Strode College complex, complete with a most active theatre, while a little further south east the world renowned Millfield School lies with its lecture halls, library, workshops, and sports facilities, centred round the memorial house built by William Stephens Clark in 1889.

Taunton Map 2 Ab

The town on the Tone – the centre of the fertile area of Taunton Deane, and administrative home of the county. An ancient castle, central market, busy rail junction and high class hotels set the seal on its importance through the ages. As a town and a market the origins are Saxon. The Castle was built in Norman times with 13th, 17th and 18th century additions. Approached through the archway known as Castle Bow, almost hidden between an electricity board showroom and a multiple tailor's shop, the Castle is now the home of the Somerset Archaeological and Natural History society and the important **Somerset County Museum**. The Great Hall, now rebuilt, was the scene of one of Lord Chief Justice Jeffrey's 'Bloody Assizes'

T

of 1685 after the Battle of Sedgemoor. Here 500 supporters of the Duke of Monmouth were arraigned.

Taunton's history has often been vicious and cruel and yet has left the town with many fine buildings and pleasant streets of which none is more surprising or delightful than the intriguing Bath Place, which is all but hidden from the High Street (now a shopping precinct) by a low arch and dark passage. This long street with most attractive low bow-fronted windows displaying the wares of antique shops, craft shops, the Women's Institute market and even dainty lingerie, emerges to face County Hall, an imposing building opened in 1936 when the County Council was transferred from Weston-super-Mare. Rising behind it the Shire Hall of 1855 seems to pout, in Tudor style, at the contemporary concrete and glass extension of local government buildings which crouch alongside.

In nearby Corporation Street which runs parallel to

River Bridge, Taunton

Bath Place are the Municipal Buildings which sprang from a Grammar School built in 1480. Further Tudor style alterations were made at the beginning of this century while at the same time a public library was built opposite to complement the whole. The town's Information Centre lies within the library complex.

Turning the corner, back into High Street, a stroll through the shopping centre, now pleasantly laid out with trees and bench seats from which one can gaze at what is left of some fine Georgian architecture, brings one to the ornate Victorian gateway of Vivary Park, so called because it was here that the Bishops of Winchester, who once had Taunton in their charge, had their vivarium – two great pools maintained for the storage of their fish. The original streams that ran into the river Tone from its tributary, the Blackbrook, once flowed through the now pleasant Vivary Park with its Victorian Bandstand continuing down the High Street and serving the market square at the bottom.

In that square – in truth it is a triangle each side of which is known as Fore Street – the Market House was built in 1770 opposite the gabled and timbered Tudor House which was refronted in 1578 and is the oldest house in Taunton because inside its structure is 14th century. It belonged to Sir William Portman who had custody of the Duke of Monmouth for his last journey to London. The rest of the triangle housed market stalls. Today the stalls have long since disappeared giving way to flower beds and a refuge for pedestrians from the three-sided traffic flow. At right angles to the eastern edge of Fore Street, one Sir Benjamin Hammet laid out the splendid Georgian street, named after him, the better to approach and view the imposing red sandstone west tower of St Mary Magdalene, rebuilt in 1862 when it was found to be unsafe.

Purists need have no fear, for the reconstruction of this great perpendicular tower was carried out stone by stone to be an exact replica of the original. The tracery and pinnacles are exquisite in their workmanship and the

T

three tiers each have twin three light windows – all of which gives a fine lacelike effect that is enchanting. The interior of the church, built at the end of the 11th century by the town's prosperous clothiers, contains some interesting memorial tablets and there is a tomb chest in the churchyard of early Tudor date. The churchyard must be one of the busiest in the kingdom for it is a direct short cut from a large municipal car park through to Hammet Street and the town's many shopping centres, including the brand new 'Old Market'!

St James, a hundred yards or so away, also has a lofty tower, a vantage point for the saints, if not the clergy, to stare down into the County Cricket Ground by which it stands. The font here is 15th century and there is some 18th century stained glass. Close to hand, opposite the shopping precinct known as the Courtyard set in the intriguingly named Coal Orchard stands The Brewhouse Theatre and Arts Centre which was first conceived by the town's citizens in 1964 and saw the light of day when public and private subscription so allowed in 1977. With an imposing and well planned auditorium and stage as well as the appropriate technical facilities there is a restaurant, buffet, and bar which are open to the general public outside of performance hours, and frequently art exhibitions are held in the gallery alongside the theatre.

Bridge Street, north of the Tone bridge, is an interesting shopping area leading to the station and the town's twin cinemas. Here are craft shops, ironmongers, fruit stalls and many other shops that are 'local' in character. This side of the river lies Taunton's British Rail Station worthy of mention. It stands on what was once the Great Western Railway line from Paddington to Exeter and Penzance but here the line up from the extreme west divides and it is also possible to catch a train to Wales, the Midlands or the far north of England. In that, it is possibly the most efficient single central station in the whole of England. A splendid enquiry and continental booking office has just been added to it.

North Street, running back from the river bridge, is

another traditional shopping centre with a large
department store and a main post office. At the top of North
Street, but with its main entrance on Castle Green,
stands the Castle Hotel, a building of some historic
importance and one which is still run as a local family
concern although it markets its amenities world wide and is
renowned for its 'salon' type of entertainment at weekends.

Taunton is noted for its schools, most of which were
established and built in the 19th century although
their respective styles would belie this. Queen's School
is imitation Tudor, while King's and Taunton both
have Gothic pretensions.

On the road from Ilminster, or off the Motorway – for
Taunton can now be bypassed on the M5 – stands a
low thatched building known as St Margaret's. Now
the busy headquarters of the Somerset Rural
Community Council, it was once a hospital for the care
of people with skin disorders.

North of the town, the village of Norton Fitzwarren has a
19th century church that has retained its medieval tower
and 14th century chancel screen. There are some rich
carvings to be found, evidence of the craftsmanship that is
ever present in the west country. Norton Court, built
around 1600, stands nearby. The most striking evidence of
local craftsmanship lies in this village where the
cider makers art is still recognised in the colour of the
buildings. Some would describe the decoration on the
walls as ochre in colour. Those who are better informed
know it to be 'Taunton Gold' for many of the buildings
are the property of a famous cider company and the
colour can even be found on their stationery.

Trull, all but part of Taunton, but nevertheless a village
of status, has much of its original 13th century church
still standing. Splendid carvings are to be found
on pulpit and bench ends and 15th century stained glass
still exists. A mid 16th-century house stands in nearby
Poundisford Park (Historic Homes). Although additions
were made in both the 17th and 18th centuries some
of the detail goes back to the time of Henry VIII.

T

Thornbury   Map 4 Ba

Half way between Bristol and Gloucester lies Thornbury, famed for its castle, even now that it is a celebrated restaurant. Built on the edge of the town by Edward Stafford, Duke of Buckingham, who pulled down a previous mansion on the same site, it is part palace and part castle. The Duke, however, was not to enjoy its completion for he was beheaded for treason in 1521. Thereafter the castle was confiscated by the King but subsequently restored to the Stafford family by Queen Mary in 1554. It ultimately passed by marriage into the hands of the Howard family who finally sold it in the sixties after a couple of centuries during which it had a somewhat chequered career.

Today the diner passes through a vineyard planted in 1972. Here stands the great gatehouse and everywhere there are reminders of Buckingham. His emblems are carved in stone, brick and on wood – on doorways and adorning some of the fireplaces. The Stafford Knot is even present on a mounting block in the courtyard.

Parts of the castle are residential and private but some of the outer structure can be seen from the windows in the north wall of the neighbouring churchyard of St Mary's. The church itself, as befits a town with a feudal residence, is a grand building with a turreted tower. A Norman church once stood on the site, but the chancel dates from the 14th century with a south aisle added later, the latter, inevitably sporting the Stafford Knot. The roof corbels also display the arms of the Lords of the Manor.

The succession of the Staffords was tenacious to say the least, the last Stafford occupant being Sir Algar Howard who died in 1970 and was Garter King of Arms from 1944 until 1950. The restaurant opened in 1966.

The town of Thornbury lies a little apart from its castle and church, situated away from the once busy turnpike and the A38. 'Infilling' due to the ever growing population is gradually bringing both together. The town thrives on a street arrangement that has existed since medieval times. The High Street, Gloucester Road and Castle Street are linked by the curiously named Plane. There is a fine collection of 15th century buildings although with the loss of its spinning industry the various fairs and markets have died out and the corn market and booth hall are no longer in use. Nevertheless an enormous swan and an equally large lion confront one another in the High Street as they adorn the respective and similar porches of the Swan and White Lion Hotels.

The town's market was once held in the open street. Today it is held by the redundant railway station. A large sports centre was added for the ever growing population in 1980.

A mile or so to the south west, Alveston, on the A38, consists mainly of modern housing estates but has a Victorian church of 1885. There is a cricket pitch near the Ship Inn, noteworthy in that it saw the rise of the first 'star' player, one W.G. Grace. Today the Thornbury Cricket Club plays on the same pitch – the club that was founded in 1872 by W.G.'s brother, 'Coroner' E.M. Grace.

Watchet   Map 1 Ba

Beneath the great 15th century church of St Decuman, high on its hill above the town, lies the little Port of Watchet with its not inconsiderable volume of shipping from foreign parts. Once, when iron ore was mined in the Brendon Hills a small railway moved the ore from the hills to the dockside en route for the steel mills of Wales across the Bristol Channel. Today trade is in car parts to Portugal and paper to North Africa. The town's paper mills now use recycled paper. A walk from the harbour along the esplanade will reveal views across the Channel to the Welsh coast but the town's Victorian buildings are the real reason for deflecting the eye towards the water for they are not the prettiest – in fact, in some respects they are somewhat alien to the county and it may

W

well be that some of those dull yellow bricks made their way to the Somerset coast from the Welsh one.

The church of St Decuman is 15th century and contains monuments to the Wyndham Family who owned Kentsford Farm, which lies slightly to the west, with a two arched packhorse bridge crossing the Washford Stream.

Further inland Old Cleeve has a 15th century church among its cottages with traces of Norman work. The red sandstone Abbey, at Washford, which now lies in ruins was commenced by an abbot and a group of monks in 1198 and largely finished before 1297. Most was lost at the time of the Dissolution (1536), but an interesting tour may be made through the gate house to the cloister and through the remains of the library, chapter house, dormitory and other remaining features.

Watchet Museum in Market Street contains relics depicting the history of Watchet.

Watchet Harbour

Wedmore Map 2 Ba

The village is today one of some substance, attracting
commuters and retired well-to-do citizens to a residential
area of quality and character. It has its place in national
history too, for King Alfred had a residence here and
it was in Wedmore that he signed the treaty which severed
the Danish hold on Southern England.

The large, important church stands imposingly in a
well-kept churchyard which rises high above a sloping
street looking down upon the adjacent coaching inn. A
massive central tower goes back to Norman times and the
south doorway still has its original ironwork. Below lies the
village with its Borough housing the main shopping area.
Many of the houses have Georgian frontages and Porch
House, one of a number round an open green, has casement
windows and a large Georgian porch. To one side lies a little
mullioned building of 1680 with an inscription to
'John Westover, Chyrurgeon'. The Westovers, father and
son, were both surgeon members of a prominent
Wedmore family.

Below the church a rambling old coaching inn,
The George, has a bar that is actually lower than the
coachyard. Watch your step as you descend into a room
with high backed antique settle against stripped stone walls
whose overhead beams are hung with gin traps, tools and
lanterns. The decor also includes a cartwheel and
stuffed birds. Outside there is a peaceful walled lawn.

The parish of Wedmore once contained five windmills
one of which was owned by the Westover family. A disused
windmill can be seen at Ashton. Another of the windmills
is incorporated into the fabric of a house in the village.

Wellington Map 2 Ac

A huge monument on the top of a steep promontory of the
Blackdowns commemorates the Iron Duke who was given
The Wellington estate in 1813. The great obelisk to

95

W

honour the victor of the battle of Waterloo was designed
by a Barnstaple man who was no doubt influenced by
the Egyptian style that was much in vogue at the time. On
the base, close to the door which leads to the small staircase
within, a winged sculpture in the Egyptian manner
stands guard.

Below the monument, which is easily reached by car
(the lanes are well sign posted), a new by-pass sweeps traffic
away from the once through route in the town towards
Devon, making Wellington the first or last port of call
in Somerset. Standing in rich agricultural country the
town has a good shopping centre to serve the light industrial
complex that lies on its north side. West country
cloth, mattresses, bricks and chemicals (the aerosol first
saw the light of day here) brought some prosperity,
while on the south side of the town Wellington school has
carried its name far across the world.

Wellington Museum, housed in a 17th century Posting
house reflects the history. The town's importance is
somewhat overshadowed by its proximity to Taunton. At
the time of Domesday it was an estate of the Bishop of
Wells. By 1279 it had become a borough. If Wellington
has a famous son it must be Sir John Popham, who
bought the estate and whose tomb rests in the parish church
at the east end of the town. He was, variously, Solicitor
and Attorney General, Chief Justice, and Speaker of the
House of Commons and was involved in the trials of
Mary Queen of Scots, Sir Walter Raleigh and the
Gunpowder Plotters.

The church in which this enthusiast of colonisation and
transportation lies in his free standing tomb with its
towering Corinthian canopy, has little to commend it
internally, although its external aspect is solid enough,
15th century, with a great pinnacled tower.

The Town Hall was given a classical façade when it was
built in 1833 at the same time as the old almshouses.
Old Court is Georgian as are many of the old houses in
Fore Street and Mantle Street, while on the edge of the
town at Tonedale there is a group of early 19th century

houses built round the square known as Five Houses, to
accommodate factory workers at the time of the battle
of Waterloo.

There are several outstanding houses around Wellington,
the most interesting being Cothay, through the
grounds of which runs the young river Tone. Today it
is the home of Taunton's Member of Parliament,
Edward du Cann, who has managed to impart a most
homely atmosphere to a 15th century manor house. It was
built by the Bluets, who also built Greenham Barton,
one mile south of Cothay. It has an open hall with a two
storey porch and inserted windows.

Wellow   Map 4 Bb

Picturesque, popular even in Roman times, to judge by the
remains of their villas which have been found scattered
within the vicinity. Perhaps they too, in common with their
present day counterparts, were commuters to
Aqua Sulis – the Roman City of Bath – or sentinels
garrisoned at this outpost.

The steep hills of Mendip fall away here leading to the
pretty Wellow Brook with its wide ford. All vehicles
must splash through the fast running waters while the
village children mount the rail on the pack horse bridge to
watch their progress. Behind the bridge, the old mill
once worked by the stream, has become a dwelling and,
from that point, a steep reverse climb up the hill brings
one to the High Street and possibly to the much needed
local hostelry.

The church of St Julian is 14th century in construction
but much earlier in origin. It is well restored, no doubt at
the expense of the Hungerford family whose Manor is
nearby. The 13th century dovecot, a fine building
belonging to the Manor, stands by the High Street.
Somewhat similar to the one at Dunster, it provided pigeon
meat during the winter months when other sources of
fresh protein were less plentiful.

To the south, back across that fast running stream, ever

in a hurry to change its name to the river Somer before
it joins the Avon, is the Neolithic tomb of **Stoney Littleton**
(Archaeological Site) with its great chambered long
barrow, 13 feet high and over 100 feet long. The keys to it
are kept at the nearby farm.

Wells Map 3 Aa

When I first came to Somerset I gazed in awe at the great
West Front of **Wells Cathedral** (Church Buildings) (at
present undergoing restoration).

Best seen from the valley road by Dulcote Hill, the
towers of the Cathedral rise majestically, framed by the
trees, but once in the Cathedral precincts the city lies, all
embracing, around you and, if there was nothing else to see
the Vicar's Close alone would make one's sojourn worth
while. Close by lies the Chain Gate archway, the **Wells
Museum**, and the Chapter House, while a door at the top
of a flight of steps at the North End of the Close leads
out onto North Liberty, a city within the city.

In the grounds of the **Bishop's Palace** (Church
Buildings) lies the pool above the natural springs which
gave the city its origin and, presumably, its name. A
drawbridge over the Palace moat leads across lawns and
cloisters back to the Cathedral, a building which needs a
book to itself, so numerous are its artefacts and
architectural features. There is an embarrassment of riches:
carved capitals, roof vaulting and the astronomical clock.
The great Crossing, looking just like an open mouthed
giant's head, is awe inspiring, but most fascinating of all
is the flight of steps curving up to the Chapter House,
time-worn by millions of feet.

The tombs and pillars blaze in many colours when
the sunlight passes through the magnificent stained glass.
The roof bosses are flowers and fruit while the carved
choir stalls portray owls, monkeys, cats (and fiddle),
griffins and even mermaids.

From the Cathedral West Front pass through Penniless
Porch into the Market Place of medieval Wells and on to

St Cuthbert's, with its lofty 15th century tower.
Between the two places of worship lie the old inns: the
Crown, late 17th century, three storeyed and with a
courtyard; cobbles and gables pinpoint the Star; the Swan
faces the Cathedral's West Front; King Charles's Bar has a
17th century staircase – and, it is said, a ghost! The
King's Head has a 15th century collar-beamed roof.

The High Street, with its wide cobbled gutters along
which flow the clear waters from the rising wells
at the top of the town, is busy at all times, but never more
so than on market day when the itinerant stall holders
fill the square outside 'Bishop's Eye', the main entrance
to the Bishop's Palace. The fountain near the centre
of the Market Place is Gothic, built on the site of an old
conduit. The Market Hall is now the Post Office, the
Town Hall dates from 1779 while the houses on the
north west side can be traced back to 1450.

Rising over the lee of the Mendips, on the stage coach
road from Wells to Bristol, lies Chewton, home of the
ancient family Waldegrave.

Wells Cathedral

W

Weston-Super-Mare Map 4 Ab

Unashamedly a holiday resort, it is almost inconceivable
that so many people should want temporary
accommodation at the same time. Nevertheless the
hundreds of houses, row upon row, bearing signs
indicating the availability of 'bed & breakfast', 'full board'
and the like have to be seen to be believed. Coming in
from the nearby motorway they seem to stretch for miles
only being brought to an abrupt end by shops and arcades
that seem to have made a desperate intervention to stop
the local inhabitants from letting off their rooms right down
to the water's edge.

But of course there are acres of fine sand, a splendid new
bathing pool, two piers, flower beds, rockeries, a Winter
Garden and theatre and all the other attributes that go
to make up a real English holiday centre. More than just a
holiday resort, however, Weston-Super-Mare has a large
proportion of retired people and the many Victorian
mansions have been converted into flats to house them.
Their presence has ensured a large and viable shopping
centre with the nation's chain stores well in evidence.
While that town centre has no particular architectural
merit, the Royal Crescent, built in 1848, is distinctive and
gives the town a reminder of Georgian attractiveness.

Those who do not seek the pleasures of the amusement
arcade and the bingo palace will find the town to be a
mine of Victoriana, both in its buildings and its
antique shops – one has the impression that many of those
seaside landladies have been 'modernising' at long last
and turning out all the old objects that used to grace
their landings.

When the railway arrived in 1841 the population of what
had once been a fishing village doubled in a decade. Since
then its growth has been nothing short of amazing –
the more so in that the water completely disappears beyond
acres of mud when the tide is out.

A mile or so away, Bleadon Hill, a magnificent feature,
seems to have detached itself from the Mendips to become a

suburb of Weston-Super-Mare. No less attractive
stands the knoll at Uphill, where the River Axe flows into
the Bristol Channel. Its Norman church of St Nicholas
was a landmark for sailors. **Worlebury Camp**
(Archaeological Sites), the Iron Age fortress with hut circles
and earthworks, stands on a headland north of the town.

Wincanton   Map 3 Bb

First or last town in Somerset according to direction – or
route – for the A303, England's south western artery
which once passed through its long main street, wide at the
top, dividing into a one way system at the bottom, has
now been removed from the town – so much the better for
those who live or wish to tarry awhile in this pleasant
border town. Some border towns have a 'no man's land'
ambience. Not so Wincanton. There are plenty of inns
and hotels here and a Victorian Town Hall of merit
which incorporates some 18th century work. The shops
look modern enough but there are some interesting early
Georgian upper storeys to be seen.

The inns and hotels give the best clue to a more recent
existence for the town built on a river crossing on the
main London to Exeter road. According to Dr. Robert
Dunning, Wincanton could offer beds for 50 guests
and stabling for 254 horses at one one time, an interesting
ratio on which to ponder.

The town was noted for cloth making and the weaving of
silk and some 200 looms were still in use at the end of
the last century. The prosperity brought by the town's
market and the weaver's trade is evidenced by the
18th century houses, many of them appearing after a
disastrous fire in 1747. Several of these houses were built
by a master builder from Warwickshire, Nathaniel Ireson,
who came to the town in 1726 and remained until his death
in 1769, although he adorned many other parts of provincial
England. His weathered statue still stands in the
local churchyard.

Today Wincanton has one claim to national fame – the

W

National Hunt meetings held on its racecourse on
the hill. It is also a transport centre maintaining a large
group of tankers and containers allied to the dairy group
that has a presence in the town making dried milk and
cheese products.

Wiveliscombe   Map 1 Bb

The first notable building as one enters this centre for
tours of the Brendon Hills is the magnificent Tudor edifice
that houses a well known bank. The building itself is a
sham, but an excellent and imposing one, erected in 1881.

In medieval times the town contained an episcopal manor
frequented by the Bishops of Bath & Wells when
touring this distant part of their diocese – the remains of
their dwelling can be seen in the 14th century archway
leading to ground appropriately designated as Palace Green.

The only remains are of the original medieval church
which was demolished in 1827 to make way for the
present red sandstone structure which played an important
role during World War II, storing ecclesiastical
treasures from all over the country. Glass, plate, records,
books, whole libraries and even furniture were assembled
from churches, cathedrals and synagogues; much of the
collection would otherwise have been destroyed by
enemy action.

Once a centre for the weaving of cloth and a
Somerset brewery, this pleasant and compact town now
manufactures modern kitchen and other tableware made
just to the north by Taunton Vale Industries.

Wookey Hole   Map 3 Aa

Not to be confused with the village of Wookey, a mile away,
Wookey Hole, always a fascinating attraction with its
great cave, has been made even more so as the home of
the famous – by decree of Madame Tussauds.

Once the home of prehistoric cave dwellers, the present
layout of the great cave and its ancilliaries, hollowed

out by the underground River Axe, was achieved by one H.E. Balch, a Post Office worker from Wells, who devoted most of his life to the task. The first chamber has a vaulted roof and contains the stalagmite form known locally as the Witch of Wookey, a creature reputedly turned to stone by one of the monks from Glastonbury as he attempted to exorcise her. The second chamber is almost 75 feet in height and there are many other interlinking chambers, not all of them open to the public, who are well catered for by the special car park and souvenir shops none of which detract from the rural wooded approach.

The village itself is of interest, mainly 19th century in character, it serves the workers at the local paper mill which harnesses the River Axe to obtain its energy. It has done so since the early 19th century and the high quality handmade paper that is made is used for documents and even for certain banknotes. Acquired by London's Madame Tussaud's Exhibition organisation in 1972, paper is still produced but extra duties have been found for the building. Part of the mill now houses a splendid collection of fairground objects, roundabout horses, organs, scenic railway cars and the like, all beautifully preserved in their gaudy colours and here seen in a better light than when flashing round in a working fairground.

Elsewhere the storeroom and studio, which Madame Tussaud has created to house some of the stock from the London Exhibition, contains row upon row of shelves of heads whose fame has faded or who have otherwise disgraced themselves. Ranged side by side irrespective of status, they are a sharp reminder that fame can sometimes be transient, or if sustained may require an older looking model.

Wrington   Map 4 Ab

It may be a far cry from Parliament Square to the Avon village of Wrington but it was the tower of All Saints church which was the inspiration Sir Charles Berry needed when he designed the Victoria Tower for the Houses of

Y

Parliament. The church has other claims to fame. One is
that Hannah More is buried here. Her name occurs so many
times in connection with her good deeds from Bristol's
Fishponds to London's Clapham Common as well as
in a good part of Somerset and Avon that it comes as a
relief to find that she has come to rest somewhere. Her
bust is to the west of the church door. To its east is the
bust of the philosopher, John Locke, who was born
in a cottage near the churchyard and there is a tablet near
the gate acknowledging the site of his birth.

The church tower, all 113 feet of it, dominates the fine
Broad Street – the same by name as by nature –
where markets were once held and travelling showmen
and stallholders once brought their fairs and their wares.
The street stands in a conservation area and there is
little evidence of traffic once the Bristol commuters
have departed for the day from this quiet romantic spot in
the Yeo Valley, which once sported its own railway line and
station. The Wrington Vale Light Railway Company
was opened in 1901 primarily to carry equipment
for the Bristol Water Works Company who were building a
vast reservoir at the Blagdon end where it abruptly
terminated. It has been closed these many years.

Yeovil Map 3 Ac

With all the trappings of a successful industrial town,
Yeovil is one of the number in the south of England that
have a common denominator – they have grown out of all
recognition over the past fifty years both in population
density and architecturally. On the eastern flank
of the town the red bricks of a thousand bungalows and
semis march inexorably towards Sherborne and the
Dorset Border while most of the quaint shops that once
lined the busy high street have long since given way to the
mass of chain stores in Middle Street while the smaller,
locally owned establishments fight for survival in the
side streets or the town's extremities.

The main street is closed to traffic, enabling the shopper

to browse in comparative safety, though the driver,
who must use the circular routes round the town, must be
alert and wary, for an attempt to park on the periphery is
like trying to steer a ball bearing on a pin table – finding the
hole rather than the hazard!

Today, owing its wealth to Westlands, with their
international connection in the construction and sale of
helicopters, Yeovil has a prosperity that demands
appropriate outlets for its spending power. Even as this
guide is being written a new shopping precinct, the
Quedam, is being opened, the third in as many years; all
this, not merely for the citizens of the town but for
the agricultural region for which it is also a centre, with
market days held twice a week. In Saxon times farmers
were bringing their dairy produce, wool and sheepskins
to the town. Today Europe's largest tannery stands
just outside the town, so close to the border with Dorset
that its employees have the choice of two counties in which
to live, in contrast to the Saxon man who went no
further than his vill in the valley beside the Yeo.

The split between citizens during the Civil War (the
Lords were for the King, the townsfolk for Parliament),
and the rioting in 1831 when the militia were called in,
have given the town an uneasy past. The one serene
spot that has survived a turbulent history is the
churchyard at the top of Middle Street in which stands the
great perpendicular church of St John the Baptist.
While the crypt may be a little earlier this parish church
was begun by one Robert Sambourne, rector between
1362 and 1382. The octagonal font and the brass lectern
are both 15th century.

In an 18th century coach house **Yeovil Museum** has a
good collection of firearms and local Roman finds. There
is also a reproduction of the Alfred Jewel which was
discovered in 1693 close to Athelney.

On the A30 from London to Lands End, the town lies
just off the Fosse Way, yet, surprisingly on such a
route there is no evidence of large coaching inns, and one of
Yeovil's really old buildings, the George, was pulled

Y

down to ease the traffic through Middle Street. That
traffic now thunders round the new roundabouts
and by-passes but quiet walks may be found such as
Nine Springs, a wooded combe with pools and waterfalls in
a rustic setting. A sandstone cutting akin to a tiny gorge
leads off Babylon Hill to Bradford Abbas. Westward Abbey
Farm and tithe barn stand resplendent in warm
Ham stone in the continuing village of Preston Plunknett.
The Abbey Farm, now occupied by a construction
company, was once a grange, belonging to Bermondsey
Abbey. The house has graceful 'turret' stacks and
although it was damaged by enemy action during the war
it has been beautifully restored.

Yeovil College, the Fire Station, the District Hospital,
the Divisional Police Headquarters, Maltravers House –
housing government offices and the Yeovil District
Council (now South Somerset District Council) –
together with the Octagon or Johnson Hall (the local
entertainment complex) are all examples of the many
buildings which did not exist a quarter of a century ago.

'Jack the Treacle Eater' is one of a number of
18th century follies standing in Barwick Park, about
1½ miles to the South of Yeovil, just off the
Dorchester Road. To the north lies the once secluded
farming village of Yeovilton which today stands by the
side of a perimeter runway of the Royal Naval Air Station
which was established soon after the outbreak of the
last war. Known locally as HMS Heron, its greater
claim to fame for the tourist lies in the **Fleet Air Arm
Museum** which houses a collection of aircraft
including the sleek but claustrophobic Concorde 002, as
as well as scale models, documents, equipment, paintings
and photographs of well known actions including the
1982 Falklands War.

Map 1

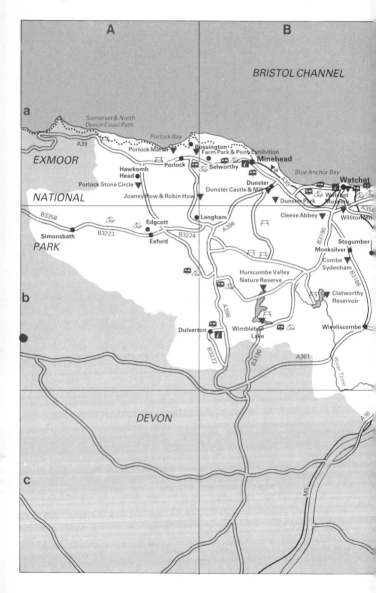

Map 2

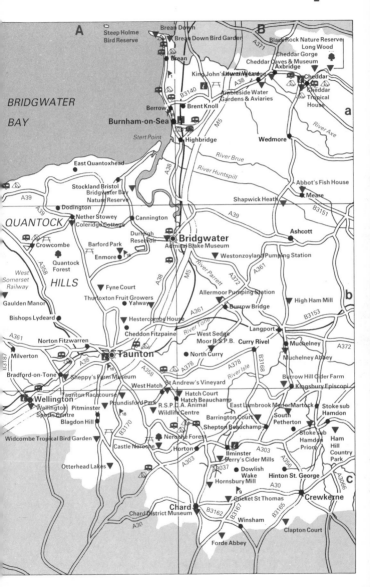

BRIDGWATER
BAY

Steep Holme
Bird Reserve

Brean Down

Brean Down Bird Garden

Black Rock Nature Reserve
Long Wood

Brean

Cheddar Gorge
Cheddar Caves & Museum
Axbridge

King John's Hunting Lodge

A38

Cheddar

Cheddar
Tropical
House

a

Ambleside Water
Gardens & Aviaries

Berrow

Brent Knoll

B3140

Burnham-on-Sea

M5

Stert Point

Highbridge

Wedmore

River Axe

River Brue

River Huntspill

East Quantoxhead

A38

Abbot's Fish House

Stockland Bristol
Bridgwater Bay
Nature Reserve

Shapwick Heath

Meare

A39

Dodington

Cannington

A39

B3151

QUANTOCK

Nether Stowey
Coleridge Cottage

Ashcott

Crowcombe

Durleigh
Reservoir

Bridgwater
Admiral Blake Museum

West
Somerset
Railway

Barford Park

Enmore

Quantock
Forest

HILLS

Westonzoyland Pumping Station

A361

Gaulden Manor

Fyne Court

Allermoor Pumping Station

High Ham Mill

Thurloxton Fruit Growers
Yalway

River Parrett

M5

River Tone

Burrow Bridge

b

Bishops Lydeard

Hestercombe House

B3153

A361

Norton Fitzwarren

Cheddon Fitzpaine

West Sedge
Moor R.S.P.B.

Langport

A372

Milverton

Taunton

North Curry

Curry Rivel

Muchelney

A372

A38

A378

River Isle

A358

Muchelney Abbey

Bradford-on-Tone

Sheppy's Farm Museum

West Hatch

St Andrew's Vineyard

A378

B3168

Burrow Hill Cider Farm

Wellington

Taunton Racecourse

Hatch Court
Hatch Beauchamp

Kingsbury Episcopi

Wellington
Sports Centre

Pitminster

Poundisford Park

R.S.P.C.A. Animal
Wildlife Centre

East Lambrook Manor Martock

Stoke sub
Hamdon

Blagdon Hill

B3170

Barrington Court

Shepton Beauchamp

South
Petherton

Stoke sub
Hamdon
Priory

Widcombe Tropical Bird Garden

Castle Neroche

Neroche Forest

Horton

Ham
Hill
Country
Park

Otterhead Lakes

Ilminster
Perry's Cider Mills

A303

A356

Dowlish
Wake
Hornsbury Mill

A303

B3037

Hinton St. George

A30

C

Chard
Chard District Museum

Cricket St Thomas

Crewkerne

A3066

B3162

B3167

Winsham

B3165

A30

Clapton Court

Forde Abbey

109

Map 3

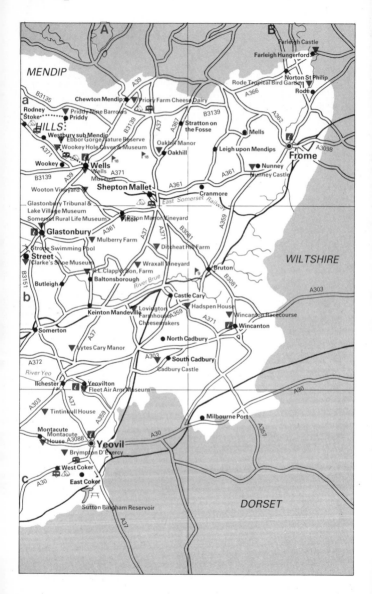

MENDIP

A38

B3135

a

Farleigh Castle

Farleigh Hungerford

Norton St Philip

Rode Tropical Bird Garden

Rode

A366

A362

Chewton Mendip

Priory Farm Cheese Dairy

Priddy Nine Barrows

Priddy

Rodney Stoke

HILLS

Westbury sub Mendip

Ebbor Gorge Nature Reserve

Wookey Hole Caves & Museum

A371

Wookey

B3139

A39

Wells

Wells Museum

A371

Wooton Vineyard

B3139

A367

Stratton on the Fosse

A37

Oakhill Manor

Oakhill

Mells

Leigh upon Mendips

Frome

A3098

Nunney

Nunney Castle

A361

Shepton Mallet

A361

Cranmore

East Somerset Railway

A359

Glastonbury Tribunal & Lake Village Museum

Somerset Rural Life Museum

Pilton Manor Vineyard

Glastonbury

A361

A37

A371

B3081

WILTSHIRE

Mulberry Farm

Ditcheat Hill Farm

Strode Swimming Pool

Street

Clarke's Shoe Museum

J.C. Clapp & Son, Farm

River Brue

Wraxall Vineyard

Bruton

B3081

A303

B3151

Baltonsborough

Butleigh

Castle Cary

b

Keinton Mandeville

Lovington Farmhouse Cheesemakers

A359

Hadspen House

A371

Wincanton Racecourse

Wincanton

Somerton

A37

North Cadbury

Lytes Cary Manor

A372

A303

South Cadbury

Cadbury Castle

River Yeo

Ilchester

Yeovilton Fleet Air Arm Museum

A359

Milbourne Port

A30

A357

Tintinhull House

A303

A37

Montacute

Montacute House

A3088

Yeovil

Brympton D'Evercy

c

West Coker

A30

East Coker

Sutton Bingham Reservoir

A37

DORSET

110

Map 4

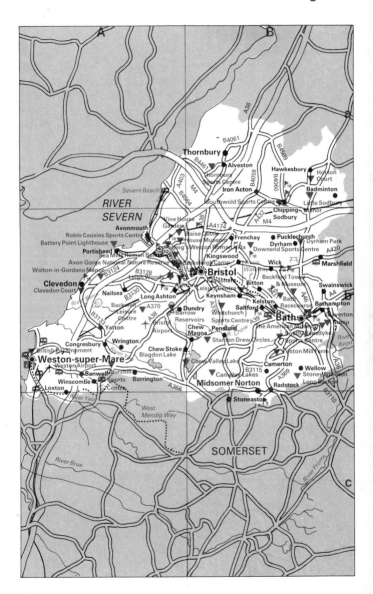

Thornbury
B4061
Alveston
Hawkesbury
Hoxton Court
Thornbury Sports Centre
Iron Acton
B4058
B4060
Badminton
Little Sodbury
Severn Beach
Manor
Southwold Sports Centre
Chipping Sodbury
A432
M4

RIVER SEVERN

Vine House Garden
A4174
Avonmouth
Robin Cousins Sports Centre
Baise Castle
House Museum
Frenchay
Pucklechurch
Dyrham Park
A420
Battery Point Lighthouse
Weston Roman Villa
Downend Sports Centre
Portishead
Sea Mills Roman Harbour
Kingswood
Wick
Marshfield
Avon Gorge National Nature Reserve
Camp
Walton-in-Gordano Manor
B3124
Beckford Tower & Museum
Bristol
Swainswick
Clevedon
Bitton
Bath Racecourse
Bathampton
Clevedon Court
Leisure Centre
Nailsea
B3130
Long Ashton
Keynsham
Kelston
Salford
Bath
Backwell Leisure Centre
A370
Dundry
A4
Yatton
B3133
Barrow Reservoirs
Whitchurch
A39
The American Museum
Claverton Camp
Bristol Airport
Chew Magna
Pensford
Sports Centre
South Wansdyke Sports Centre
Congresbury
Wrington
Stanton Drew Circles
Claverton Manor
River Avon
British Encampment
Chew Stoke
A38
Sports Centre
Weston-super-Mare
Blagdon Lake
Chew Valley Lake
Weston Mill Farm
Weston Airport
Camerton
Wellow
Banwell
Murchill
Camerley Lakes
B3115
Stoney Littleton Long Barrow
Winscombe
Sports Centre
Burrington
A366
Midsomer Norton
A369
Radstock
A362
Loxton
River Yeo
Stoneaston
B3110

West Mendip Way

River Brue
SOMERSET
River Frome

River Brue

111

Town Directory

BATH
Map 4 Bb

Art Gallery: Victoria Art Gallery
Boat Trips: Bath Boating Station
Church Building: Bath Abbey
Events: Bath Festival, Historical Pageant, Autumn Antiques Fair
Historic Homes: Herschel House, No 1 Royal Crescent
Horse Racing: Bath Horse Racing Course
Museums: Burrows Toy Museum, Museum of Bookbinding, Camden Works Museum, Carriage Museum, Museum of Costume, Fashion Research Centre, Geology Museum, Halls of the Heroes, Holburne of Menstrie, Postal Museum, Roman Baths Museum, RPS Centre of Photography
Other Historic Building: The Guildhall

Roman Sites: Roman Baths & Pump Room
Sports Centre: Bath Sports & Leisure Centre
Nearby
Archaeological Site: Stoney Littleton Long Barrow
Country Park: Dyrham Park
Mill: Priston Mill

BRIDGWATER
Map 2 Ab

Museum: Admiral Blake Museum
Sports Centre: Sydenham Sports Centre
Events: Bridgwater Fair
Early Closing: Thursday
Market Day: Wednesday
Nearby
Garden: Barford Park
Nature Reserve: Bridgwater Bay National Nature Reserve

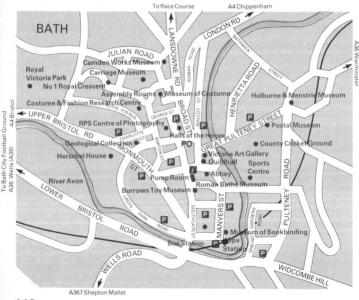

Spa Sutton

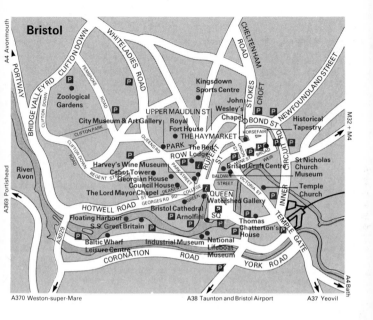

BRISTOL

Map 4 Bb

Air Sports & Pleasure Flights Bristol & Wessex Aeroplane Club, Bristol Airport Pleasure Flights, Skysales Ltd
Art Galleries: Arnolfini Gallery, Bristol Museum & Art Gallery, Watershed Gallery
Country Park: Ashton Court Estate
Church Buildings: Bristol Cathedral, The Lord Mayor's Chapel, Temple Church, John Wesley's Chapel
Crafts: Bristol Craft Centre
Events: Distribution of Tuppeney Starvers, Bristol Promenade Concerts, Horse Show, Harbour Regatta, World Wine Fair & Festival, Bristol Flower Show, Bristol Water Carnival
Historic Homes: Georgian House, Red Lodge, Royal Fort House
 Museums: Bristol Historical Tapestry, City Museum, Harveys' Wine Museum, Industrial Museum, National Lifeboat Museum, St Nicholas Church Museum
Other Historic Buildings: Cabot Tower, Thomas Chatterton's House, Council House
Sports Centres: Baltic Wharf Leisure Centre, Kingsdown Leisure Centre
Unusual Outings: SS Great Britain
Zoos: Bristol Zoo
Early Closing Day: Wednesday
Nearby
Archaeological Site: Stokleigh Camp
Garden: Vine House Garden
Museum: Blaise House Castle Museum
Nature Reserves: Avon Gorge National Nature Reserve, Leigh Woods
Roman: Kings Weston Roman Villa, Sea Mills Roman Buildings

CHARD
Map 2 Bb
Event: Chard Show
Museum: Chard District Museum
Mill: Hornsbury Mill
Nearby
Garden: Forde Abbey
Unusual Outing: Cricket St Thomas
Wildlife Park

CHEDDAR
Map 2 Ba
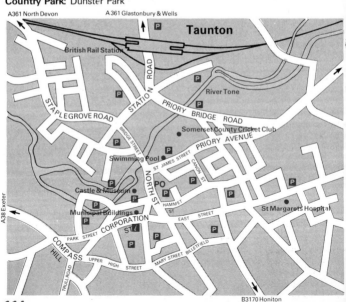
Museum: Cheddar Caves Museum &
Exhibiton
Nature Reserve: Black Rock Nature
Reserve
Unusual Outing: Cheddar Caves
Zoo: Cheddar Tropical House

DUNSTER
Map 1 Ba
Castle: Dunster Castle
Country Park: Dunster Park

Events: Horse & Agricultural Show
Other Historical Buildings: Yarn
Market, Old Dovecote
Picnic Site: Croydon Hill Picnic Place
Early Closing: Wednesday

FROME
Map 3 Ba

Castle: Nunney Castle
Bird Park: Rode Tropical Bird Garden
Events: Carnival, Cheese Show
Sports Centre: Frome Sports Centre
Early Closing: Thursday
Market Day: Wednesday

GLASTONBURY
Map 3 Ab

Archaeological Site: Chalice Well
Church Building: Glastonbury Abbey
Events: Cage Bird Show, Beltane
(Druid Celebration of Spring)

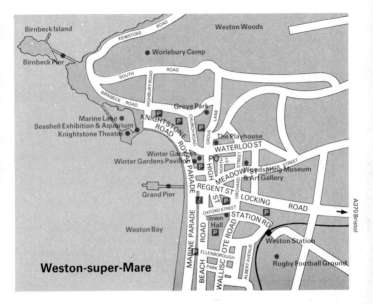

Weston-super-Mare

Museums: The Tribunal, Somerset
Rural Life Museum
Other Historic Building: The
Tribunal
Early Closing: Wednesday
Market Day: Tuesday
Nearby
Farms: R.L. Clapp & Son Ltd.,
Mulberry Farm
Museum: Clark's Shoe Museum
Vineyards: Wooton Vineyard, Wraxall
Vineyard, Pilton Manor Vineyard

MINEHEAD
Map 1 Ba

Crafts: J. Wood & Sons
Events: Hobby Horse Celebrations
National Morris Ring Meeting
Railway: West Somerset Railway
Early Closing: Wednesday
Nearby
Castles: Dunster Castle
Mill: Dunster Mill

SHEPTON MALLET
Map 3 Aa

Events: Royal Bath & West Show,
Antiques Fair
Historic Home: Oakhill Manor
Railway: East Somerset Railway
Nearby
Farm: Ditcheat Hill Farm
Vineyard: Pilton Manor Vineyard

TAUNTON
Map 2 Ab

Castle: Taunton Castle
Crafts: Knitknacks, W R & J Steele,
Blagdon Forge, Church Farm Weavers
Events: Medieval Fair, Flower Show,
Carnival & Cider Barrel Race,
Marathon
Horse Racing: Taunton Racecourse
Museum: Somerset Country &
Military Museum

115

Market Days: Saturday & Tuesday
Nearby
Bird Reserve: West Sedgemoor
Gardens: Gaulden Manor,
Hestercombe Garden
Historic Homes: Hatch Court,
Poundisford Park
Mill: Orchard Mill
Vineyard: St Andrew's Vineyard

WELLS
Map 3 Aa
🔲 ⛄ 🚐 ()

Church Buildings: Bishop's Palace,
Wells Cathedral
Events: May Fair
Museum: Wells Museum
Early Closing: Wednesday
Market Day: Saturday & Wednesday
Nearby
Archaeological Site: Priddy Nine
Barrows
Nature Reserve: Ebbor Gorge
National Nature Reserve
Unusual Outing: Wookey Hole Caves

WESTON-SUPER-MARE
Map 4 Ab
🔲 ⅄ 🚐 ()

Archaeological Site: British
Encampment
Air Sports: Mendip Gliding Club
Events: County Cricket Festival,
International Hockey Festival
Museums: Woodspring Museum
Unusual Outing: Model Village
Early Closing: Thursday:
Market Day: Sunday

YEOVIL
Map 3 Ac
🔲 ⅄ 🚐

Historic Homes: Brympton D'Evercy,
Tintinhull House
Museum: Brympton D'Evercy,
Wyndham Museum
Sports Centre: Buckler Mead Sports
Centre
Market Day: Friday
Nearby
Archaeological Site: Cadbury Castle
Church Building: Stoke-sub-Hamdon
Priory
Historic Home: Montacute House
Museum: Fleet Air Arm Museum
Picnic Site: Sutton Bingham
Reservoir

Leisure A-Z

Details given have been carefully checked but are subject to change. Last admission can be half an hour before stated closing time.
Symbols: see p5.
Abbreviations: ch children
ch16 children to age 16
OAP old age pensioners
m mile
N north
S south
E east
W west

Air Sports and Pleasure Flights

Flying Lessons

BRISTOL & WESSEX AEROPLANE CLUB
Map 4 Ab
Lulsgate (027 587) 2514/2174
Bristol Airport, 8m SW Bristol city centre on A38
Open: all year, daily 9.00-17.30
Courses: PPL, IMC, Night, Aerobatics, RT, RAD/NAV, Multi
Aircrafts: Cessna 150, 152; Piper PA28, 140; PA28, 181; PA32 R; Saratoga; Beech 55
Membership: £40 per year
Lessons: from £50 per hour

Gliding

MENDIP GLIDING CLUB
Map 4 Ab
Weston-super-Mare (0934) 833722
Weston-super-Mare Airport, 2m E
Weston- super-Mare city centre on A371
Open: w/ends and some evenings (phone for details)
Air Experience Flight: £5
Membership: phone for details

Hot Air Ballooning

SKYSALES LTD.
Bristol (0272) 501196
Ashton Court Estate, Bristol
Open: April-Oct, daily by arrangement
Charge: from £60 per person per hour

Pleasure Flights

BRISTOL AIRPORT PLEASURE FLIGHTS
Map 4 Ab
Lulsgate (027 587) 4204
Bristol Airport, 8m SW Bristol city centre on A38
Open: all year, w/ends 10.00 -18.00 by arrangement only. Also school holidays, Mon-Fri 14.00-18.00
Charges: from £8.95 per person
Variety of flights ranging from short flights around Bristol and Cheddar to longer flights around the whole county

Angling

Organisations

NATIONAL FEDERATION OF ANGLERS
Derby (0332) 362000
Halliday House, 2 Wilson St, Derby
DE1 1PG
The governing body for coarse angling in Britain. Membership is through clubs and associations. 420 such organisations are affiliated representing some 450,000 coarse anglers

NATIONAL FEDERATION OF SEA ANGLERS
Uckfield (0825) 3589
General Secretary: R W Page
26 Downsview Crescent, Uckfield, East Sussex TN22 1UB
Governing body for Sea Angling in Britain. 800 clubs are affiliated and the federation represents the interests of nearly two million sea anglers

SALMON & TROUT ASSOCIATION
01-283 5838
Fishmongers Hall, London Bridge, London EC4R 9El
National body for game fishing with over 70 branches in Britain and over 200,000 members

NATIONAL ANGLERS COUNCIL
Peterborough (0733) 54084
11 Cowgate, Peterborough PE1 1LZ
Governing body for angling (all types) in England. Runs National Angling Coaching scheme and a Proficiency Awards' scheme, designed to improve the proficiency of anglers, with special emphasis on ecology and protection of the water environment

CENTRAL ASSOCIATION OF LONDON & PROVINCIAL ANGLING CLUBS
01-686 3199
Kemble Rd, Croydon, Surrey
Members and affiliated clubs can use the waters which the association either owns or rents. They also provide an Anglers' Guide to these waters
See also: Angling Clubs

Rod Licences

WESSEX WATER AUTHORITY
Bristol (0272) 290611
Passage St, Bristol, BS2 0JQ
The rivers and inland waters of Somerset and Avon are controlled by the Wessex Water Authority. Anglers using these waters must first obtain an official rod licence. In Somerset rod licences are available from distributors throughout the region. A list of these locations is available from the Fisheries Information office

BRISTOL AVON DIVISION
Bath (0225) 313500
P.O. Box 95, Broad Quay, Bath, Avon BA1 2YP

SOMERSET DIVISION
P.O. Box 9, King Square, Bridgwater Somerset TA6 2EA

Permits

Almost all rivers and stillwaters are privately owned or controlled by the authority. One important reason for joining an angling club is that members will have access to good waters which are not open to the public

Some waters are accessible only to members of particular clubs but in many cases a permit can be Obtained which allows fishing.

These permits are for a day, week or a season and are usually available from bailiffs on the banks or from local tackle shops

In the following section, where to fish, the clubs, or others, who control the waters are listed below each entry

For the address and telephone numbers of the club secretaries see Angling Clubs

If permits can be obtained elsewhere this information is also given

Where to Fish

Some of the following information is taken from the **Fishing Handbook** (1983 edition), a comprehensive annual guide to all angling organisations and locations in Britain and Ireland. It includes a guide to day permit fishing and to sea fishing, a list of angling clubs and a directory of suppliers. Three smaller publications separate information for Coarse Fishing, Game Fishing and Sea Fishing

For further details contact Beacon Publishing Northampton (0604) 407288 Jubilee House, Billing Brook Rd, Weston Flavell, Northampton

Coarse Fishing: Rivers

AVON

RIVER AVON

The Avon rises in the Cotswolds near Tetbury and flows via Chippenham, Bath & Bristol to the Severn Estuary west of Bristol. Mostly known for coarse fishing and some trout which is mostly in the upper reaches. The river is unique in the amount of fishing controlled solely by associations and therefore offering

little or no ticket fishing. The only way for a visitor to gain real access to it is by taking out seasonal membership of one of the associations involved. Easily done by calling at nearest tackle shop. **Free fishing:** Hanham weir to Estuary, towpath between Newbridge and Pulteney Weir, and for a short distance upstream from Bathampton Weir

Permits: Bathampton AA; Day permits from Crudingtons, Broad St, Bath; Fishcraft, Brougham Hayes, Bath; Bath AA, monthly tickets only available by writing to secretary; Bradford & Avon District AA; Weekly permits from Smith & Ford Sports, Bradford on Avon; West Tackle, Trowbridge; Bristol & District Amalgamated Anglers, season permits only; Ushers AC; Hendersons Tackle, Trowbridge

RIVER CHEW

Rises near Chewton Mendip and flows through Bristol waterworks reservoirs at Litton and Chew Valley Lake. Continues through Chew Magna, Stanton Drew, Publow, Woollard and Compton Dando to its confluence with the River Avon at Keynsham. Coarse fishing predominates from confluence to Compton Dando but thereafter trout become numerous. Species include bream, dace, eel, grayling, perch, roach, and tench

Free Fishing: juveniles only on public path at Keynsham

Permits: Bristol and District Amalgamated Anglers, season permits only

RIVER FROME (BRISTOL)

Rises at Dodington and offers coarse fishing of a fair standard

Species include bream, carp, dace, eel, perch, roach, tench and trout

Free Fishing: Contact Bristol City Council for details

Angling

SOMERSET

RIVER AXE
Emerges from the Mendip Hills at Wookey Hole. Upper reaches preserved for trout but coarse fish, especially roach, chub, dace and pike occur where the river begins to cross the lowlands at the foot of the Mendips
Permits: day and week permits, Omnia Sports, Chapel Hill, Clevedon; W. Evans, Orchard Street, Weston-super- Mare; season permits only, Bristol & District Amalgamated Anglers; day and season permits, Chard Cycle Co., Holyrood St., Chard

RIVER BRUE
Rises in Mendip Hills above Bruton. Trout fishing down to West Lydford but from here to Glastonbury there is plenty of coarse fish including chub, roach, dace and pike
Permits: Nicholas Sports, Street; day and week permits from G. Jotcham,

RIVER FROME (SOMERSET)
Main tributary of the Bristol Avon. Rises in Burton Forest and flows north through Frome, joining the Bristol Avon above Trowbridge. Trout fishing in upper reaches but lower down, coarse fish, especially good roach predominate
Permits: Bristol and Amalgamated Anglers, season permits only

RIVER MARDEN
Fed by springs rising from Marlborough Downs the River Marden joins the Avon upstream of Chippenham. Trout occurs naturally in the upper reaches but downstream of Calne, coarse fish predominate. Barbel are found near confluence with River Avon
Permits: day and weekly permits from Calne AA; Dumb Post Inn, Bremhill; L Wilkins, Tackle Dealer, 3 Wood Street, Calne

High Street, Burnham; season permits, Bristol and Amalgamated Anglers

RIVER CONGRESBURY, YEO
Rises in the Mendips and feeds into Blagdon reservoir. Coarse fishing below Wrington. Species include dace, roach, rudd
Permits: season only, Bristol & District Amalgamated Anglers

RIVER HUNTSPILL
See other waters

RIVER ISLE
Rises near Chard and flows into and out of Chard Lake. Coarse fish, including roach, rudd, chub & dace, are found where the river meets the Parrett near Drayton
Permits: season and day permits, Chard Cycle Co., Chard; Clapps Newsagents, Ilminster; Rules Tackle Shop, Langport and from the Bailiff on the bank at Ilminster. Also from most tackle shops in the district

RIVER KENN AND NEW BLIND YEO
The New Blind Yeo is an artificial drainage channel carrying most of the diverted waters from the River Kenn. Both these waters are noted for good quality roach
Permits: Omnia Sports, Clevedon; W. Evans, Orchard St, Weston-super-Mare and local tackle shops

RIVER PARRETT
Rises in Dorset near Crewkerne and flows in a northerly direction toward Langport where it is joined by the the River Isle and the Somerset Yeo. It continues its journey northward and enters the Bristol Channel through a long estuary just below Bridgwater. Coarse fish predominate below Petherton Bridge. Species include roach, bream, rudd, chub, dace, carp and pike

Permits: Day, week and season permits from A.W. Rule Fishing Tackle Specialists, Parrett Close, Langport; Langport & District AA; Wessex Federation of Angling Clubs and most tackle shops in the region; Weekly permits from Haggs Tackle, Princes St, Yeovil or Stoke-sub-Hamdon & District AA

RIVER TONE
A major tributary of the River Parrett, the Tone rises near Exmoor National Park and almost immediately enters Clatworthy Reservoir. From here to Taunton it offers trout, grayling, dace and roach. Coarse fish, especially chub, dace and roach are found in the deeper waters in Taunton
Permits: Day, week and month permits available from tackle shops in Taunton; Topp Tackle, Station Road, Taunton; Bridge Sports, Bridge Street, Taunton; A Woodbury, High Street, Wellington

RIVER YEO
Rising in hills south of Yeo, the river enters Sherborne Lake. From here to Yeovil, it is mixed fishing for trout and coarse fish. Below Yeovil, the river becomes deeper and coarse fish predominate by the time it joins the River Parrett at Langport
Permits: Day permits from Tony Coles Florist, The Square, Ilchester and local tackle shops in Yeovil. Also Hagas Tackle, Yeovil or Marney Sports, Yeovil

Coarse Fishing: Stillwaters

AVON

ABBOTS POND
Abbots Leigh
Permits: Woodspring District Council, Leisure Services Department
Weston-super-Mare (0934) 413040

BERKLEY LAKE
Frome
Permits: Brian Neale, Fosters Menswear, Frome

BITTERWELL LAKE
2m S Frampton Cotterell
Permits: available on site

BRISTOL CITY DOCKS
Bristol
Permits: Baltic Wharf Leisure Centre, Cumberland Road, Bristol

BROOKERS WOOD
Woodland Park, Nr Westbury
Permits: must be booked in advance as only 5 permits available per day
Westbury (0373) 822238

DODINGTON HOUSE
Chipping Sodbury, Avon
Lower lake contains coarse fish species including bream, carp, dace, roach and tench
Permits: information available from the Agent, Dodington House, Chipping Sodbury
Chipping Sodbury (0454) 318899

DUNKIRK POND
Devizes
0.8 hectare clay pit
Permits: Day permits available on site

EASTVILLE PARK LAKE
Free fishing

EDEN VALLEY LAKE
Westbury
Permits: available on site

HENLEAZE LAKE
Bristol
Permits: available on site from mid June-end Oct

LAKESIDE
Devizes
Permits: available on site

Angling

ST GEORGE'S PARK LAKE
Bristol
Owned and managed by Bristol City Council
Free fishing: enquiries to Recreations Office, Parks Department, Bristol City Council

STATION POND
Westbury
Permits: Eden Vale AA, Tuesday and Thursday only

WITHAM FRIARY PONDS
Frome
2 ponds covering 1.2 hectares. Carp, crucian carp and roach
Permits: E.D.H. Miles, Witham Hall Farm (037384) 239

SOMERSET

APEX POND
Burnham
Permits: Day and week permits from G. Jotcham, High Street, Burnham-on-Sea

ASHFORD RESERVOIR
Bridgwater
Permits: Day and week permits from local tackle shops

ASH POND
Chard
Permits: Day and season permits from Chard Cycle Co., Holyrood Street, Chard

BRICKYARD PONDS
Prawlett, Bridgwater
Permits: season permits only from Bristol & District Amalgamated Anglers

BRIDGWATER DOCKS
Bridgwater
Permits: day and week permits from L.A. Williams, 7 Webber Way, Puriton, Bridgwater (0278) 684027

COMBWICH PONDS
Cannington
Permits: day and week permits from L.A. Williams, 7 Webber Way, Puriton, Bridgwater (0278) 684027; or local tackle shops

DUNWEAR PONDS
Bridgwater
Permits: L.A. Williams, 7 Webber Way, Puriton Bridgwater (0278) 684027

NEWTOWN PONDS
Highbridge
Bream, carp, roach and rudd
Permits: day and week permits from Chard Cycle Co., Holyrood Street, Chard

PERRY STREET POND
Chard
Permits: season and day permits from Chard Cycle Co., Holyrood Street, Chard

RED LYNCH LAKE
Bruton
Permits: available on site

SCREECH OWL PONDS
Bridgwater
Permits: L.A. Williams, 7 Webber Way, Puriton Bridgwater (0278) 684027

TAUNTON ROAD POND
Taunton
Permits: L.A. Williams, 7 Webber Way, Puriton Bridgwater (0278) 684027

Coarse Fishing: Other Waters

SEMINGTON BROOK
Rises S of Devizes and flows NW to link with the Avon near Holt. Mixed Fishing
Permits: day and week permits from Smith & Ford Sports, Bradford on Avon; Wests Tackle, Roundstone Street, Trowbridge; Bradford on Avon & District AA

RIVER HUNTSPILL
Man-made drainage channel excavated in the 1940's and connected to river Brue & South Drain via the Cripps River. Bream, carp, dace, eel, perch, pike, roach, rudd, ruff and tench
Permits: Local tackle shops or L.A Williams, 7 Webber Way, Puriton Bridgwater (0278) 684027

KING'S SEDGEMOOR DRAIN
Artificial drainage channel dug around 1790. It carries diverted waters of river Carey. Notable coarse fishery and used for local and national match fishing competitions. Bream, carp, eel, perch, pike, roach, rudd and tench
Permits: L.A. Williams, 7 Webber Way, Puriton
Bridgwater (0278) 684027

EIGHTEEN FOOT RHYNE
An arm of King's Sedgemoor Drain. Contains usual coarse fish species encountered in this area
Permits: day and week from L.A. Williams, 7 Webber Way, Puriton Bridgwater (0278) 684027

LANGACRE RHYNE
Drainage channel which carries excess water from the moors into the King's Sedgemoor Drain. Contains most species of coarse fish
Permits: local tackle shops and L.A. Williams, 7 Webber Way, Puriton Bridgwater (0278) 684027

NORTH DRAIN
Excavated in late 18th century to drain moorland to the north of River Brue. Bream, rudd, perch
Permits: day and week permits from local tackle shops and L.A. Williams, 7 Webber Way, Puriton Bridgwater (0278) 684027

SOUTH DRAIN
Known locally as the Old Glastonbury Canal the South Drain begins at Edington and is linked to the Huntspill River via the pumping station at Gold Corner. Contains a good head of bream, roach, perch, tench and carp
Permits: L.A. Williams, 7 Webber Way, Puriton; G. Jotcham, High St., Burnham-on-Sea; Nicholas Sports, Street

WESTMOOR/SOUTHMOOR/THORNEYMOOR AND LONG LOAD DRAINS
Permits: Local tackle shops and L.A. Williams, 7 Webber Street, Puriton, Bridgwater

Coarse Fishing: Canals

KENNET AND AVON CANAL
The finest canal fishery in British Isles. Contains all the major coarse fish species. Started in 18th century and completed in 1810. Extends 57 miles, linking the Thames at Reading with the Bristol Avon at Bath
Permits: day and week permits from Smith & Ford Sports, Bradford on Avon; Wests Tackle, Roundstone Street, Trowbridge; Bradford on Avon District AA; Day permits from Crudingtons, Broad Street, Bath; Fishcraft, Brougham Hayes, Bath; Bathampton AA

FEEDER CANAL
Bristol
Permits: Veals Tackle Shop, Bristol

BRIDGWATER AND TAUNTON CANAL
Permits: day and week permits from local tackle shops and L.A. Williams, 7 Webber St., Puriton; day permits from Bridge Sports of Topp Tackle, Taunton

Angling

Game Fishing: Rivers

AVON

RIVER CHEW
Trout fishing from Compton Dando to confluence with River Avon at Keynsham
See also: Coarse Fishing
Permits: Bristol & Avon Amalgamated Anglers, season permits only

SOMERSET

RIVER CHEDDAR, YEO
Finds its source in Cheddar Gorge and from here through the town of Cheddar it offers trout fishing
Permits: day permits available from local tackle shops

RIVER ISLE
Trout fishing from source near Chard down to Ilminster
See also: Coarse Fishing
Permits: day permits from Chard Cycle Co., Holyrood Street, Chard; Clapps Newsagents, Ilminster; Rules Tackle Shop, Langport

RIVER PARRETT
Upper reaches preserved for trout fishing
See also: Coarse Fishing
Permits: day permits from Rules Tackle Shop, Langport, Hoggs Tackle, Yeovil and most of the major clubs and tackle shops in the region

RIVER TONE
Trout found in the 20 mile stretch of river from Clatworthy Reservoir to Taunton
See also: Coarse fishing
Permits: Bridge Sports, Taunton; Topps Tackle, Taunton; most tackle shops in Wellington

RIVER YEO (YEOVIL)
See: Coarse Fishing
Permits: Tony Coles Florist, The Square, Ilchester; Hagas Tackle, Yeovil; Marney Sports, Yeovil

Game Fishing: Stillwaters

AVON

BARROW RESERVOIRS
Bristol
Least popular of Bristol Reservoirs. Restocked with yearling fish only. Fishing from the bank
Permits: day and season permits available on site

BLAGDON LAKE
Bristol
Fishing from the bank and boats. Brown and Rainbow trout
Permits: day and season available from lake

CAMELEY LAKES
Temple Cloud
Fly fishing only. Privately owned
Permits: information from Mr J. Harris, Hillcrest Farm, Cameley, Temple Cloud (0761) 52423

CHEW VALLEY LAKE
Chew Stoke, Bristol
Popular trout fishery. Brown and Rainbow trout. Fishing from banks and boats
Permits: season and day permits available on site

DODINGTON HOUSE
Chipping Sodbury
Upper lake contains trout
Permits: information from; The Agent, Dodington House, Chipping Sodbury (0454) 318899

ST ALGAR'S FARM LAKE
West Woodlands, Frome
Permits: advance booking required. Warminster (0985) 3233

SOMERSET

CLATWORTHY RESERVOIR
Wiveliscombe, Taunton
Lying on the edge of Exmoor, this
reservoir offers 5 miles of shoreline in
a water well-stocked by the Wessex
Water Authority
Permits: available from fishing lodge
on site
Reservoir Ranger, Wivelscombe
(0984) 23549

DURLEIGH RESERVOIR
Bridgwater
80 acre lowland reservoir well
stocked with brown and rainbow
trout. Boat and bank fishing
Permits: available from angling lodge
at reservoir
Reservoir Ranger, Bridgwater (0278)
424786

HAWKRIDGE RESERVOIR
Spaxton, 5m W Bridgwater
32 acres. Well stocked reservoir lying
under Quantock Hills. Rainbow trout
Permits: available on self-issue basis
at the shelter near the car park

NUTSCALE RESERVOIR
Owned by Wessex Water Authority,
leased to syndicate for trout fishing
Permits: limited permits only by
advance booking from T C B Guy, The
Great House, Timberscombe (064
384) 345

OTTERHEAD LAKES
Churchingford, Taunton
2 small lakes on South side of
Blackdown Hills linked by stream.
Well stocked with rainbow and brown
trout. Bank fishing only
Permits: available from Otterhead
lodge

SUTTON BINGHAM RESERVOIR
Yeovil
142 acres with more than 5 miles
shoreline. Excellent bank and boat

fishing for brown and rainbow trout
Permits: day permits from fishing
lodge on site
Reservoir Ranger: Yetminster (0935)
872389

Sea Fishing

WESTON SUPER MARE
Shore and boat fishing. During winter
the best catches are pout, cod and
whiting. During spring and summer,
flounder, bass, dabs, skate, conger
and sole are the main catches to be
had
Boat Charter
'Weston Star'
Skipper: Ivan Nash
Weston-super-Mare (0934) 22788

MINEHEAD
Beach fishing reasonable for flounder,
dabs and bass. Boat fishing mainly for
conger, cod, bass and dogfish. Some
good catches of mackerel in summer.
Harbour fishing for mullet, codling
and bass
Boat Charter
'Joseph-Marrie II'
Skipper: Dave Roberts
Minehead (0643) 3892
'Pelican II' Minehead (0643 5272
'Searcher'
Minehead (0643) 3687
'Gay Spartan'
Minehead (0643) 2701
'Sundown'
Minehead (0643) 5361
'Minehead Angler'
Skipper: T. Arnold
Minehead (0643) 5730/4158
'Michael I'
Skipper: Roger Baker
Minehead (0643) 3974
'Miss Tilley'
Minehead (0643) 2674

WATCHET
Good boat fishing location with lots of
excellent marks. Steart Flats, near
Watchet are productive with good

Angling

catches of flounders, dabs and rays. Shore fishing from Bassington and Dunster beaches are reasonable for dogfish and conger

Coarse Angling Clubs

Abbreviations
A   Angling
AA   Angling Association
C   Club
F   Fishing
P   Preservation
S   Society

AVON

BATHAMPTON AA
Secretary: D. Crookes 25 Otago Terrace, Larkhill, Bath
Bath (0225) 27164
Membership: unrestricted
Formed: 1930
Members: 2300 **Facilities:** 10 miles of fishing on Bristol Avon, 5 miles of trout fishing on tributaries of the Bristol Avon, 10 ponds and lakes offering carp, tench, etc

BLANDFORD & DISTRICT AC
Secretary: D. Stone
4 Cadley Close, Blandford Forum
Blandford (0258) 54054
Membership: unrestricted
Formed: 1952
Members: 275
Facilities: slow moving fishing in and around Blandford. Dorset Stour

BRISTOL AVON & DISTRICT ANGLERS CONSULTATIVE ASSOCIATION
Secretary: C.F. Sutton
147 Sheridan Road, Twerton, Bath
Bath (0225) 28210

BRISTOL GOLDEN CARP AA
Secretary: C. Golding
24 Queen Street, Two Mile Hill, Kingswood, Bristol
Bristol (0272) 677379

BRISTOL & DISTRICT AMALGAMATED ANGLERS
Secretary: I.S. Parker
16 Lansdown View, Kingswood, Bristol
Bristol (0272) 67977
Membership: unrestricted
Members: 600

BRISTOL & WEST OF ENGLAND FEDERATION OF ANGLERS
Secretary: V.D Tyrell
16 Falcon Close, Westbury-on-Trym
Bristol (0272) 500165
Membership: restricted
Formed: 1902
Members: 7,500 anglers represented
Facilities: Bristol Avon, 3 miles right bank downstream from confluence of Pipley Brook, Swineford to confluence of Willsbridge Brook, Willsbridge, Bristol including weir and scours at Keynsham. Feeder canal from Avon St Bridge to Netham Lock

RIDGEWAY & DISTRICT AA
Secretary: R.J. Walker
17 Birch Court, Keynsham, Bristol
BS18 2QR
Membership: unrestricted, junior membership available
Members: 60
Facilities: Many stretches of River Avon, Bristol stretches on River Brue, River Yeo, River Chew, River Axe, Somerset, Frome, Tockenham reservoir, Pawlett Ponds and Nailsea Ponds. Hiring available on 40 peg limit application in writing at least 6 months in advance. For larger venue apply to Bristol & District Amalgamated Anglers

STALBRIDGE AS
Secretary: A.M. Cairns
33 Park Road, Stalbridge
Stalbridge (0963) 62562
Membership: unrestricted
Members: 180
Formed: 1950
Facilities: 2 miles of the River Stour

containing chub, roach, pike, perch, dace, gudgeon; 1 mile River Lydden also containing chub, roach, eels, etc

STURMINSTER & HINTON AA
Secretary: T.J. Caines
Coombe Gate, The Bridge, Sturminster
Sturminster Newton (0258) 72355
Membership: restricted
Members: 300
Formed: 1905
Facilities: 7 miles on both banks of River Stour

WESTON-SUPER-MARE & DISTRICT AA
Secretary: J.A. Morgan
57 Earlham Grove, Weston-super-Mare
Membership: unrestricted
Members: 1000
Formed: 1902

SOMERSET

BATHAMPTON AA
Secretary: A. Adams
38 Beech Avenue, Shepton Mallet
Membership: unrestricted
Members: 3,500
Formed: 1920
Facilities: coarse fishing on the Bristol Avon and ten ponds and lakes in Bath and the surrounding area. Trout fishing on the tributaries of the Bristol Avon

BRIDGWATER AA
Secretary: P.D. Summerhayes
4 Raleigh Close, Bridgwater
Bridgewater (0278) 56340
Membership: unrestricted
Members: in excess of 1840
Formed: 1905
Facilities: virtually all waters within a ten mile radius of Bridgwater, including Huntspill and Cripps Rivers, South Drain, Bridgwater and Taunton Canal between the River Parrett and bridge on A361. Local Rhynes and ponds. Season, weekly and day tickets are all entitled to use all waters and are listed on licence

CHARD & DISTRICT ANGLING CLUB
Secretary: D Lemon
38 Glanvill Avenue, Chard, TA20 1EU
Membership: unrestricted, junior membership available
Members: 150
Facilities: coarse fishing at Perry Street Pond, Perry Street, nr Chard and Ash Pond, Ash. Coarse and trout fishing at River Isle at Donyatt and Ilminster, and River Axe, Chard

CHEDDAR AC
Secretary: N.C. Cordery
'Applegarth' Mill Lane, Wedmore
Membership: unrestricted
Members: 200
Facilities: fishing on River Axe, Hixham Rhyne, North Drain and Cheddar Clay Pits

FROME & DISTRICT AA
Secretary: R.J. Lee
103 The Butts, Frome BA11 4AQ
Membership: unrestricted
Formed: 1931
Members: 350
Facilities: Approx. 7 miles of River Frome above and below town. A small trout stream and 1 lake containing tench, bream, roach etc

ILCHESTER & DISTRICT AA
Secretary: R.M Hughes
32 St Cleers Orchard, Somerton
Membership: unrestricted. Junior membership available
Formed: 1957
Members: 280
Facilities: River Yeo Ilchester, members also permitted to fish Wessex Federation of Anglers water, river Parret, Isle Langport and shared water Westmoor/Southmoor, Thorney Moor and Long Load drains Langport area

ILMINSTER & DISTRICT AA
Secretary: A. Green
10 Hill View Terrace, Ilminster
Membership: unrestricted

Angling

Formed: 1953
Members: 100 seniors, 100 juniors
Facilities: About 6 miles of water from downstream of Ilminster. The water from downstream of Ilminster. The water holds roach , chub, dace, gudgeon, rudd and some perch. A relatively fast flowing river. A better winter river than a summer one

LANGPORT & DISTRICT AA
Secretary: Mrs I. Barlow "Florissant" Northfield, Somerton TA11 6SJ
Membership: unrestricted
Formed: 1957
Members: 336 adults & juniors
Facilities: River Parrett, Yeo Corner to Oath Lock on opposite bank to that held by Wessex Federation. Slow to medium flow

NORTH SOMERSET ASSOCIATION OF AC
Secretary: R. Newton
64 Clevedon Road, Tickenham, Clevedon
Membership: unrestricted
Members: 2000
Facilities: Association of Weston-super-Mare & District AA,Highbridge AA and Clevedon & District FAC

STOKE-SUB-HAMDON & DISTRICT AA
Secretary: M. Prescott
'Homemead' Rimpton Road, Marston Magna, Yeovil
Membership: unrestricted
Formed: 1955
Members: 250
Facilities: River fishing, coarse and trout, on upper reaches of River Parrett

TAUNTON FLY FC
Secretary: J.S. Hill
21 Manor Road, Taunton
Membership: unrestricted. Junior membership available
Formed: pre 1900
Members: approx 95

Facilities: 10 miles of River Tone upstream of French Weir, Taunton. Three separate stretches totalling 2 miles on River Axe, Devon

WESTLAND FRESHWATER AC
Secretary: B.E. Swain
108 Beechwood, Yeovil
Membership: restricted
Formed: 1965
Members: 250
Facilities: Stretch of River Yeo at Mudford. 2 miles. Also a pool at Charlton Mackral. Good dace and roach. Most other coarse fish in small quantities

YEOVIL AND SHERBOURNE AA
Secretary: N. Garrett
18 Springfield Road, Yeovil
Membership: unrestricted

Game Angling Clubs

AVON

BATHAMPTON AA
Secretary: D. Crookes, 25 Otago Terrace, Larkhill, Bath
Bath (0225) 27164
Membership: unrestricted
Formed: 1930
Members: 2300
Facilities: 10 miles of fishing on Bristol Avon, 5 miles of trout fishing on tributaries of the Bristol Avon, 10 ponds and lakes offering carp, tench etc

SOMERSET

BATHAMPTON AA
Secretary: A. Adams
38 Beech Avenue, Shepton Mallet
Membership: unrestricted
Formed: 1920
Members: 3,500
Facilities: coarse fishing on the Bristol Avon and ten ponds and lakes in Bath and the surrounding area. Trout fishing on the tributaries of the Bristol Avon

CHARD & DISTRICT ANGLING CLUB

Secretary: D. Lemon
38 Glanvill Avenue, Chard TA20 1EU
Membership: unrestricted. Junior membership available
Members: 150
Facilities: Coarse fishing at Perry Street Pond, Perry Street. Coarse and trout fishing at River Isle at Donyatt and Ilminster, and River Axe, Broom Bridge

NORTH SOMERSET ASSOCIATION OF AC

Secretary: R. Newton
64 Clevedon Road, Tickenham, Clevedon
Facilities: Association of Weston-super-Mare & District AA; Highbridge AA and Clevedon & District FAC

STOKE-SUB-HAMBON & DISTRICT AA

Secretary: Mr M. Prescott
'Homemead' Rimpton Road, Marston Magna, Yeovil
Membership: unrestricted
Formed: 1955
Members: 500
Facilities: River fishing, coarse and trout, on upper reaches of River Parrett

TAUNTON FLY FC

Secretary: J.S. Hill
21 Manor Road, Taunton
Membership: unrestricted. Junior membership available
Formed: pre 1900
Members: approx 95
Facilities: 10 miles of River Tone upstream of French Weir, Taunton. Three separate stretches totalling 2 miles on River Axe, Devon

Sea Angling Clubs

AVON

ALBATROSS SAC

Secretary: C.J.C. Wood
33 Stanbury Avenue, Fishponds, Bristol
Bristol (0272) 570421
Membership: unrestricted
Members: 40 **Formed:** 1975
Facilities: full year of booked trips for deep sea angling to venues on the South and West coasts, also Wales. Shore and competitions section taking part in club and federation organised trips and matches

BRISTOL SA

Secretary: M.J. Bacon
41 Grass Meers Drive, Whitchurch, Bristol (0272) 830621
Membership: restricted
Formed: 1950
Members: 45
Facilities: the club concentrates on boat fishing at South West Coastal venues. 2 trips per month on a regular basis catering for up to 10 members at a time

BRISTOL SHARK CLUB

Secretary: W.J. Dunstone
Home Farm, Courtlands Lane, Bower Ashton
Weston-super-Mare (0934) 862063
Membership: restricted
Formed: 1963
Members: 30
Facilities: Deep sea fishing in Bristol Channel and South Coast

BRUNEL SAC

Secretary: K. Reed
27 St Michaels Avenue, Clevedon BS21 6LL
Bristol (0272) 872101
Membership: restricted
Formed: 1971
Members: 35

MERCHANT ARMS SAC
Secretary: H.E Rushton
23 Cornish Walk, Stockwood
Bristol (0272) 837511
Membership: unrestricted
Formed: 1973
Members: 70
Facilities: wide range of sea angling, wreck, reef and shark. Also very keen to enlarge beach casting section. Fish mostly in Devon & Cornwall

PIONEER SAC
Secretary: C. Jones
11 Longway Avenue, Whitchurch, Bristol (0272) 837191
Membership: unrestricted
Formed: 1975
Members: 120
Facilities: anywhere on the English or Bristol Channels, Welsh Coast and Irish Sea. Both boat and shore fishing

WESTON-SUPER-MARE AA
Secretary: G.A. Crossman
3 Little Orchard, Uphill
Weston-super-Mare (0934) 31129
Membership: unrestricted
Formed: 1952
Members: 200
Facilities: club house and organised boat and shore matches in Devon, Somerset and Avon

SOMERSET

3 BS SAA
Secretary: R. Lambert
14 Julians Acres, Berrow
Membership: unrestricted
Formed: 1976
Members: 120
Facilities: coastal waters of the Bristol Channel along the Burnham and Berrow shore line. Charter boat facilities available from Burnham-on-Sea. Fishing the reefs of Hinkley point and Brean Down

BLACKDOWN SAC
Secretary: P.F. Milton
13 Churchfields, Wellington TA21 8SD
Wellington (082347) 6453
Membership: restricted
Formed: 1975
Members: 75
Facilities: sea angling only

BRIDGWATER SAC
Secretary: O. Syms
101 Holford Road, Bridgwater
Bridgwater (0278) 423043
Membership: unrestricted
Formed: 1965
Members: 87
Facilities: 16 charter boat trips annually from Plymouth, Minehead and Ilfracombe. Boat Festival at Ilfracombe. Beach and boat matches under auspices of Bristol Channel Federation of Sea Anglers. Monthly club beach matches in local area

CHARD & DISTRICT ANGLING CLUB
See Coarse Angling Clubs

HINKLEY POINT SAC
Secretary: J.A. Fidoe
9 Willow Walit, Bridgwater
Bridgwater (0278) 55896
Membership: restricted
Formed: 1970
Members: 60
Facilities: fishing throughout the country. Particularly the south side of the Bristol Channel (Hinkley Reefs) near power station. Own boat for club members moored at Porlock for deep fishing in the Channel

KINGS BILLY SAC
Secretary: M. Patrick
7 Woodland Road, Frome
Frome (0373) 71534
Membership: unrestricted
Formed: 1976

Members: 35
Facilities: deep sea venues from
Dartmouth to SW Wales to 60 miles
out when wrecking. Beach from Poole
to Weston-super-Mare

N.F.S.A. MISTERTON AC
Secretary: J. Bloomfield
16 Southmead Crescent, Crewkerne
Membership: unrestricted
Formed: 1971
Members: 24
Facilities: Westbay Bridport, Lyme
Regis, Weymouth, Brixham,
Dartmouth, Bere Regis

RAINBOW SAC
Secretary: P.N. Southword
16 Howard Road, Yeovil
Yeovil (0935) 21438
Membership: unrestricted
Formed: 1974
Members: 60
Facilities: Poole Harbour to Brixham.
Everybody welcome

TAUNTON VALE SA
Secretary: K. Dawe
90 Belmont Road, Taunton
Taunton (0823) 74433
Membership: unrestricted
Formed: 1975
Members: 75
Facilities: beach and boat fishing
from Dorset, Somerset, Devon and
Cornwall

TOR SAC
Secretary: R.W.G. Musgrave
18 Mildred Road, Walton
Street (0458) 42957
Membership: unrestricted
Formed: 1958
Members: 60

WESTLANDS SPORTS SAC
Secretary: J. Robinson
15 Crofton Park, Yeovil
Yeovil (0935) 71818
Membership: unrestricted
Formed: 1965
Members: 50
Facilities: club matches are fished

mainly on Chesil Beach, Poole, Bristol
Channel and Weymouth Bay areas

Aquariums

**SEA SHELL EXHIBITION AND
AQUARIUM**
Weston-super-Mare (0934) 417117
Marine Lake, Marine Parade, Weston-
super-Mare
Open: March-Oct, daily 10.00- 20.00
Charge: 50p (ch 35p)
Variety of species from all over the
world including tropical and marine
fish, aquatic animals, S American
piranahs, alligators. Also interesting
sea shell exhibition
🅿 ♿ ♿

Archaeological Sites

BRITISH ENCAMPMENT
Map 4 Ab
Worlebury Hill, Weston-super-Mare
Open: anytime
Free
British hill fort covering 10/2 acres,
where local Saxons inflicted a heavy
defeat on the Romans in 577AD

Archaeological Sites

CADBURY CASTLE
Map 3 Ab
7m NE Yeovil S of A303
Open: all year, daily
Free
18 acre hill fort believed to be site of King Arthurs Camelot. Extensive excavations have revealed that the site was inhabited before 3,000BC and that it was fortified by Iron Age, British & Anglo Saxon tribes. Most of the surviving structure dates from 11th century when it was defended against the danes by Ethelred the Unready
Guides available during summer months when excavations are in progress
Excellent views

CASTLE NEROCHE
5m NW Chard off unclassified Chard-Widcombe road
Map 2 Ac
Open: all year, daily
Free
Remains of impressive 11th century earth-work castle situated in a conifer wood
See also woodlands: Castle Neroche Wood

CHALICE WELL
Glastonbury, at the foot of Glastonbury Tor
Open: March-Oct, daily, 9.00- 17.00; Nov-April, daily, 13.00-16.30
Also known as Blood Spring, the Chalice Well has an ancient tradition of healing and its symbolic association with blood connects it in early Christian and Arthurian legend with the Quest for the Holy Grail

HAM HILL CAMP
Map 3 Ac
3m W Yeovil off A3088
Open: anytime
Free: Large L- shaped Iron Age and Roman hill fort of about 200 acres situated within Ham Hill Country Park

JOANEY HOW AND ROBIN HOW
Map 1 Ba
Dunkerey Hill, 3m S Porlock off the unclassified Porlock-Langham road
Open: anytime
Free
Two cairns over 70ft wide, Robin being 10ft high and Joaney about half that. Names thought to have derived from Robin Hood and Little John

KINGS WESTON ROMAN VILLA
See Roman Sites

PORLOCK STONE CIRCLE
Map 1 Aa
2m SW Porlock on unclassified Hawkomb Head-Edgcott road
Open: anytime
Free
Bronze Age site 80ft across with 10 standing and fallen stones. All quite small

PRIDDY NINE BARROWS
Map 3 Aa
North Hill, 4m N Wells on B3135
Open: anytime
Group of Bronze Age burial mounds one of which yielded several finds now exhibited in Bristol City Museum

SEA MILL'S ROMAN BUILDINGS
See Roman Sites

STANTON DREW CIRCLES
Map 4 Bb
Stanton Drew, 6m S Bristol off B3130
Open: all year, Mon-Sat, at discretion of the owners
Free
Most important prehistoric monument in Avon. 3 Bronze Age circles, 2 avenues of standing stones and a burial chamber. Thought to be smaller version of Stonehenge

STOKLEIGH CAMP
Map 4 Ab
Avon Gorge, 2m W Bristol city centre
off A369
Open: anytime
Free
Iron Age hill fort within Leigh Woods.
Largest of 3 promontory forts which
controlled passage up the River Avon
See also Woodlands: Leigh Woods

**STONEY LITTLETON LONG
BARROW**
Map 4 Bb
Wellow, 6m S Bath off B3770
Open: all year, daily, at any
reasonable time (keys and candles
from Stoney Littleton farm)
Free
The finest prehistoric tomb of its kind
in Avon, it is 107ft long, 13ft high
and includes a passage grave some
50ft long. Restored in 1858

**RPS NATIONAL CENTRE OF
PHOTOGRAPHY**
Three main galleries of changing
photographic exhibitions
See Museums

VICTORIA ART GALLLERY
Bath (0225) 61111 ext 324
Bridge Street, Bath
Open: all year, Mon-Fri 10.00-
18.00; Saturdays 10.00-17.00.
Closed Sundays and BH's
Free
Collection includes European Old
Masters and 18thc-20thc British
paintings, drawings and watercolours

WATERSHED GALLERY
Bristol (0272) 276444
1 Cannons' Road, Bristol
Open: all year, Mon-Sat, 12.00-
20.00. Telephone for exhibition
programme details
Free
Gallery within Britain's first media and
communications centre. Programme
of changing contemporary exhibitions
🅿 ♿ 🍴

Art Galleries

ARNOLFINI GALLERY
Bristol (0272) 299191
Narrow Quay, Bristol
Open: all year, Tues-Sat 11.00-
20.00; Sun 14.00-19.00
Free
Arts complex with exhibitions of
painting and sculpture. Also
performances of contemporary music,
theatre, dance and film
🅿 🍴 🍽 🍴

**CITY MUSEUM AND ART
GALLERY**
Good collection of English, Italian and
Dutch masters, sculpture, glass and
excellent ceramics
See Museums

Bird Parks

**AMBLESIDE WATER GARDENS
AND AVIARIES**
Map 2 Ba
Axbridge (0934) 732362
Lower Weare, 1m SW Axbridge on
A38
Open: Easter-early Oct, Tues-Sun &
BH's 10.30- 17.30; end Oct-Easter,
w/ends 10.30-17.30
Charge: 60p (ch40p)

Natural walk through aviary with over 250 species of birds. Also attractive garden containing shrubs, rabbits, guinea pigs and pheasants
Dogs on leads
🅿 ♿ 🚻 ☕

BREAN DOWN BIRD GARDENS
Map 2 Aa
Brean Down (027 875) 209
Brean Down, 2m S Weston-super-Mare off A370
Open: early Apr-end Oct, daily 10.00-18.00
Charges: 75p (ch 40p)
Collection over 100 birds from all over the world
Dogs on leads
🅿 ♿ 🚻☕

BRITISH BIRDS OF PREY CENTRE
Centre where sick and injured birds of Prey (Hawks and Owls) are cared for in the hope that they can be returned to the wild. Also a Barn Owl conservation programme is in operation
See Country Parks: Combe Sydenham Country Park

TROPICAL AVIARY
Finest of its kind in the country. Enables visitors to watch a wide variety of free-flying birds from America, Asia and North and South America. Designed to give the birds conditions which are as close as possible to their natural habitat
See Unusual Outings: Cricket St Thomas Wildlife Park

RODE TROPICAL BIRD GARDENS
Map 3 Ba
Beckington (0373) 30326
Rode, 4m N Frome off A36
Open: all year, daily 10.00-18.00 or dusk if earlier (closed 25, 26 Dec)
Charge: £1.65 (ch 80p, OAP's £1.30)

Brilliant collection of almost 180 species of exotic birds in 17 acres of gardens. Larger birds include penguins, vultures, macaws and flamingoes
Pets corner, butterfly & insect exhibition, aquarium, reptile house
No Dogs
🅿 🚻 ♿ ☕🍴

WIDCOMBE TROPICAL BIRD GARDENS
Map 2 Ac
Blagdon Hill (082342) 268
Blagdon, 6m S Taunton off B3170
Open: April-Oct, daily 10.30- 17.30
Charge: £1.25 (Ch 70p)
Tropical birds shown in park-like grounds
🅿 🚻 ♿ ☕

Bird Watching

This section includes areas specially designated as bird reserves and information concerning the relevant bodies controlling those reserves. Also included are areas which because of their particular environment offer ideal habitats for particular species and are therefore good places for ornithological observation

When visiting any of the places listed remember that they are there for the birds so do nothing which would in any way disturb them or harm their environment. Always keep to marked paths

Organisations

ROYAL SOCIETY FOR THE PROTECTION OF BIRDS

The lodge, Sandy, Beds SG19 2DL
The RSPB is a charity and part of its work involves managing 85 bird reserves in Great Britain. The aim of these reserves is the conservation of birds and their habitat. The RSPB organises birdwatching and bird conservation. There is a special organisation for young people: Young Ornithologists' Club (YOC)

If you would like to know more about the RSPB and YOC, if you would like to make a donation or become a member contact the address above

Reserves and Sites of Ornithological Interest

BREAN DOWN
Map 2 Aa
2m S Weston-super-Mare off A370
Access: anytime
300 ft high limestone headland with variety of birds including gulls, kestrels, chats and redshanks. Ideal migration watching point, especially during October

BRIDGWATER BAY NATIONAL NATURE RESERVE
Map 2 Aa
5m NW Bridgwater
Access: Apr-Oct by permit only
Permits: available on application to the Warden, D'Arches, Stolford, Stogursey
Excellent for mallard, wigeon, teal and shelduck. Only place in Britain where shelduck gather in large numbers to moult in mid-summer. White-fronted geese visit the reserve occassionally during winter. Hides are provided from which good views of the birds

can be obtained
NCC

CHEW VALLEY LAKE
Map 4 Bb
Chew Stoke, 8m S Bristol on unclassified Bristol-Chew Stoke road
Access: anytime
One of the best areas for winter wildfowl in Britain. During Autumn the lake attracts numerous waders, divers and Grebes. Large Gull roost in winter
WWA

DURLEIGH RESERVOIR
Map 2 Ab
2m W Bridgwater off unclassified Bridgwater-Enmore road
Access: by permit only
Permits: available on application to Wessex Water Authority
West end of reservoir has been designated as a bird sanctuary. Shallow lake attracts dabbling duck and passage waders in autumn and mute swans in July and August
WWA

LEIGH WOODS
Map 4 Ab
3m SW Bristol city centre off B3129
Access: anytime
159 acre mixed broadleaf wood in Avon Gorge provides habitat for woodpeckers, nightingales, redstart and hawfinch
See also Nature Reserves
NT

PORLOCK MARSH
Map 1 Aa
West Porlock, 6m W Minehead off A39
Access: anytime
Area of gorse, reed beds and shallow pools supporting winter duck, waders and frequent passage waders

Boat Trips

STEEP HOLME
Map 2 Aa
off the coast, 5m W Weston-super-Mare
Access: details from Steep Holme Trust, 11 Kendon Drive, Westbury-on-Trym, Bristol
Breeding colony for gulls and cormorants

WEST SEDGEMOOR BIRD RESERVE
Map 2 Bb
West Sedgemoor, 7m E Taunton off unclassified Taunton-North Curry road
Open: Feb-June, Saturdays, by arrangement with warden (groups of 20 only)
Charge: £1.00
Lowland flood meadow attracting variety of species. Reserve is owned and managed by RSPB (see above)
RSPB

Boat Trips

This section includes most of the well known cruises available in Avon. Where possible departure times and charges have been included. However, it is always advisable to check. Local tourist information offices will have a list of all the cruises available and their departure times and they will be happy to assist you

BATH BOATING COMPANY
Bath (0225) 66407
Forester Road, Bath
Open: April-end Sept, daily 10.00-dusk

Passenger launch operates from Pulteney Weir-Bathampton. Telephone for details of departure times and fares
Skiffs and punts for hire

BRISTOL & BATH CRUISERS
Bristol (0272) 214307
Phoenix Wharf, Bristol
Open: all year
Operates a variety of cruises on the Bristol Harbour and the River Avon in modern well furnished, weatherproof vessels the 'Flower of Bristol', the 'Avon Queen' and the 'Enterprise of Bristol'
Candlelight Cruise: 2 hour candlelight cruise of Bristol Harbour operating from Narrow Quay
Departs: 20.00
Charge: £7.00 per person, including choice of meal
Sunday River Cruise: 6 hour trip on River Avon
Departs: Apr-Oct, on some Sundays
Charge: £8.00 with lunch, £6.00 without lunch (Ch14 £5.00, £3.00)
Trips also operate from Narrow Quay on BH's at hourly intervals. Boats may be hired for group bookings
✗ ♀

BRISTOL FERRY BOAT COMPANY
Bristol (0272) 558986
Open: April-Sept, daily 11.00-18.00
Ferry boats 'Margaret' and 'Independence' operate a daily scheduled ferry service around Bristol City Docks calling at 14 landing stages between Hotwells and Bristol Bridge
Charge: single 50p; return £1.00 (ch & OAP's 25p and 50p)
Boats are also available for private bookings and school/educational trips at special rates. For further information and timetables contact bookings office

KENNET AND AVON CANAL WATERBUS
Bristol (0282) 48135
Kennet and Avon Canal Trust, The
Wharf, Crouch Lane, Devizes
12 seater, enclosed waterbus
'Dragonfly' operates 45 minute trips
on the Kennet and Avon Canal from
Bath to Folly Bridge
Departures: Easter-Sept, Sundays;
May- August, Saturdays 14.30 and
then at 45 minute intervals thereafter
Charge: 80p (ch 40p)
One and a half hour trips from Bath to
Claverton Pumping Station
Departs: April-Oct, pumping days
10.30 (telephone for exact dates)
Charge: £2.50 (ch £1.75)
Also Charter Trips for groups 12
people by arrangement
Kennet and Avon Canal Trust
Information Centre
Open: Easter-end Sept, Sun and
BH's; May-Aug, Saturdays only
14.15- 17.30
Information on the canal, maps,
guides, souvenirs

Caravan & Camping Sites

CARAVANS
Any reference in this section to
caravans is to touring vans, not to
permanent vans. Some of the sites
will have permanent vans for hire
(often very large holiday camp caravan
parks) while others are open only to
touring caravans, dormobiles & tents.
If you have a preference for a
particular type of caravan park always

telephone in advance to check
There are many other sites which
have only permanent caravans for hire
(usually on a weekly basis). Contact
local tourist information centres for
details.
Listed below is a selection of
touring caravan parks and camping
sites.

TENTS
Tents are admitted to the following
camping and caravan sites where
indicated.

CHARGES
Charges given are for one day/night.
Unless otherwise indicated charges
for caravans and tents include a car;
charges for caravans, tents and
dormobiles include two people. There
may be a range of charges for tents
depending on size

LOCATIONS
Locations are listed under the nearest
town

Avonmouth

VILLA CARAVAN PARK
Map 4 Aa
Pilning (04545) 2540
Severn Beach, Pilning, 4m N
Avonmouth off A403
Open: March-Oct
Pitches: 25 tents or caravans
Charges: available on application
Childrens play area

Bath

BURY VIEW FARM
Map 4 Bb
Saltford (02217) 3672
Corston Fields, 1m W Bath on A39
Open: Easter-end Sept
Pitches: 15 caravans or tents
Charges: available on application
Dogs on leads

NEWBRIDGE CARAVAN PARK
Marshfield (0225) 28778
Brass Mill Lane, Bath
Open: all year
Pitches: 72 caravans
Charges: from £5.00
Dogs on leads, childrens play area
🐾

Bridgwater

HUNTWORTH GATE CARAVAN PARK
Map 2 Ab
Bridgwater (0278) 56823
Taunton Road, 2m S Bridgewater off A38 or M5
Open: March-Oct
Pitches: 15 caravans; 45 dormobiles or tents
Charges: from £2.50
Dogs on leads, childrens play area

LAKESIDE PARK
Map 2 Ab
Bridgwater (0278) 423352
121 Taunton Road, Bridgwater
Open: March-Nov
Pitches: 10 caravans
Charge: £2.50
Dogs on leads
🐾

Burnham-on-Sea

HOME FARM CARAVAN & CAMPING PARK
Map 2 Ba
Burnham-on-Sea (0278) 783632
Edithmead, 1 m E Burnham-on-Sea on B3140
Open: all year
Pitches: 120 caravans; 50 tents; 50 dormobiles
Charges: £3.50 (peak times July-Sept); £2.50 (off-peak); Dogs 60p
Childrens adventure playground, coarse fishing lake, bicycle hire, pony rides, picnics, rambles and many other activities and entertainments organized throughout the summer
🐾 ☕ ♀ 🚻

LAKESIDE HOLIDAY PARK
Map 2 Ba
Burnham-on-Sea(0278) 783379
Westfield Road, 1m S Burnham-on-Sea on B3140
Open: April-Sept
Pitches: 100 caravans
Charges: from £1 (offpeak) to £5 (peak times)
No Dogs
Play area, outdoor swimming pool
🐾 ☕ ♀ 🚻

UNITY FARM HOLIDAY CENTRE
Map 2 Aa
Burnham-on-Sea (0278) 75235
Coast Road, 1 m N Berrow, 2m N Burnham- on-Sea on unclassified Berrow-Brean road
Open: March-Nov
Pitches: 800 caravans or tents
Charges: from £3.00
Dogs on leads
Childrens play area, games room, indoor swimming pool, access to adjoining leisure centre
🐾 ✕ 🚻

Chard

FIVE ACRES HOUSE
Map 2 Ac
Buckland St Mary (046 034) 364
Buckland St Mary, 5m NW Chard on A303
Open: all year
Pitches: 6 caravans or tents
Charge: caravans £1.75; tents £1.50
🐾

Cheddar

BROADWAY HOUSE CARAVAN & CAMPING SITE
Map 2 Ba
Cheddar (0934) 742610
1 m NW Cheddar on A371
Open: March-Oct
Pitches: 192 caravans & tents
Charges: available on application
Children's adventure playground,
heated outdoor swimming pool,
special facilities for disabled
🛁 ✕ ♿

CHURCH FARM CAMPING SITE
Map 2 Ba
Cheddar (0934) 743048
The Bungalow, Church Farm, Church
Street, Cheddar
Open: March-Oct
Pitches: 70 caravans & tents
Charge: caravans from £3.50; tents
from £3.00; awnings 50p extra
No dogs
🛁 ♿

FROGLANDS FARM CARAVAN & CAMPING PARK
Map 2 Ba
Cheddar (0934) 742058
Froglands Farm, 1 m SE Cheddar city
centre on A371
Open: Easter-Oct
Pitches: 18 caravans; 42 tents
Charges: available on application
🛁 ♿

NETHERDALE CAMPING GROUND
Map 2 Ba
Winscombe (093 484) 3481
Sidcot, 1 m N Cheddar on A38
Open: April-Oct
Pitches: 25 caravans & tents
Charges: £4.00
Dogs on leads

Clevedon

COLEHOUSE FARM CAMP SITE
Map 4 Ab
Clevedon (0272) 872680
Kenn, 1 m S Clevedon off B3133
Open: April-Sept
Pitches: 36 caravans & tents
Charges: £2.00
Dogs on leads

Dulverton

EXE VALLEY CARAVAN SITE
Map 1 Ab
Winsford (064 385) 206
Mill House, Bridgetown, 2m NW
Dulverton on A396
Open: April-Oct
Pitches: 20 caravans & 10 tents
Charges: available on application
Dogs on leads

EXMOOR HOUSE CARAVAN CLUB SITE
Dulverton (0398) 23268
Dulverton, 10m S Minehead on
B3223
Open: 2 Easter-end Oct
Pitches: 70 caravans
Charges: from £2.20 (peak times);
£1.80 (offpeak times); £1.00
surcharge for non-caravan club
members
Dogs on leads

HALSE FARM CAMP SITE
Map 1 Bb
Winsford (064 385) 259
Halse Farm, Winsford, 2m N
Dulverton off A396
Open: Mar-Oct
Pitches: 12 caravans; 12 tents
Charges: £2.00
Childrens play area
🛁

Caravan and Camping Sites

LOWTRON CROSS INN
Map 1 Bb
Brompton Regis (039 87) 220
Upton, 3m E Dulverton on B3190
Open: March-Oct
Pitches: 11 caravans & tents
Charges: £3.00 (peak times); £2.00
(off peak)
Adjoining pub & beer garden

Minehead

BEECHES HOLIDAY PARK
Map 1 Ba
Washford (0984) 40391
Blue Anchor Bay, 4m E Minehead on
B3191
Open: April-Sept
Pitches: 35 caravans & tents
Charges: from £3.50
Childrens play area, outdoor
swimming pool
🖢

MINEHEAD & EXMOOR CARAVAN
& CAMPING SITE
Map 1 Ba
Minehead (0643) 3074
1m W Minehead off A39
Open: all year
Pitches: 25 caravans & 25 tents
Charges: caravans £2.50; tents
£1.50; 50p per person
Dogs under control
Childrens play area, special facilities
for disabled

Porlock

BURROWHAYES CARAVAN &
CAMPING SITE
Map 1 Aa
1m E Porlock on A39
Open: March-Oct
Pitches: 40 caravans; 80 tents
Charges: available on application
Dogs on leads
Childrens play area
🖢

DOWNSCOMBE FARM CAMP
SITE
Map 1 Ab
Exford (064 383) 239
Downscombe Farm, 6m SW
Minehead off B3224
Open: April-Oct
Pitches: 30 tents
Charges: available on application

PORLOCK CARAVAN PARK
Porlock (0643) 862269
High Bank, Porlock
Open: March-end Oct
Pitches: 65 caravans & tents
Charges: available on application
Dogs on leads
🖢

WESTERMILL FARM
Map 1 Aa
Exford (064 383) 238
Exford, 4m SW Porlock off B3223
Open: May-Oct
Pitches: 60 tents
Charge: £3.50
🖢

Taunton

ANCHOR INN
Map 2 Ab
Bradford-on-Tone (082346) 334
Hillfarrance, S Norton Fitzwarren, 4m
W Taunton off A361
Open: April-Oct
Pitches: 5 caravans; 2 tents
Charges: caravans £2.00; tents
£1.00
Dogs under control
🗙 ፌ

ASHE FARM CARAVAN & CAMP
SITE
Taunton (0823) 442567
Thornfalcon, 1m SE Taunton on
A358
Open: April-Oct
Pitches: 15 caravans; 15 tents
Charges: £1.25 per person; £3.50
per family (2 adults and any number
of children)

ST QUENTIN HOTEL CARAVAN & CAMPING PARK
Map 2 Ab
Taunton (0823) 73016
Bridgwater Road, Bathpool, 1m NE
Taunton on A38
Open: all year
Pitches: 125 caravans & tents
Charges: from £5.00; reduced rates
for cyclists, hikers and children
🐾 ✗

STEWLEY CROSS CARAVAN SITE
Map 2 Ab
Hatch Beauchamp (0823) 480314
Stewley Cross filling station, Ashill,
3m SE Taunton on A358
Open: April-Oct
Pitches: 5 caravans & tents
Charges: £3.00
🐾

SQUARE & COMPASS INN
Map 2 Bc
Hatch Beauchamp (0823) 480467
Windmill Hill, 1/2m SW Ashill, 4m
SE Taunton off A358
Open: all year
Pitches: 5 caravans; 5 tents
Charges: £2.50
Dogs by arrangement
✗ ♀

Watchet

BLUE ANCHOR BAY CARAVAN PARK
Map 1 Ba
Dunster (064 382) 360
Blue Anchor Bay, 2m E Watchet on
B3191
Open: March-Oct
Pitches: 75 caravans
Charges: available on application
🐾 ♿

DONIFORD BAY HOLIDAY VILLAGE
Map 1 Ba
Williton (0984) 32423:P Doniford,
2m E Watchet off A39

Open: April-Sept
Pitches: 125 caravans & 38 tents
Charges: available on application
Childrens adventure playground
🐾 ♿

HOME FARM HOLIDAY CENTRE
Map 2 Aa
Williton (0984) 32487
St Audries Bay, Williton, 3m E
Watchet
Open: all year
Pitches: 35 caravans; 5 tents
Charges: £3.75
Private beach
🐾 ♀

QUANTOCK ORCHARD CARAVAN PARK
Map 2 Ab
Crowcombe (098 48) 618
Crowcombe, 3m SW Watchet on
A358
Open: all year
Pitches: 48 caravans & tents
Charges: caravans from £3.75; tents
from £3.75
Childrens playground
🐾

SUNNYBANK CARAVAN PARK
Map 1 Ba
Williton (0984) 32237
Doniford, 2m E Watchet on A39
Open: March-Nov
Pitches: 16 caravans & tents
Charge: available on application
Dogs on leads
Games room, heated outdoor
swimming pool
🐾

Caravan and Camping Sites

Weston-super-Mare

ARDNAVE CARAVAN & CHALET PARK
Map 4 Ab
Banwell (09934) 22319
Crooks Lane, Kewstoke, 2m NE
Weston- super-Mare on unclassified
Weston-super- Mare-Kewstoke road
Open: March-end Oct
Pitches: 20 caravans or tents
Charges: £4.50 (peak season);
£3.50 (off-peak); awnings 50p extra
🛦

CHANNEL VIEW CARAVAN & CAMPING SITE
Map 2 Aa
Brean Down (027 875) 241
Brean Farm, Brean Down, 2m SW
Weston- super-Mare off A370
Open: April-Oct
Pitches: 95 caravans & tents
Charges: available on application
Dogs on leads

MANOR FARM CARAVAN PARK
Map 4 Ab
Banwell (0934) 29731
Grange Road, Uphill, 1m S Weston-
super- Mare on A370
Open: Easter-end Sept
Pitches: 40 caravans
Charges: available on application
Dogs by arrangement

OAK TREE & WEST END CARAVAN PARK
Map 4 Ab
Banwell (0934) 822529
3m E Weston-super-Mare town
centre off A 371
Open: all year
Pitches: 30 caravans & tents
Charges: available on application
Dogs on lead
Childrens play area, special facilities
for disabled
🛦 ♿

PURN FARM CARAVAN PARK
Map 4 Ab
Bleadon (0934) 812342
Bleadon, 2m S Weston-super-Mare
city centre on A370
Open: March-Oct
Pitches: 150 caravans & tents
Charges: from £3.50
Swimming pool, children's play area
🛦 ♀

WARREN FARM CARAVAN & CAMPING PARK
Map 4 Ab
Brean Down (027 875) 227
Warren Road, Brean Down, 2m SW
Weston- super-Mare off A370
Open: April-Oct
Pitches: 300 caravans; 250 tents
Charges: £3.50
Dogs on leads
🛦

Wells

BUCKLEGROVE CARAVAN & CAMPING PARK
Map 3 Aa
Wells (0749) 870261
Wells Road, Rodney Stoke, 3m NW
Wells on A371
Open: March-Sept
Pitches: 98 caravans & tents
Charges: £5.00 (peak times); £4.50
(off-peak)
No Dogs, children's play area, indoor
swimming pool
🛦

HOMESTEAD PARK
Map 3 Aa
Wells (0749) 73023
Wookey Hole, 1/2m NW Wells off
A371
Open: Easter-Oct
Pitches: 55 caravans & tents
Charges: caravans £4.40; tents
£4.60
Post office & general store adjacent to
site

MANLEAZE CARAVAN PARK
Map 3 Aa
Shepton Mallet (0749) 3671
Cannards Grove, Shepton Mallet, 5m
SE Wells on A371
Open: all year
Pitches: 25 caravans and tents
Charges: caravans £2.50; dormobiles
£2.50-£3.00; tents from £2.00
Dogs on leads
🐾

**OLD DOWN HOUSE CAMPING
SITE**
Map 3 Aa
Stratton-on-the-Fosse (0761)
232355
Emborough, 3-4m NE Wells at the
junction of B3139 & A37
Open: mid March-early Nov
Pitches: 30-40 caravans and tents
Charge: £3.00
Children's play area
🐾

Yeovil

HIGHLANDS HOTEL
Map 3 Ac
West Coker (0935 86) 2318
175 West Coker Rd, 1/2m W Yeovil
on A30
Open: all year
Pitches: 5 caravans
Charge: £1.50
Children's play area

PARTWAY LANE CARAVAN PARK
Map 3 Ac
Yeovil (0935) 862863
West Coker Hill, West Coker, 1m SW
Yeovil on A30
Open: April-Oct
Pitches: 20 caravans and tents
Charge: caravans from £3.00; tents
from £2.50 (50p each extra person in
July & Aug)
Dogs on leads

Castles

CADBURY CASTLE
See Archaeological Sites:

DUNSTER CASTLE
Map 1 Ba
Dunster, 3m SE Minehead off A39
Open: Apr-end Sept, Sat-Wed 11.00-
17.00; Oct-Nov, Sat-Wed 12.00-
16.00 (last admission half hour
before closing time)
Charge: castle, grounds and park
£2.00; reductions for groups by
arrangement
Fortified home of the Luttrell family
for 600 years. Dates from the 13th
century with 19th-century additions.
Fine 17th-century staircase and
plaster ceilings. Also terraced garden
of rare shrubs and 28 acre park
Dogs in Park only
NT 🅿 🐾 ♿

FAIRLEIGH CASTLE
See Historic Homes

NUNNEY CASTLE
Map 3 Ba
Nunney, 3/2m SW Frome off A361
Open: standard DofE times
Free
Unusual late 14th-century castle more
French th North wall was pierced by a
shell in the Civil War in 1920. The
site has been well restored

TAUNTON CASTLE
12th century Norman castle with
massive walls. Notable gatehouse
added in 1495. Great Hall was the
scene of Judge Jeffrey's Bloody
Assize in 1685. Now the home of the
Somerset County Museum. **See
Museums**

Church Buildings

BATH ABBEY
Bath (0225) 330289
Abbey Churchyard, Bath
Open: March- Sept, daily 9.00-
17.30; Oct-Feb, daily 9.00-16.30
Free
Late 15th century abbey built on the
site of a Saxon and Norman abbey.
Fine example of the perpendicular
period of English Gothic architecture.
Notable features include fine tower;
west facade, portraying the ladder
dream of Bishop Oliver King; heavily
carved west door set in a triple arch;
elaborate and striking fan vaulting in
the chancel; prior Bryde's Chantry and
enormous clerestory windows

BISHOPS PALACE
Wells (0749) 78691
Wells, 6m NE Glastonbury on A39
Open: Easter & end April-Oct, Thurs,
Sun & BH's; Aug, daily 14.00-18.00
(last admission 17.30)
Charge: £1.00 (ch 30p; OAP's 75p)
Official residence of the Bishops of
Bath & Wells, the Bishop's Chapel
and the ruins of the banqueting hall
date from the 13th century. The
undercroft remains virtually
unchanged from this date. State
Rooms with Long Gallery contain
portraits of former Bishops.
Surrounded by fortifications and a
moat, access is gained through 14th-
century Gatehouse
🅿 🚻 ♿

BRISTOL CATHEDRAL
Bristol (0272) 24879
College Green, Bristol
Open: all year; daily 8.00-18.00
Free: donations welcomed
Originally built as an Augustine
monastery in 1140, little remains

from that time except the chapter
house. The abbey church was started
in 1298 and received cathedral
status from Henry VIII in 1542.
Interesting features include complex
aisle vaulting, stalls with misericords
and a 14th-century skeleton vault in
the anteroom of the Berkley Chapel
🅿 ♿

CLEEVE ABBEY
Map 1 Bb
Washford, 2m S Watchet off A39
Open: Standard DofE; also Sundays
during April-Sept
Charge: 60p (ch & OAP's 30p)
Ruined 13th-century Cistercian house
noted for gatehouse, dormitory and
refectory with traceried windows,
timbered roof and wall paintings
DofE 🅿

FORDE ABBEY
See Historic Homes

THE LORD MAYOR'S CHAPEL
College Green, Bristol
Open: all year, Sat-Thurs 10.00-
12.00 & 13.00- 16.00
Free
Official place of worship of Lord
Mayor, originally medieval hospital of
the Gaunts founded by Maurice de
Gaunt. Hospital lasted 300 years until
its dissolution by Henry VIII who
sold it to the Corporation of Bristol.
Remarkable 16th-century French &
Flemish painted glass

MUCHELNEY ABBEY
Map 2 Bb
2m S Langport off unclassified
Langport-Shepton Beauchamp road
Open: standard DofE
Charge: 40p (ch 40p; OAP's 20p)
One of the oldest abbeys in Somerset,
church has now vanished but Abbot's
house is still intact
DofE 🅿

STOKE-SUB-HAMDON PRIORY
Map 2 Bc
Stoke-sub- Hamdon, 6m W Yeovil off
A3088
Open: all year, daily 10.00-18.00 or
dusk if earlier
Free
15th-century Ham-stone house, once
a chantry and retaining original
screens and part of great hall
NT

TEMPLE CHURCH
Temple Street, Bristol
Open: any reasonable time .
Free
Only the exterior remains of this 15th-
century church

DofE

WELLS CATHEDRAL
Wells (0749) 78691
Wells, 6m NE Glastonbury on A39
Open: all year, daily 7.30-18.00 or
dusk if earlier
Free: donations gratefully accepted
Cathedral dates from two main
periods- 1180-1240 & 1290-1340-
the east end of the nave being the
earliest part. On the west front is the
most extensive array of medieval
sculpture to survive in Britain also of
note is the inverted arches under the
crossings that support the massive
weight of the central tower; the 13th-
century octagonal Chapter House; a
14th-century astronomical clock with
knights that joust every hour and
14th-century glass & vaulting in the
Lady Chapel
🅿 &

WESLEY'S CHAPEL
Bristol (0272) 24740
The Horsefair, Bristol
Open: all year, Mon, Tues & Thurs-
Sat 10.00- 13.00 & 14.00-16.00
(closed BH's); groups by arrangement
Free

The oldest Methodist chapel in the
world, built in 1739, rebuilt 1748, by
John Wesley. Both the chapel and
John Wesley's living rooms are
preserved in their original form
No dogs
🅿 ⊟ &

Country Parks

This section includes recreational
areas which offer the opportunity to
enjoy relatively unspoiled countryside

ASHTON COURT ESTATE
Map 4 Ab
Bristol (0270) 663702
3m SW Bristol city centre off B3128
Open: all year, daily
Free
840 acre estate landscaped in the
early 1800's and containing formal
gardens, park and woodlands
featuring self-guided nature trails and
orienteering course. Ashton Court
Mansion was the Smyth family home
for over 400 years and is now owned
by the Bristol City Corporation
Various events held here throughout
the year: **See Events**
🅿 ⊟ &

COMBE SYDENHAM COUNTRY
PARK
Map 1 Bb
Stogumber (09846) 284
Combe Sydenham, Monksilver, 3m S
Watchet off A358
Open: Apr,June,Sept & Oct, Tues,
Wed & Fri; May BH's; July & August,

Mon- Fri 11.00-17.00
Charge: £1.20
Ancient deer park and trout farm
surrounding Combe Sydenham Hall.
Woodland walks and excellent views
of Exmoor and the Quantocks. British
Birds of Prey Centre
See also Historic Homes: Combe
Sydenham Hall
🅿 🐾🍴🚻♿

DUNSTER PARK
30 acres of woodland around Dunster
Castle with 3m walk through
enclosed 18thc deer park
See Castles: Dunster Castle

DYRHAM PARK
Map 4 Bb
Dyrham, 8m N Bath off A46
Open: all year, daily 12.00-18.00 or
dusk
Charge: 50p
263 acres of ancient parkland with
herd of fallow deer
See also Historic Homes: Dyrham
Park
Dogs on leads
NT🅿 🚻🍴

HAM HILL COUNTRY PARK
Map 2 Bc
Stoke-sub-Hamdon, 5m W Yeovil on
A3088
Open: all year, daily
Free
Scenic beauty spot covering 154
acres overlooking the flood plain of
the rivers Yeo & Parrett. Excellent
views of the Mendips, Quantocks and
Dorset Hills
Iron Age & Roman hill fort: **See
Archaeological Sites:** Ham Hill
Camp
Lavatories
🅿 🍴♿

WIMBLEBALL LAKE
Map 1 Bb
Brompton Regis, 10m S Minehead
off A396
Open: all year, daily

Charge: 20p (parking fee)
374 acre reservoir set amidst the
beautiful scenery of Exmoor offering
picnic areas with glorious views,
woodland walks, nature reserve, small
camp site and fly fishing
Information kiosk, Lavatories
🅿 🍴🚻♿

Crafts

This section lists workshops, craft
centres, galleries and craft shops
where craft work, ancient as well as
modern, can be seen and bought, and
often commissioned

Craftsmen can normally be seen at
work at these workshops, potteries
and forges. However, working
craftsmen are not 'exhibits' and must
earn their living by their craft.
Although you may enter their place of
work at their discretion they may not
always have time to stop, talk and
explain their work at length

Where possible opening times have
been given but they may well vary
according to circumstances. It is
therefore advisable to check the
opening times in advance

Basketware

P.H. COATES & SON
Taunton (0823) 490249
Meare Green Court, Stoke St Gregory,
Taunton
Open: all year, weekdays, 10.00-
13.00 & 14.00-16.00; groups by
arrangement
Locally made baskets of fine
Somerset willow. Full range of

baskets can be seen in their making. Also demonstrations of the preparation and burning of willow charcoal for artists

W. GADSBY & SON
Burrowbridge (082 369) 259
Burrowbridge, SE Bridgwater on A361
Open: all year, weekdays 9.00-17.00; Saturday 10.00-17.00
Basket manufacturers making a large range of basketware and willow furniture from their own willows grown on the Somerset Levels

Clothing

DULVERTON WEAVERS
See Weaving

J WOOD & SONS (EXMOOR) LTD
Washford (0984) 40291
Old Cleeve, Minehead
Open: April-Oct, w/days
Factory tours: 10.45, 11.30, 14.15 & 15.00
Free
Sheepskin factory which processes skins from raw article to finished product. Large range of clothing and rugs

KNITKNACKS
Taunton (0823) 72193
41 Bridge Street, Taunton
Produces individually designed knitwear including co-ordinated separates, day dresses and unusual eveningwear

Furniture

STOGUMBER WOODWORK
Stogumber (098 46) 205
Wayshill, Stogumber
Ralph Farrer makes furniture to commission in quality hardwood, also stools, coffee tables, games boards and other small pieces which can be bought from his showroom

Horncraft

W.R. & J. STEELE
Dobbins Farm Cottage, Bagborough, Taunton
Horn products made from stag antler, cattle horn and buffalo horn

Ironwork

BLAGDON FORGE
Blagdon Hill (082 342) 669
Blagdon Hill, Taunton
Open: all year, daily 9.00-18.30
Mainly modern ironwork with some traditional pieces made to order

Leatherwork

McCOY SADDLERY AND LEATHERCRAFT
Minehead (0643) 862518
High Street, Porlock
Manufacturers selling all kinds of saddlery and bridles as well as small leather goods and handbags. Workshop not open to the public

Pottery

ABBEY ST POTTERY
Crewkerne (0460) 74438
14 Abbey Street, Crewkerne
Pottery shop selling the work of Rory McLeod. Using clays from Devon, Dorset and Cornwall, he makes stoneware cooking pots, plates, mugs, bowls, teapots, etc

BATH CRAFTS & BATH POTTERY
Bath (0225) 62192
Broad Street Place, Bath
Open: all year, Mon-Sat 9.00- 18.00
Combined craft shop and workshops. The workshop houses two potters whose work includes thrown and decorated stoneware, slipware, garden pots and silk screens on ceramics. Also jeweller specialising in silver and titanium coloured by electrolysis

Crafts

VELLOW POTTERY
Stogumber (098 46) 458
Lower Vellow, Williton, Taunton
Wide range of handthrown ovenproof
stoneware kitchenware, decorated
with brushwork or wax-resist
decoration. Also individual pieces in
stoneware and porcelain

WALCOT POTTERY
Bath (0225) 64789
Walcot Street, Bath
Work of four potters who share a
workshop, ranging from table and
kitchenware from table and
kitchenware and gardening pots of all
kinds, to decorative individual pieces

WEST MONKTON POTTERY
West Monkton (0823) 412626
Robins, Greenway, West Monkton
Studio pottery, mainly useful pots for
the kitchen

Weavers

CHURCH FARM WEAVERS
Taunton (082345) 267
Kingston St Mary, Taunton
Open: all year, Tues-Sat 14.00-18.00
Hand-loom weaving workshop in cider
barn where John Lennon and Talbot
Potter design and weave individual
tweeds, rugs, furnishing fabrics, wall-
hangings, stoles, etc using their hand-
spun wool, plant dyes

DULVERTON WEAVERS
The studio, Dulverton
Open: all year, w/days 9.00- 18.00
Specially designed clothes woven and
made up in a range of wools and
fibres, including wool from Jacob
sheep and tussah silk

JACQUIE BAKER
Boltonsborough (0458) 50584
Weaver's Dream, Mill Road, Barton St
David, Somerton
Using wool from her own Dorset
Horn sheep, Jacquie Baker spins and
weaves it into tapestries. Also sells
handpainted lace bobbins. Courses in
spinning and weaving

Woodworking

JOHN BRIGHTWELL
Hatch Beauchamp (0823) 480548
Crinkle Birr Cottage, Higher West
Hatch, Taunton
Open: all year, w/days 9.00-17.30;
w/ends by appointment
Maker of spinning-wheels of several
types. Work baskets, needlework
chests, also occasional furniture and
fine woodwork. Commissions
welcomed

RALPH FARRER
Stogumber (098 46) 205
Stogumber Woodwork, Wayshill,
Stogumber
Open: all year, Mon-Sat 9.00-13.00
& 14.00-17.00
Hand-made furniture in quality
hardwoods, also smaller low-priced
articles such as stools, solataire
boards, bread boards and turnery

General

BRISTOL CRAFT CENTRE
Bristol (0272) 297890
6 Leonard Lane, Bristol
Open: all year, w/days 10.00-17.00;
Sat 10.00-17.00
Craft centre with resident craftsmen
working in stained glass, hardwood
furniture, leatherwork, applique, lace,
embroidery and patchwork, porcelain,
jewellery, exotic wood inlay and
pottery. Gallery has monthly
exhibitions selling a variety of crafts

CLEVEDON CRAFT CENTRE
Clevedon (0272) 872567
Newhouse Farm, Moor Lane East,
Clevedon
Open: all year, daily
14 studios include workshops for
silver and jewellery, tile tables, wax
flowers, wood turning and furniture
making, leatherwork, wood-carving,
sculpted glass, weaving and spinning,
glass engraving, caligraphy, printing,
cabinet making. Also small
countryside museum and tearooms

HAVEN POTTERY & CRAFT CENTRE
Burnham-on-Sea (0278) 783173
West Huntspill, Highbridge
Open: all year, Mon-Sat 9.30-13.00
& 14.00-18.00
Workshop containing hand-made
stoneware pottery, silversmith,
leatherworker & glass blower

Cricket

County Cricket

SOMERSET COUNTY CRICKET CLUB
Taunton (0823) 72946
Secretary: A S Brown
County Ground
St James St, Taunton
Although success in the form of a
county championship title has eluded
Somerset, their contribution to cricket
has been in the colourful characters
the have provided. Among them are
Harold Gimlett, Arthur Wellard, Bill

Andrews, Maurice Tremlett and Ian
Botham and such overseas
personalities as the Australians Colin
McCool and Bill Alley, and the West
Indians Peter Wright, Viv Richards
and Joel Garner
   The County ground at Taunton is
one of the most attractive in the
country
Membership: £34.00 (ch 18
£10.00)
Scores & Prospects of Play:
Taunton (0823) 70007

GLOUCESTERSHIRE COUNTY CRICKET CLUB
Bristol (0272) 45216
County Ground
Nevil Rd, Bristol
The county of Avon does not have a
county cricket team but comes under
the auspices of Gloucestershire CCC
   Gloucestershire has a tradition for
producing powerful stroke-makers
and none more famous than William
Gilbert Grace who dominated first
class cricket in this country in the late
1880's and Walter Hammond, the
outstanding all- round cricketer of his
day. Other famous names associated
with Gloucestershire are C. L.
Townsend and Gilbert Jessop, who
captained Gloucestershire for 12
years
Membership: Single £30; Husband
& Wife £43.00. Membership
includes free ground admission and
full use of pavilion and members'
enclosure at all Gloucestershire home
grounds (except Nat-West Trophy
Matches and Benson & Hedges
Knock-Out rounds
Scores & Prospects of Play: Bristol
(0272) 45216

League Cricket

BRISTOL & DISTRICT CRICKET ASSOCIATION
Keynsham (027 56) 4177
Secretary: R Abraham
42 Dunster Rd, Keynsham
The ruling body for all levels of cricket in Bristol and surrounding areas

SOMERSET CRICKET ASSOCIATION
Taunton (0823) 81892
Secretary: R Snelling
Affiliated to the NCA the association is the ruling body for all levels of cricket in Somerset

SOMERSET CRICKET LEAGUE
Taunton (0823) 82300
Secretary: Mr Mockridge
The league consists of 132 teams which play one day fixtures on Saturdays during the season. Able to give any advice required to teams and individuals requiring information about league cricket in Somerset

Disabled

This section highlights those places and organisations in Somerset & Avon which offer special facilities for disabled people. There are many other places which are accessible to disabled vistors and these will be found in the various sections and are marked with the symbol &

Sports Organisations

BRITISH SPORTS ASSOCIATION FOR THE DISABLED
Secretary (South West Region): Miss D Wilkinson
Cheltenham (0242) 31231
36B Wards Road, Hatherley, Cheltenham, Glos. GL51 6JW
Specialist advice and encouragement from organisation that co-ordinates activities, facilities, and clubs for disabled people. The following clubs are affiliated to the association

AVON COUNTY ASSOCIATION
Secretary: Miss L Strobridge
Swindon (0793) 724262
35 Whatley Road, Clifton, Bristol BS8

SOMERSET COUNTY ASSOCIATION
Chairman: Mr R.T. Webb
Taunton (0823) 72478
5 Mount Nebo, Taunton

AVON PHAB CLUB
Mr G. West
14 Frederick Place, Bristol BS8 1AS

KINGSWOOD DISABLED ANGLING CLUB
Mr D. Allen
24 Mulberry Drive, Kingswood, Bristol

BERWICK LODGE SPORTS ASSOCIATION
Mr G.A.C. Miller
13 Oakfield Road, Clifton, Bristol, BS8

BRISTOL SOCIETY FOR THE M.H.
Mrs P. Hannam
3 Market Chambers, St Nicholas Street, Bristol, BS1 1UB

DIPPERS CLUB, YATE, BRISTOL
Karen Brown
The House in the Hill, Latteridge Iron Acton, Bristol

AVON EAGLES PARASCENDING CLUB
Mr R.G. Druce
19 Burycourt Close, Lawrence Weston, Bristol

AVON RECREATION FOR VH
Mr D. Le Poldevin
10E Alfred Place, Kingsdown
Bristol BS2 8HD

AVON SWIFTS SPORTS CLUB
Mrs M. Ralfs
111 Clover Ground, Eastfield Road, Westbury-on-Trym, Bristol BS9 4UL

BATH POLIO FELLOWSHIP
Mrs E. Banwell
109 Gilda Crescent, Wells Road
Bristol, BS14 9LD

BRISTOL BLIND BOWLERS
Mr J. Thomas
215 Ambleside Avenue, Southmead
Bristol BS10 6HG

VALLEY GATEWAY CLUB
Mr E. Appleton
54 Griffin Road, Clevedon

SARAS FOUNDATION
Mr A. Whitlock
The Clubhouse, off the Shallows
Saltford, Bristol BS18 3HA

APOLLO SWIMMING CLUB, YEOVIL & SHERBORNE
Mr J. Maunder
'Alpha', Limington Road
Ilchester, BA22 8LX

FROME & DISTRICT RECREATION & SPORTS CLUB FOR THE DISABLED
Mr W. Roberts, 'Barbican', The Copse, Frome, Somerset

HALCON CENTRE
Halcon Day Centre
Hamilton Road, Taunton, Somerset

MENCAP
Mr P. Friend
17 High Street, Taunton, Somerset

BRIDGWATER ENTERPRISES
Northgate, Bridgwater, Somerset

FROME ENTERPRISES CENTRE
Mr F. Evans
Manor Road, Frome, BA11 4BS

HIGHFIELD CENTRE
Mr J. Duffy
103A Highfield Road, Yeovil, BA21 4RJ

MENDIP DISABLED ASSOCIATION
Mrs L. Franklin
37 Ashcott Road, Meare, Glastonbury
Somerset, BA6 9SU

PENGUIN SWIMMING CLUB FOR THE DISABLED
Mrs K. Butcher
18 Maple Drive, Burnham-on-Sea, Somerset

Riding for the Disabled

RIDING FOR THE DISABLED ASSOCIATION
Coventry (0203) 56107
Miss C Haynes, Avenue Road, National Agriculture, Stonleigh, Kenilworth, Warwickshire
Established to co-ordinate riding activities and groups. The following groups are all members of the association

BRIDGWATER GROUP
Mrs Stebbing
Nether Stowey (0278) 732492
Group rides at Enmore

FROME GROUP
Mrs Soames
Frome (0373) 66023
Group rides at Frome

Events

PRINCESS MARGARET SCHOOL GROUP
Mrs Hunter
Hatch Beauchamp (0823) 480781
Group rides at Wrongtange, Curland

SANDHILL PARK GROUP
Major Nume
West Monkton (0823) 412206
Group rides at Sandhill Park, Taunton

SHEPTON MALLET GROUP
Mrs Taylor
Bourton (0747) 840406
Group rides at Shepton Mallet

SPARKFORD GROUP
Mrs Olive
Charlton Mackrell (045 822) 3289
Group rides at Sparkford

YEOVIL & SHERBORNE GROUP
Lady Koelle
Holnest (096 321) 417
Group rides at Closworth

ABBOTS LEA GROUP
Mrs Jefferson
Bitton (027 588) 3125
Group rides at Wirrelsbridge

AVON GROUP
Mrs Harrington
Bristol (0272) 590266
Group rides at Avon Centre

BAYTREES SCHOOL GROUP
Mrs Pratt
Weston-super-Mare (0934) 416408
Group rides at Baytree School

BEAUFORT ADVENTURE GROUP
Mrs Sparks
Didmarton (045 423) 265
Group rides at Kilcott

CLAVERHAM GROUP
Mrs Lewis
Yatton (0934) 832558
Group rides at Claverham

HIGHER HORIZONS GROUP
Mrs Hullbert
Bristol (0272) 654836
Group rides at Henfield

LINCOMBE LODGE GROUP
Mrs Cheshire
Banwell (0934) 822771
Group rides at Churchill

ROCKHAMPTON GROUP
Mrs Ford
Falfield (0454) 260256
Group rides at Falfield

ROYAL UNITED HOSPITAL GROUP
Miss Monkton
Bath (0225) 28331 ext 541
Group rides at Weston

SELLWOOD GROUP
Mrs Rawlington
Limpley Stoke (022 122) 2161
Group rides at Bath

STOKE PARK HOSPITAL GROUP
Mr Button
Bristol (0272) 655261
Group rides at Stapleton

WILLIAM KNOWLES GROUP
Mrs Morris
Weston-super-Mare (0934) 27392
Group rides at Weston-super-Mare

WINFORD HOSPITAL GROUP
Mrs Lett
Chew Magna (027 589) 2378
Group rides at Winford

Events

Events are listed under the month in which they normally occur but for exact dates and further details of

events contact local Tourist
Information Centres

April

BRISTOL
Distribution of the Tuppeney Starvers'
Sugared buns

TAUNTON
Marathon

WESTON-SUPER-MARE
International Hockey Festival
Veteran & Vintage Car Show

YEOVIL
West Country Book Fair

May

BATH
Festival

BRISTOL
Bristol Proms
North Somerset Agricultural Show

CLEVEDON
Clevedon Air Club Sea Front
Exhibition

CRICKET ST THOMAS
Custom Car Show

GLASTONBURY
Beltane: Order of British Druids
celebration of Spring

MINEHEAD
Hobby Horse Celebrations

WELLS
May Fair & Folk Festival

June

BATH
Historical Pageant

BRISTOL
Horse Show

DRAYCOTT
Strawberry Fair

SHEPTON MALLET
Royal Bath & West Show

WESTON-SUPER-MARE
Annual Open Bowling Tournament

July

BRISTOL
World Wine Fair & Festival
Harbour Regatta & Rally of Boats
Grand Prix Power Boat Racing

CHARD
Chard Show

MINEHEAD
National Morris Ring Meeting

SHEPTON MALLET
Antiques Fair

TAUNTON
Siege of Taunton

WESTON-SUPER-MARE
Summer Carnival

August

BRISTOL
Flower Show
Steam Rally
International Balloon Festival
Water Carnival

DUNSTER
Horse & Agricultural Show

KINGSWOOD
Annual Flower Show
Miss Kingswood Competition

PRIDDY
Sheep Fair

TAUNTON
Medieval Fair
Flower Show

WESTON-SUPER-MARE
County Cricket Festival

WINCANTON
Horse Show

September

BRISTOL
International Balloon Festival

BRIDGWATER
Bridgwater Fair

FROME
Carnival
Cheese Show

WELLINGTON
Annual Wellington to Taunton River
Tone Struggle

WINCANTON
Flower Show

October

BATH
Autumn Antiques Fair

TAUNTON
Annual Carnival & Cider Barrel Race

November

NORTH PETHERTON
Guy Fawkes Carnival

GLASTONBURY
Cage Bird Show

Farms

BURROW HILL CIDER FARM
Map 2 Bb
South Petherton (0460) 40782
Kingsbury Episcopi, 6m NW Yeovil off
B3165, 4m S Kinsbury Episcopi-
Langport unclassified Rd
Open: By arrangement only
Producers of natural dry cider, winner
of more prizes than any other in
Britain in last three years. Visitors
invited to watch cider making process
🐄

CRICKET ST THOMAS DAIRY FARM
Modern dairy farm surrounding
Cricket St Thomas Wildlife Park;
milking demonstrations
See Unusual Outings: Cricket St
Thomas Wildlife Park

DITCHEAT HILL FARM
Map 3 Ab
Ditcheat (074 986) 213
5m S Shepton Mallet on A371
Open: by arrangement
Dairy farm producing traditional
Somerset cheese and butter
🐄

FORDE ABBEY FRUIT GARDENS
South Chard (0460) 20272/20384/
20575
Forde Abbey, 4m SE Chard off
B3167
Open: farm visits by arrangement
50 acres of pick your own soft fruit
and vegetables
See also Historic Homes: Forde
Abbey
🐄

LOVINGTON FARMHOUSE
Map 3 Ab
Wheathill (096 324) 262
Lovington, 3m W Castle Cary off
B3153

Open: by arrangement. Please phone
mornings for details
Cheesemakers producing Cheddar
cheese made from specially selected
milk

MULBERRY FARM
Map 3 Ab
Glastonbury (0458) 34414
West Pennard, 4m E Glastonbury off
A361
Open: by arrangement
Traditional farmhouse cheese and
butter
🐾

PERRY BROS CIDER MILLS
Tours of cider makers including
demonstrations of cider making
processes Sept-Nov
See Museums

PRIORY FARM
Map 3 Aa
Chewton Mendip (076 121) 666
Chewton Mendip, 6m NE Wells on
A39
Open: all year, daily (phone for details
of times)
Charge: 50p
Cheese dairy where cheese and butter
are made and sold
🐾 ⛄🍴

R.L. CLAPP & SON LIMITED
Map 3 Ab
Boltonsborough, 4m SE Glastonbury
on unclassified Glastonbury-
Boltonsborough road
Open: by arrangement. Phone for
details
Traditionally made farmhouse
cheddar, butter and cream
🐾

SHEPPEY'S FARM
Map 2 Ab
Bradford-on-Tone (082 346) 233
Bradford-on-Tone, 2m W Taunton off
A38
Open: April-Dec, Mon-Sat 8.30-
dusk; Sun 12.00-14.00

Free
Traditional farm cider makers with
their own apple orchards. Visitors can
watch every stage of the cidermaking
process and view the machinery and
equipment from past generations
including thatchers' and coopers'
tools. Also small cider & agricultural
museum
🅿 🐾

SOMERSET FARM PARK
Map 1 Aa
Porlock (0643) 862816
1m E Porlock off A39
Open: Easter-Sept, w/days 14.00-
16.30
Charge: £1.00 (ch 50p)
Saxon farm with over 120 breeds of
old English farm animals including
working shire horses, pigs, goats,
sheep and rabbits
Hand ploughing demonstrations,
rides, adventure playground, Exmoor
pony exhibition
No dogs
🅿 🐾 ⛄🍴

THURLOXTON FRUIT GARDENS
Map 2 Ab
West Monkton (0823) 412348
Kierles Farm, Thurloxton, 4m S
Bridgwater W of A38
Open: early season tours by
arrangement
Charges: vary accordingly
Soft fruit & vegetable farm allowing
visitors to 'pick their own'

Gardens

The counties of Somerset & Avon
have many beautiful gardens which
are open to the public. Many of them
are owned by the National Trust or
are attached to historic homes or
castles. Others are privately owned

Gardens

NATIONAL GARDEN SCHEME
01-730 0359
57 Lower Belgrave St, London,
SW1W OLR
This charitable trust receives its funds
from many gardens throughout
England and Wales. Most of them are
small, private gardens which open
only a few times a year. Some larger
gardens also contribute their takings
on particular days. Money raised helps
many causes, but particularly district
nurses in need, either because of old
age or illness or because of the stress
and pressure of their work

Those gardens which support the
scheme are indicated by the initials
NSG

It is not possible to list here all the
gardens in Somerset & Avon which
support the scheme since many of
them open only once a year. Included
here is a selection of those open more
often. The NGS publishes a booklet
describing all the gardens in Somerset
& Avon that support the scheme, as
well as a booklet giving a complete
list of all NGS gardens in England and
Wales. To obtain copies of these
booklets and further information
contact the address above

BARFORD.PARK
Map 2 Ab
Spaxton (027867) 309
4m W Bridgwater on unclassified
Bridgwater-Enmore road
Open: May-Sept, Wed & Thurs,
14.00-18.00; other times by
arrangement
Charge: 40p (ch 10p)
Small stone and red-brick country seat
surrounded by a four acre formal
garden, including a water garden, and
a five acre woodland garden
No dogs
See also Historic Homes
NGS &

BARRINGTON COURT
Map 2 Bc
Barrington, 10m W Yeovil off B3168
Open: end April-end Sept, Sun-Wed
14.00-17.30
Charges: £1.00; reductions for
groups by arrangement
Tudor mansion surrounded by series
of walled gardens laid out in 1920's
by Gertrude Jekyll: lily, iris, and rose
gardens with wall shrubs and borders
No dogs
See also Historic Homes
NT & NGS ⊊ &

BISHOP'S PALACE
7 acres of well-established trees,
shrubs, lawns & flower beds. Jubilee
Arboretum contains wide range of
young indigenous and exotic trees
See Church Buildings

BRYMPTON D'EVERCY
Map 3 Ac
10 acre formal garden with daisy,
potpourri, herbaceous and shrub
beds, extensive lawns, vineyards and
lake
See Historic Homes
NGS

CLAPTON COURT GARDENS
Map 2 Ac
Crewkerne (0460) 73220/72200
3m SW Crewkerne on B3165
Open: all year, w/days 10.00-
17.00; Suns, 14.00-17.00; also
open Easter Sat and all Sats in May
14.00- 17.00
(closed BH's)
Charges: £1.20 (ch 30p); reductions
for groups by arrangement
One of Somerset's most beautiful
gardens with a fine collection of rare
and unusual trees and shrubs of
botanical interest in formal and
woodland settings. Outstanding
display of spring bulbs and glorious
autumn colours
No dogs
NGS ▣ 🐾 ⊊

CLAVERTON MANOR
Replica of George Washington's flower garden at Mount Vernon; fine specimen trees and pleasant lawns and borders form the rest of the garden
See Museums: American Museum

CLEVEDON COURT
18thc terraced garden with rare shrubs
See Historic Homes

CRICKET ST THOMAS WILDLIFE PARK
16 acres of informal gardens containing hundreds of rare shrubs and magnificent trees
See Unusual Outings

DUNSTER CASTLE
Terraced gardens with rare shrubs
See Castles

EAST LAMBROOK MANOR GARDENS
Map 2 Bc
South Petherton (0460) 40328
South Petherton, 6m W Yeovil off A3088
Open: all year, daily 9.00-17.00
Charges: 30p (ch 20p)
Interesting cottage-style garden designed by the well-known gardening writer, Mrs Margery Fish. Includes a bog garden, a herb garden and many unusual plants
No dogs
See also Historic Homes: East Lambrook Manor
🅿 🛉 ᵹ

FORDE ABBEY GARDEN
Map 2 Bc
Chard (0460) 20231
4m SE Chard off B3167
Open: May-Sept, Sun, Wed & BH's, 14.00-18.00; April & Oct, Sun 14.00- 18.00
Charge: £1.00

12th-century Cistercian monastery surrounded by 30 acres of gardens and lakes including water and rock gardens and a fruit farm **See Farms:** Forde Abbey Fruit Gardens
See also Historic Homes: Forde Abbey
🅿 🛉 ᗑ

GAULDEN MANOR GARDENS
Map 2 Ab
Lydeard St Lawrence (09847) 213
Tolland, 11m NW Taunton on Taunton- Exmoor road
Open: early May-early Sept, Thurs, Sun & BH's 14.00-18.00; July & Aug, Wed 14.00-18.00
Charge: 60p
12th-century manor with rose, herb, bog and secret gardens
See also Historic Homes: Gaulden Manor
No dogs, plants for sale
NGS 🅿 🛉 ᗑ ᵹ

HADSPEN HOUSE GARDEN
Map 3 Bb
Castle Cary (0963) 50200
2m SE Castle Cary on A371
Open: all year, Tues & Thurs 10.00-17.00; also April-end Oct, Suns & BH's 14.00-17.00 (closed January)
Charge: £1.00 (ch 50p)
Sheltered south-sloping garden of 8 acres containing many interesting trees, shrubs and rare plants in a delightful 18th-century setting. Also nursery growing an extensive range of plants specialising in unusual varieties of Hostas
No dogs
NGS 🅿 🛉 ᵹ

HESTERCOMBE HOUSE GARDENS
Map 2 Ab
Taunton (0823) 87222
Cheddon Fitzpaine, 3m N Taunton off Taunton-Yalway road

Open: May-Aug, Thurs only 12.00-17.00. Also May-July, last Sun in each month 14.00-18.00
Free
Garden designed by Sir Edwin Lutyens and Gertrude Jekyll

LYTES CARY MANOR
Formal garden with yew hedges and herbaceous border
See Historic Homes
NGS

MANOR HOUSE GARDEN
Map 4 Ab
Clevedon (0272) 87067
Walton-in-Gordano, 2m E Clevedon off B3124
Open: beg April-end Sept, Mon, Wed, Thurs 10.00-16.00; Apr-June, Aug, Sept, 1st Sun of each month & BH's 14.00-18.00
Charge: 50p (ch 25p)
4 acre garden consisting largely of shrubs and trees
No dogs
🅿 ⌣

MIDELNEY MANOR:
3 acres of wall gardens, wild garden
See Historic Homes
NGS

MONTACUTE HOUSE
Fine example of Jacobean garden which slopes from the house through a series of yew hedges and stone terraces
See Historic Homes

NORTH WOOTTON VINEYARD
Peaceful cottage garden & stream; also well-known vineyard with winery and vineyard shop
See Vineyards
NGS

OAKHILL MANOR
8 acres of gardens in an estate of 45 acres
See Historic Homes

TINTINHULL HOUSE GARDEN
Map 3 Ac
Tintinhull, 4m SE Yeovil off unclassified Yeovil-Tintinhull road
Open: April-end Sept, Wed, Thurs, Sat & BH's 14.00-18.00 (last admissions 17.30)
Charges: £1.30
17th-century house surrounded by 4 acre formal garden with mixed shrubs and herbaceous borders, immaculate lawns, flagstone paths and water gardens
No dogs
NT & NGS 🅿 ♿

TROPICAL BIRD GARDENS
17 acres of woodland, flower gardens and ornamental lake
See Bird Parks

VINE HOUSE GARDEN
Bristol (0272) 503573
Henbury, 5m NW Bristol city centre off B4057
Open: all year, by arrangement only
Charge: 50p (ch, OAP's 25p)
2 acre garden with small water garden and many rare species collected by owners on botanical expeditions abroad
♿

Golf Courses

BATH GOLF CLUB
Map 4 Rb
Bath (0225) 63834
Sham Castle, 2m SE Bath city centre off A36
18 holes/ parkland/ 6369 yds
Par 71/ SSS 71/ pro

Visitors: welcome but must have recognised handicap certificate. Advance phone bookings preferred
Charge: w/days £6.50; w/ends £8.00
🅿 🍺 ⛽ ✕ ♀

BREAN GOLF CLUB
Map 2 Aa
Brean Down (027875) 409
Coast Rd, Brean, 4m N Burnham-on-Sea off M5
14 holes/ level moorland/ 5470 yds
Par 69/ SSS 67/ Pro
Visitors: welcome anytime except Sun mornings until midday
Charges: w/days £3.00 per day; w/ends £4.00 per day
🅿 🍺 ⛽ ✕ ♀

BRISTOL & CLIFTON GOLF CLUB
Map 4 Ab
Long Ashton (027239)
Beggar Bush Lane, Bristol, 5m SW Bristol city centre off A370
18 holes/ downland/ 6294 yds
Par 70/ SSS 70/ pro
Visitors: welcome anytime
Charge: w/days £7.50; w/ends £9.00
🅿 🍺 ⛽ ✕ ♀

BURNHAM & BERROW GOLF CLUB
Map 2 Aa
Burnham (0278) 783137
St Christopher's Way, Burnham-on-Sea, 2m N Burnham off B3139
18 holes/ championship links course/ 6608 yds
Par 71/ SSS 73/ pro
Visitors: must be recognised members of another golf club and should telephone in advance
Charge: w/days £8.00 per day; w/ends £9.00 per day
🅿 🍺 ⛽ ✕ ♀

CHIPPING SODBURY GOLF CLUB
Map 4 Ba
Chipping Sodbury (0454) 319042
The Common, 1m NW Chipping Sodbury off B4060
9 & 18 holes/ parkland/ 6194 yds & 6937 yds
Par 70 & 73/ SSS 73/ pro
Visitors: welcome anytime except Sun mornings
Charge: w/days £6; w/ends £7
🅿 🍺 ⛽ ✕ ♀

CLEVEDON GOLF CLUB
Map 4 Ab
Clevedon (0272) 874057
Walton-in-Gordano, 1m N Clevedon off B3124
18 holes/ parkland with estuary views/ 5835 yds
Par 69/ SSS 68/ pro
Visitors: welcome on w/days only
Charge: w/days £7; w/end & BH's £10.00
🅿 🍺 ⛽ ✕ ♀

ENMORE PARK GOLF CLUB
Map 2 Ab
Enmore, 3m W Bridgwater
18 holes/ parkland/ 6444 yds
Par 71/ SSS 71/ pro
Visitors: advisable to phone in advance
Charge: w/days £6.50 VAT; w/ends £8 VAT
🅿 🍺 ⛽ ✕ ♀

FILTON GOLF COURSE
Map 4 Bb
Bristol (0272) 694169
Golf Course Lane, Bristol, 4m N Bristol off A38 & B4056
18 holes/ parkland/ 6025 yds
Par 69/ SSS 69/ pro
Visitors: welcome but must have recognised handicap certificate. Must play with member at w/ends
Charge: w/days £7
🅿 🍺 ⛽ ✕ ♀

Golf Courses

FOSSEWAY COUNTRY CLUB
Map 2 Ba
Midsomer Norton (0761) 412214
Charlton Lane, Midsomer Norton, 2m
SW Radstock on A367
9 holes/ parkland/ 4194 yds
Par 62/ SSS 61/
Visitors: welcome Sundays after
13.00 & Wednesdays until 17.00
Charge: w/days £3.50 per day; w/
ends £4.50
🅿 🍴 🛏 🍴 ♀

HENBURY GOLF COURSE
Map 4 Ab
Bristol (0272) 500044
Westbury-on-Trym, 3m N Bristol at
Junction of B4057 & B4056
18 holes/ parkland/ 6039 yds
Par 70/ SSS 70/ pro
Visitors: welcome but necessary to
phone in advance
Charge: w/days £7; w/ends £7.50
🅿 🍴 🛏 🍴 ♀

LANSDOWN GOLF CLUB
Map 4 Bb
Bath (0225) 22138
4m NW Bath city centre off A431
18 holes/ flat parkland/ 6235 yds
Par 71/ SSS 70/ pro
Visitors: welcome but must
telephone in advance
Charge: w/days £7; w/ends £8
🅿 🍴 🛏 🍴 ♀

MANGOTSFIELD GOLF CLUB
Map 4 Bb
Bristol (0272) 565501
Carsons Rd, Mangotsfield, N Bristol
city centre
18 holes/ parkland/ 5537 yds
Par 68/ SSS 66/
Visitors: welcome anytime
Charge: w/days £3.50; w/ends £5
🅿 🍴 🛏 🍴 ♀

MENDIP GOLF CLUB
Map 3 Aa
Oakhill (0749) 840205
Gurney Slade, 3m N Shepton Mallet
on A37

18 holes/ undulating downland/
5982 yds
Par 69/ SSS 69/ pro
Visitors: welcome on w/days but
must play with member at w/ends
Charge: w/days £5; w/ends £6.50
🅿 🍴 🛏 🍴 ♀

MINEHEAD & WEST SOMERSET GOLF CLUB
Map 1 Ba
Minehead (0643) 4378
The Warren, Minehead, E Minehead
town centre off A39
18 holes/ level links/ 6130y yards
Par 70/ SSS 69/ pro
Visitors: welcome anytime but
advisable to phone in advance
Charge: w/days £6.85; w/ends
£8.45
🅿 🍴 🛏 🍴 ♀

SALTFORD GOLF CLUB
Map 4 Ab
Saltford (022 17) 3220
Golf Club Lane, Saltford, 3m W Bath
off A39
18 holes/ parkland/ 6051 yds
Par 69/ SSS 69/ pro
Visitors: welcome anytime
Charges: w/days £6; w/ends £7
🅿 🍴 🛏 🍴 ♀

SHIREHAMPTON PARK
Map 4 Ab
Avonmouth (0272) 822083
Park Hill, Shirehampton, 3m N Bristol
on A4
Par 68/ SSS 67/ pro
Visitors: welcome but advisable to
phone in advance
Charge: w/days £6; £5 if introduced
by a member
🅿 🍴 🛏 🍴 ♀

TAUNTON & PICKERIDGE GOLF CLUB
Map 2 Ac
Blagdon Hill (082342) 537
Corfe, 5m S Taunton on B3170
18 holes/ downland/ 5927 yds
Par 69/ SSS 68/ pro

Visitors: must have recognised handicap certificate. Advisable to phone in advance
Charge: w/days £6.50; w/ends £8
🅿 ☕ ⊑ ✕ ♀

TOWER HILL GOLF CLUB
Map 3 Bb
Burton (074981) 3233
Alma House, Tower Hill, Burton, 5m N Wincanton on A359
9 holes/ parkland/ 4272 yds
Visitors: welcome anytime
Charge: w/days £3.75; w/ends £4.75
🅿 ☕ ⊑ ✕ ♀

TRACY PARK GOLF CLUB
Map 4 Bb
Abson (027 582) 2251)
Wick, 5m NW Bath off A420
18 holes/ undulating/ 7003 yds
Par 73/ SSS 74/ pro
Visitors: welcome anytime
Charge: w/days £6; w/ends £8
🅿 ☕ ⊑ ✕ ♀

VIVARY PARK GOLF CLUB
Map 2 Ab
Taunton (0823) 73875
Vivary Park, Taunton, S of Taunton town centre at junction of A38 & B3170
18 holes/ level parkland/ 4233 yds
Par 63/ SS 61/ pro
Visitors: advance bookings necessary and course is not available after 16.30 on Wednesdays
Charge: w/days to 17.00, £2 per round; 17.00-19.30, £3; after 19.30, £1.20; w/ends £3.00

WELLS GOLF CLUB
Map 3 Aa
Wells (0749) 75005
East Harrington Rd, Wells, E of Wells city centre off B31 139
18 holes/ hilly & well wooded/5800 yds
Par 69/ SSS 66/ pro

visitors: advisable to phone in advance
Charge: w/days £4; w/ends £5
🅿 ☕ ⊑ ✕ ♀

WINDWHISTLE GOLF, SQUASH & COUNTRY CLUB
Map 2 Bc
Wincanton (046030) 231
Cricket St Thomas, 3m NE Chard on A30
12 holes/ level parkland/ 6055 yds
Par 70/ SSS 69/ pro
Visitors: welcome but advance phone booking necessary
Charge: w/days £4.50; w/ends £6.00
🅿 ☕ ⊑ ✕ ♀

Historic Homes

ASHTON COURT MANSION
Smyth family home for over 400 years, acquired by the Bristol City Corporation and undergoing renovation
See Country Parks: Ashton Court Estate

BARFORD PARK
Map 2 Ab
Spaxton (027867) 269
Enmore, 4m W Bridgwater on unclassified Enmore-Bridgwater road
Open: May-Sept, Wed, Thurs & BH's 14.00-18.00 or by arrangement
Charge: £1.00 (ch Free); reductions for groups by arrangement
A stone and red-brick Queen Anne house set in park with fine trees, a formal garden, water garden and woodland garden :See also Gardens
No dogs

BARRINGTON COURT
Map 2 Bc
Barrington, 10m NW Yeovil off
A3088
Open: end April-end Sept, Wed
14.00-17.00; groups by arrangement
Charge: 50p
Extensively restored 16th- century
Ham- stone house with E-shaped
ground plan, Gothic & Renaissance
features
See also Gardens
No dogs
NT 🖿 ☲

BLAISE CASTLE HOUSE
18th-century mansion now a social
history museum situated in extensive
grounds
See Museums: Blaise Castle House
Museum

BRYMPTON d'EVERCY
Map 3 Ac
West Coker(093586) 2528
Brympton, 2m W Yeovil off A3088
Open: 2 Easter & May-Sept, Sat-Wed
14.00-18.00
Charges: £2.00 (ch £1.00;
reductions for OAP's on w/days only)
Tudor and Stuart mansion in superb
setting, state rooms; also Country Life
Museum and vineyard
No dogs
🅿 🖿 ☲ ♿

CLAVERTON MANOR
Greek revival house high above the
Avon Valley with rooms furnished to
show life in 17th & 19th-century
America
See Museums: American Museum

CLEVEDON COURT
Map 4 Ab
Clevedon (0272) 872257
1 /2m E Clevedon on B3130
Open: April-end Sept, Wed, Thurs,
Sun & BH's 14.30-17.30; groups by
arrangement (last admission 17.00)
Charge: £1.30

Home of the Elton family; a 14th-
century manor incorporating a 12th-
century tower & 13th-century hall.
Collection of Nailsea glass and
Eltonware. Terraced gardens and rare
shrubs
NT ☲

COLERIDGE COTTAGE
Map 2 Ab
35 Lime St, Nether Stowey, 8m W
Bridgwater off A39
Open: April-end Sept, Tues, Thurs &
Sun 14.00-17.00; groups by
arrangement
Charge: 50p
Home of Samuel Taylor Coleridge
from 1797-1800
NT

COMBE SYDENHAM HALL
Map 1 Bb
Stogumber (098 46) 284
Monksilver, 11m NW Taunton off
A358
Open: June & Sept, Tue, Wed, Fri
13.00-17.00; July & Aug, w/days
13.00- 17.00. (last admissions
16.30)
Charges: £1.60 (ch 80p, OAP's
£1.30)
Home of Elizabeth Sydenham wife of
Sir Francis Drake features Elizabethan
walled garden and ornamental tree
nurseries plus ancient deer park. Also
Country Park Trout Farm and Britsh
Birds of Prey Centre
🅿 🖿 ☲

DYRHAM PARK
Map 4 Bb
Dyrham, 8m N Bath off A48
Open: Apr, May & Oct, Sat-Wed
14.00-18.00; June-end Sept, Sat-
Thurs 14.00-18.00; other times by
written arrangement
Charge: £2.00; reductions for groups
by arrangement
Mansion built for William Blathwayt,
Secretary at War and Secretary of
State to William 111, between 1691
& 1702; the rooms have been little

changed since they were furnished by
Blathwayt and their contents recorded
in his housekeeper's inventory. Also
263 acres of ancient parkland with
herd of fallow deer
No dogs
NT 🅿 ⌷🎄

EAST LAMBROOK MANOR
Map 2 Bc
South Petherton (0460) 40328
South Petherton, 6m W Yeovil off
A3088
Open: March-Oct, Thurs 14.00-
17.00 or other times by arrangement
Charge: 50p (ch 25p)
15th-century medieval house with
16th- century additions and panelling.
Interesting cottage style garden with
rare plants **See also Gardens**

FARLEIGH CASTLE
Farleigh Hungerford, 6m SE Bath off
A36
Open: standard of DofE times and
April-Sept, Sun 9.30-dusk
Charge: 40p (ch & OAP's 20p)
Original manor house fortified by Sir
Thomas de Hungerford
DofE

FORDE ABBEY
Map 2 Bc
Chard (0460) 20231
4m SE Chard off B3167
Open: May-Sept, Sun & Wed & BH's
14.00-18.00
Charges: £1.75 (ch 75p); reductions
for groups by arrangement
12th-century Cistercian monastery
containing a medieval great hall and
many fine tapestries, now a private
home set in 30 acres of gardens and
lakes
See also Gardens
🐾 ⌷

FYNE COURT
Map 2 Ab
Broomfield, 5m N Taunton off
unclassified Taunton-Enmore Rd

Open: all year, daily 9.30-18.00 or
dusk if earlier
Charge: 20p (car parking fee)
Former pleasure grounds of the now
demolished home of pioneer
electrician Andrew Crosse now
headquarters of Somerset Trust for
Nature Conservation and Quantock
Vistors Centre
Nature reserve; nature trails;
exhibition of wildlife of the Quantocks
NT 🅿 🐾 ⌷

GAULDEN MANOR
Map 2 Ab
Lydeard St Lawrence (09847) 213
Tolland, 11m NW Taunton
Open: beg May-end Sept, Thurs-Sun,
14.00-18.00
charges: £1.40 (ch 60p)
Small historic manor originating from
the 12th-century, past home of the
Turbeville family and the Wolcotts of
the USA. Also herb garden and bog
garden **See also Gardens**
No dogs
🅿 🐾 ⌷ ♿

GEORGIAN HOUSE
7 Great George Street, Bristol
Open: all year, Mon-Sat 10.00-13.00
& 14.00-17.00
Free
Typical Georgian town house built
c1790 for wealthy merchant and
furnished in the style of the period

HATCH COURT
Map 3 Bc
Hatch Beauchamp (0823) 480208
Hatch Beauchamp, 6m NW Taunton
off A358
Open: July-mid Sept, Thurs 14.30-
17.30
Charge: £1.00; reductions for groups
by arrangement

Historic Homes

Palladian style Bath-stone mansion dating from 1755 with impressive stone staircase and early 19th-century decoration. Good collections of furniture, china and paintings; also small Canadian Military Museum, China Room, Deer Park affording superb views of Somerset

HERSCHEL HOUSE
Bath (02225) 336228
19 New King St, Bath
Open: March-Oct, Wed, Sat, Sun 14.00-17.00; other times by arrangement
Charges: 50p (ch 25p)
Georgian home of William Herschel, musician & astronomer built in 1766. Three rooms open to public including a music room, an astronomical room and Herschel's workshop. Also garden of medicinal and culinary herbs
🍵

HORTON COURT
Map 4 Ba
3m NE Chipping Sodbury off unclassified Chipping Sodbury-Hawkesbury road
Open: April-Oct, Wed & Sat 14.00-18.00 or dusk if earlier
Charge: 50p
Cotswold manor house with 12th century Norman hall and late perpendicular ambulatory in garden
No dogs, no coaches
NT

LITTLE SODBURY MANOR
Map 4 Ba
Chipping Sodbury (0454) 312232
2m NE Chipping Sodbury off unclassified Chipping Sodbury-Hawkesbury road
Open: April-Oct, by arrangement only
Charge: £1.00
15th-century manor house with 16th-century and 17th-century additions

LYTES CARY MANOR
Map 3 Ab
Charlton Mackrell, 4m SW Somerton off A37
Open: March-end Oct, Wed & Sat 14.00-18.00 (last admissions 17.30 or dusk if earlier)
Charges: £1.30
Manor house with 14th-century chapel; 15th-century hall and 16th-century great chamber; home of Henry Lyte, translator of 'Niewe Herball'
NT &

MIDELNEY MANOR
Langport (0458) 251299
Drayton, 3m SW Langport on A376
Open: early June-mid Sept, Weds & BH's 14.00-17.30
Charge: £1.00
16th & 18th-century home, originally the island manor of the Abbots of Muchelney, has been in the hands of the Trevilian family since the dissolution. Georgian and Louis XV furniture, porcelain and armorial china, paintings and family mementoes including high sheriff's banners. Also 17th-century falcon mews in the flower-filled garden
🅿

MONTACUTE HOUSE
Map 3 Ac
Montacute, 4m W Yeovil on A3088
Open: House: April-early Nov, Wed-Mon 12.30-18.00 (last admissions 17.30 or dusk if earlier); other times by written arrangement
Garden & Park: all year, Wed-Mon, 12.30- 18.00
Charge: House, Garden & Park £2.00 (ch £1.00); Garden & Park: June-end Sept 80p, Oct-end May 40p; reductions for groups by arrangement
Late 16th-century house with an H-shaped ground plan and many Renaissance features, including contemporary plasterwork,

chimneypieces and heraldic glass; fine 17th-century and 18th-century furniture; Elizabethan and Jacobean portraits from the National Portrait Gallery displayed in the Long Gallery and adjoining rooms; formal garden and landscaped park
No dogs
NT 🅿 🏷 � ⌕ 🖢

OAKHILL MANOR
Map 3 Ac
Oakhill (0749) 840210
Oakhill, 3m N Shepton Mallet on A 367
Open: Easter-Oct, daily 12.00- 18.00
Charge: £2.40 (ch & OAP's £1.70)
Country estate of 45 acres situated high in Mendip Hills. Fine example of one of England's smaller country house set in 8 acres of delightful gardens. Features one of the world's finest collections of models relating to transport, displayed in a furnished setting. Miniature steam railway transports visitors through the grounds to the house
🅿 🏷 � ⌕ 🖢

POUNDISFORD PARK
Map 2 Ac
Blagdon Hill (082 342) 244
4m S Taunton on unclassified Taunton- Pitminster road
Open: May-mid Sept, Wed, Thurs & BH's 11.00-17.00; also July-Aug, Fridays
Charges: £1.25 (ch & disabled 60p); reductions for groups by arrangement
Small Tudor House in former deer park of Taunton Castle; moulded plaster ceilings, fine furniture, displays of porcelain and costumes. Tudor Kitchen converted to restaurant. Gardens with brick Gazebo and views to the Quantock and Blackdown Hills
No dogs
🅿 🏷 ⌐ 🖢

RED LODGE
Bristol (0272) 299771
Park Row, Bristol
Open: all year, Mon-Sat 10.00-13.00 & 14.00-17.00 (closed BH's)
Free
16th-century house altered early in the 18th-century, with fine oak carvings and furnished in the style of both periods
🅿

ROYAL FORT HOUSE
Bristol (0272) 24161
Open: August, w/days 14.00-17.00 (closed BH's)
Free
Georgian house designed by Thomas Paty with stone carvings and decorative rococo plaster work

TINTINHULL HOUSE
Attractive 17th-century house, with fine pedimental facade, surrounded by modern formal gardens
See Gardens: Tintinhull House Garden

Horse Racing

BATH HORSE RACING COURSE
Map 4 Bb
Bath (0226) 24609
Lansdown, 2m NW Bath off unclassified Bath-Wick Rd
Meetings: approx 10 per year telephone for exact dates
Charges: Daily Membership £6.50; Tatterstalls £4.50; Silver Ring £2.50
🅿 ⌐ 🍴 ⚲

TAUNTON NATIONAL HUNT RACECOURSE
Map 2 Ac
Taunton (0823) 75575
2m S Taunton off B3170
Meetings: approx 11 per year (ring for details)
Charges: Club Stand £5; Tattersalls £4; Car Park £1
Membership: Double £45; Single £30; Junior £21
🅿 ⊐ ✕ ♀

WINCANTON NATIONAL HUNT RACECOURSE
Map 3 Bb
Wincanton (0963) 32548: P Charlton Musgrove, 2m N Wincanton off B3081
Meetings: approx 12 per year
Charges: from £4.50
Membership: £44 per year
🅿 ⊐ ✕ ♀

Lifeboats

ROYAL NATIONAL LIFEBOAT INSTITUTE
Poole (0202) 671133
Headquarters: West Quay Road, Poole, Dorset BH15 1HZ
The RNLI was founded in the 1820's in order to provide a rescue service for Britain's coastal waters. Since then over 90,000 lives have been saved as a result of this charity

When the local coastguard calls out a lifeboat, a crew of mainly volunteers could be risking their lives to save others. Yet there is never any shortage of local sailors to crew the lifeboats and many volunteers follow a family tradition of service

There are 200 lifeboat stations on Britain's coast and they cost the RNLI £17 million a year to run. This vast sum of money comes entirely from contributions given by the public. Volunteers are always needed to help raise these funds. If you would like to help raise money, or if you wish to make a donation, or if you want to know more about the RNLI contact the address above.

Somerset and Avon have two lifeboat stations both of which are open to the public

MINEHEAD
The 'Catherine Plunbley' is an Atlantic 21 Lifeboat. These 21 foot boats are quick and easy to launch, and very fast in the sea (up to 30 knots). They also require less maintenance and space for docking. In addition there is a 'D' class inflatable. The boats can be viewed in the boathouse on most days during the summer and some w/ends throughout the year

WESTON-SUPER-MARE
The lifeboat station is situated on Birbeck island which is reached via Victoria pier. Two lifeboats; the 'Weston Centenary', an Atlantic 21 and a 'D' class inflatable. Boat house is open most days during the summer and it is possible to watch the crew exercising on most Sundays

Mills

DUNSTER CASTLE MILL
Map 1 Ba
Dunster, 2m SE Minehead off A39

Open: Easter-end Oct, Sat-Wed
11.00-17.00; daily during July &
Aug
Charge: 60p
Restored medieval mill producing
wholewheat stoneground flour
See also Castles: Dunster Castle
NT🏛

HIGH HAM MILL
Map 2 Bb
Langport (0458) 250818
Sedgemoor Hill, 2m N Langport on
unclassified Langport-High Ham road
Open: Easter-end Sept, Sun & BH's
14.30-17.30
Charge: 50p
Last survivor of many such mills in
the area, this blue lias stone building
has an unusual thatched roof. Built in
1822, it was in use until 1910

HORNSBURY MILL
Map 2 Bc
Chard (046 06) 3317
2m N Chard off A358
Open: all year, w/days 10.30-
18.00; Sat 9.00-13.00 & 14.00-
16.00 (closed Dec 25-Jan 1)
Charge: 50p (ch 25p)
Restored 19th-century corn mill on 4
floors with displays of equipment and
fine 18ft water wheel
🅿 🍴 ⊐✗

ORCHARD MILL
Map 1 Bb
Williton (0984) 32133
Williton, 2m S Watchet off A39
Open: all year, daily 11.00- 17.00
Charge: 50p (ch 25p)
Renovated water mill with museum
containing many agricultural antiques
🅿 🍴 ⊐✗

PERRY'S CIDER MILLS
See Museums & Farms

PRISTON MILL & FARM
Map 4 Bb
Bath (0225) 23894
Priston, 5m SW Bath off B3115

Open: mid April-end Oct, Fri-Tue
14.15-17.00
Charge: 60p
Historic corn mill driven by a
waterwheel. Records in the Domesday
Book indicate that flour has been
milled on this site for over a thousand
years
🅿 🍴 🎋

WOOKEY HOLE PAPER MILL
Restored papermaking mill producing
hand-made paper
See Unusual Outings: Wookey Hole
Caves

Museums

ADMIRAL BLAKE MUSEUM
Map 2 Ab
Bridgwater (0278) 56127
Blake Street, Bridgwater, 6m NE
Taunton on M5
Open: all year, Tues, Fri-Sun 11.00-
17.00; Wed 11.00-20.00 (closed
Mon & Thurs)
Free
Birthplace of Admiral Blake, this 15th-
century house now contains relics of
the admiral; also items from the Battle
of Sedgemoor, watercolours, local
history and archaeology
🅿

**ALLERMOOR PUMPING STATION
MUSEUM**
Map 2 Bb
Burrowbridge (08 2369)324
6m S Burrowbridge off A 361
Open: by arrangement
Free
Small museum alongside the River
Parrett containing steam pumping
engines dating from 1864 & 1869.
Also hand pumps and other
equipment

Museums

AMERICAN MUSEUM
Bath (0225) 60503
Claverton Manor, 1 m E Bath
Open: end March-end Oct, Tues-Sun
14.00-17.00; also BH's and Sundays
before BH's 11.00-17.00
Charge: £2.00 (ch £1.80 & OAP's
£1.60); reductions for groups by
arrangement
Furnished rooms decorated in period
style; also fascinating collections
depicting aspects of American society,
including red indians, the Shaker
religious sect. Displays of painting,
glass, metalwork, costumes, folk
sculpture
No dogs
🅿 🍴 ⌓ ♿

AXBRIDGE MUSEUM
See King John's Hunting Lodge

BECKFORD TOWER & MUSEUM
Map 4 Bb
Bath (0225) 336228
Lansdown, 2m NW Bath on
unclassified Bath-Wick road
Open: April-Oct, w/ends 14.00-
17.00; groups by arrangement only
Charge: 50p (ch 25p)
Neo-classical building built 1827 by
H.E. Goodridge for William Beckford
of Fonthill. Small museum on first
floor contains exhibits relating to his
life and interests in Fonthill and Bath.
🅿 🍴 ⛩

BLAISE CASTLE HOUSE MUSEUM
Map 4 Ab
Bristol (0272) 506789
Henbury, 4m NW Bristol city centre
on B4C55
Open: all year, Sat-Wed 10.00-13.00
& 14.00-17.00
Free
Late 18th-century house containing
museum of West Country rural and
urbane life situated in extensive
grounds which include remains of an
Iron Age hill fort, and a mid 18th-
century Gothic castle
🍴 ⌓

BRISTOL HISTORICAL TAPESTRY
Bristol (0272) 24809
Quakers Friars, Bristol
Open: all year, w/days 13.00-
16.30; Sat 9.30-12.30
Free
Tapestry consisting of four sections,
each 18ft by 4ft depicting the city's
history over the last 1,000 years

BURROWS TOY MUSEUM
Bath (0225) 61819
York Street, Bath
Open: all year, daily 10.00-17.30
(closed Dec 25 & 26)
Charge: 80p (ch 50p)
Only museum in West of England
entirely devoted to children toys. The
collection records the pastimes of
children over the past century and a
half. Books, games, mechanical and
constructional toys, dolls, doll's
houses, carriages and accessories
No dogs
🅿 🍴 ♿

CAMDEN WORKS MUSEUM
Bath (0225) 318348
Julian Road, Bath
Open: Easter-end Sept, w/days
14.00-17.00; Oct-Easter, Sat-Thurs
14.00-17.00
Charges: £1.00 (ch, OAP's &
students 50p)
Authentic reconstruction of the entire
works of J.B. Bowler a Victorian
engineer, brass founder and mineral
water manufacturer. Unique collection
of working machinery, hand tools,
brasswork, bottles, documents
🅿 🍴 ⌓

CARRIAGE MUSEUM
Bath (0225) 25175
Circus Mews, Bath
Open: Apr-Sept, Mon-Sat 9.30-
17.30 & Sun 10.00-17.30; Oct-
March, Mon-Sat 11.00-16.00 & Sun
11.00-17.00
Charge: 80p (ch 60p)

FASHION RESEARCH CENTRE
Bath (0225) 61111
4 the Circus, Bath
Open: all year, w/days 10.00-13.00
& 14.00-17.00
Free
Extension of the Museum of Costume
with an extensive reference library and
a collection of costumes for study

FLEET AIR ARM MUSEUM
Map 3 Ab
Ilchester (0935) 840565
Yeovilton, 4m N Yeovil on unclassified
Yeovil-Yeovilton road
Open: all year, daily 10.00- 17.30 or
dusk if earlier (closed Dec 24 & 25)
Charge: £1.70 (ch & OAP's 85p);
reductions for groups by arrangement
Collection of more than 40 historic
aircraft, ship and aircrat models,
paintings and photographs of the
Royal Naval Air Service and the Fleet
Air Arm tracing the development of
naval aviation from 1903. Concorde
002 is on view in an exhibition hall
where the development of passenger
supersonic flight is graphically
portrayed
Childrens play area, flying view area
P ፤ ▭ ⌁ ⅊

GEOLOGY MUSEUM
Bath (0225) 28144
18 Queen Square, Bath
Open: all year, w/days 10.00-18.00;
Sat 10.00-17.00. (closed BH's)
Free
Museum based on the works of
geologist Charles Moore. Collection
includes wealth of fossils from the
Jurassic rocks of North Somerset and
some of these specimens can be seen
on display

Free
Regional and world wide collections,
representing ancient history, natural
sciences, fine & applied arts
P ፤ ▭ ⅊

CLARKE'S SHOE MUSEUM
Map 3 Ab
Street (0458) 43131
High St, Street, 2m SW Glastonbury
Open: Easter-end Oct, Mon-Sat
10.00-16.45; other times by
arrangement
Free
Museum housed in oldest part of
Clarke's Shoe Factory and contains
shoes from Roman times to the
present. Georgian shoe buckles,
caricatures and engravings of
shoemakers, costume illustrations,
shoe machinery and documents and
photographs illustrating early history
of the firm
No dogs
P ፤ ⅊

COUNTRYSIDE MUSEUM
Museum of countryside artefacts at
working craft centre
See Crafts: Clevedon Craft Centre

CRICKET ST THOMAS COUNTRY LIFE MUSEUM
Collection of agricultural equipment
and farming practices of the past
See Unusual Outings: Cricket St
Thomas Wildlife Park

FAIRLEIGH CASTLE MUSEUM
Collection of weapons & armour
mostly dating from the Civil War;
15th-century wall painting; 17th-
century stained glass
See Historic Homes: Fairleigh Castle

Collection of horse-drawn carriages in an 18th-century mews. Display includes over 40 vehicles with a collection of harnesses, liveries and whips

ⓅⓍ♿

CANADIAN MILITARY MUSEUM
See Historic Homes: Hatch Court

CHARD & DISTRICT MUSEUM
High Street, Chard, 14m SW Taunton on A358
Open: mid May-Sept, Mon-Sat 10.30- 16.30
Free
Collection illustrating the history of Chard including the Stringfellow collection, inventors of the first power driven aircraft

CHEDDAR CAVES MUSEUM & EXHIBITION
Map 2 Ba
Cheddar (0934) 742343
Cheddar, 7m NW Wells on A371
Open: Easter-Oct, daily 10.00-18.00; Oct-Easter, daily 11.00-17.00
Charge: 30p (ch & OAP's 20p)
Museum depicting how the caves were utilised by early man 10,000 years ago includes Stone Age weapons, 12,000-year- old skeleton, flints, amber and engraved stones
See also Unusual Outings: Cheddar Caves

Ⓟ 🍵

CIDER & AGRICULTURAL MUSEUM
Cider & farm museum containing machinery and equipment from past generations. Cider making demonstrations in Autumn
See Farms: Sheppey's Farm

CITY MUSEUM & ART GALLERY
Bristol (0272) 299771
Queens Road, Bristol
Open: all year, Mon-Sat 10.00-17.00 (closed Good Friday; Dec 25, 26, 27; Jan 1st)

GLASTONBURY ABBEY MUSEUM
Small museum in medieval gatehouse containing model of the Abbey as it stood in 1539, and remains of the original wattle & daub church which according to legend was founded in AD61 by Joseph of Arimathea
See Church Buildings: Glastonbury Abbey

GLASTONBURY LAKE VILLAGES MUSEUM
See The Tribunal

HALLS OF THE HEREOS
Bath (0225) 25519
28 Broad St, Bath
Open: all year, daily 10.00-18.00 (closed Dec 24, 25 & 26)
Charges: 80p (ch & OAP's 40p)
Large dioramic model of the Battle of Waterloo with 20,000 figures and son-et- lumiere effects. Also a model of the defence of Rourke's Drift

Ⓧ

HARVEY'S WINE MUSEUM
Bristol (0272) 277661
12 Denmark Street, Bristol
Open: all year, Fridays, 10.00- 12.00 & 14.00-16.30 (closed Good Friday)
Charge: 50p
Museum is housed in 13th-century wine cellars and contains a variety of wine related antiques including silver bottles, corkscrews and a fine collection of 18th-century English wine glasses
Guided tours by arrangement

Ⓧ

HATCH COURT
Two rooms converted into a small museum containing English fine china and mementoes of Princess Pat's Regiment and early aviation
See Historic Homes

HOLBURNE OF MENSTRIE MUSEUM
Bath (0225) 66669
Great Pulteney Street, Bath
Open: March-Dec, Tues-Sat & BH's 11.00-17.00; Sun 14.30-18.00
Charges: 80p (ch 40p)

Originally built as a hotel in the 18th century this elegant building now contains pictures, furniture and miniatures from 16th-20th century
🅿 🔋 ⌷ 🚻 &

INDUSTRIAL MUSEUM
Bristol (0272) 299771
Princes Wharf, Princes Street, Bristol
Open: all year, Sat-Wed 10.00-13.00 & 14.00-17.00
Free
Opened in 1978 this museum contains a comprehensive range of exhibits connected with the rich industrial history of Bristol. Various items of machinery and large collection of water, air and land vehicles, aero engines, instrumented cockpit mock-up of Concorde and model railway collection
🅿 &

KING JOHNS HUNTING LODGE
Map 2 Ba
Axbridge (0934) 732012
Axbridge, 8m SE Weston-super-Mare on A371
Open: April-Sept, daily 14.00- 17.00
Free
Restored early Tudor house with old photographs and exhibits of local interest. Town stocks and constables' staves also displayed
NT 🅿

LADY BANGORS FAIRGROUND COLLECTION
Wonderful collection of gallopers, spinners, old bioscope fronts, fascias, gods, horses, dragons and peacocks which were made for the travelling fairgrounds of 1870
See Unusual Outings: Wookey Hole Caves

MADAME TUSSAUD'S STOREROOM
Over 2,000 moulds of the funny, the famous and the unspeakable line the shelves

See Unusual Outings: Wookey Hole Caves

MUSEUM OF BOOKBINDING
Bath (0225) 66055
Manvers Street, Bath
Open: all year, w/days 9.00-13.00 & 14.15-17.30. (closed w/ends & BH's)
Charge: 35p
Museum depicting the historical & contemporary practice of bookbinding includes a reconstruction of a 19th century bindery and examples of the art
🅿 🔋 &

MUSEUM OF COSTUME
Bath (0225) 61111
Assembly Rooms, Alfred Street, Bath
Open: April-Oct, daily 9.30-18.00, Sun 10.00-18.00; Nov-March, daily 10.00- 17.00, Sun 11.00-17.00
Charge: £1.20 (ch 70p); reductions for groups by arrangement
World famous collection with fashions from 17th century to modern times displayed in period rooms and settings; also toys, dolls and and important collection of jewellery
No dogs
🅿 🔋 &

NATIONAL LIFEBOAT MUSEUM
Bristol (0272) 213389
Princes Wharf, Wapping Rd, Bristol
Open: April-Oct, w/days 10.30-16.30, w/ends 11.00-17.00
Charge: 20p (ch & OAP's 10p)
Collection of different types of lifeboat, engines, photographs and models depicting the history of lifeboats and lifeboatmen
🅿

PERRY'S CIDER MILLS MUSEUM
Map 2 Bc
Dowlish Wake, 4m N Chard off A3037
Open: all year, Mon-Sat 9.00-13.00 & 14.00-17.30; Sun 9.30-13.00
Free

Housed in a 16th century thatched barn the museum contains fascinating collection of small farming equipment
🅿 ⚲

POSTAL MUSEUM
Bath (0225) 60333
51 Great Pulteney Street, Bath
Open: all year, w/days 11.00- 17.00, Sun 14.00-17.00 (closed Dec 25, 26)
Charge: 75p (ch & OAP's 50p)
Depicts history of the mail service, with particular emphasis on the Royal Mailcoach era. Special philatelic displays regularly featured
🅿 ⚲ ☐ &

PRIESTS HOUSE COUNTRY LIFE MUSEUM
Illustrates role of agriculture in supporting a large country house with displays of cider and wine making, tools, etc
See Historic Homes: Brympton d'Evercy

ROMAN BATHS MUSEUM
Bath (0225) 61111
Abbey Churchyard, Bath
Open: April-Oct, Sun-Fri 9.00-18.00; July & Aug, 9.00-19.00; Nov- March, 9.00-17.00
Charge: £1.40 (ch 80p); reductions for groups by arrangement
Remains of Roman baths of 'Aquae Sulis', with museum devoted to the Roman history of Bath and containing mosaics and stone monuments from the Roman town and surrounding area, votive offerings thrown into the sacred spring. Finest of all the exhibits is the gilt-bronze head of the goddess Minerva
No dogs
See also Roman Sites: Roman Baths & Pump Room
🅿 ⚲ ✕ &

RPS NATIONAL CENTRE OF PHOTOGRAPHY
Bath (0225) 62841
The Octagon, Milson Street, Bath
Open: all year, w/days 10.00-17.30; mid July-end Aug, Sun & BH's 11.00-16.45
Charge: £1.00 (ch, OAP's, unemployed 60p); reductions for groups
Created by the Royal Photographic Society in one of Bath's most noted buildings. The centre has exhibition galleries showing the best historic and contemporary photographs, and a museum of photography including a collection of early photographic equipment
No dogs
🅿 ⚲ &

ST NICHOLAS CHURCH MUSEUM
Bristol (0272) 299771 ext 245
St Nicholas Street, Bristol
Open: all year, w/days 10.00- 17.00
Free
Depicts history of Bristol from its beginning until the Reformation including church art and silver. Changing exhibitions showing topographical features of the city mainly during the 18th and 19th century and the Hogarth altarpiece originally painted for St Mary Redcliffe Also contains a Brass Rubbing centre
🅿 ⚲

SOMERSET COUNTY & MILITARY MUSEUM
Taunton (08323) 55504
Taunton Castle, North Street, Taunton
Open: all year, w/days 10.00-17.00; also end June-beg Sept, Sat 10.00-17.00
Charge: 40p (ch & OAP's 15p)
Situated in castle the museum contains exhibits of local antiquities, archaeology, natural history and relics of the Somerset Light Infantary from 1685-1959 including uniforms, medals etc
🅿 ⚲

SOMERSET MILITARY MUSEUM
See Somerset County & Military Museum

SOMERSET RURAL LIFE MUSEUM
Map 3 Ab
Glastonbury (0458) 32903
Abbey Farm, Chilkwell Street, Glastonbury
Open: all year, w/days 10.00-17.00; also Easter-Oct, w/ends 14.00- 1830 & Nov-Easter, w/ends 14.30-17.00 (closed Good Friday & Dec 25)
Charge: 50p (ch & OAP's 20p)
New museum interpreting Somerset's rural history includes 14th-century Abbey Barn, farm buildings and machinery; also cider making, peat digging and other aspects of farm life demonstrated
🅿 🖵🅛🎋 ⛬

THE TRIBUNAL
The Tribunal, High Street, Glastonbury, 6m SW Wells on A39
Open: mid March-mid Oct, w/days 9.30-18.30 & Sun 14.00-18.30; mid Oct- mid March, w/days 9.30-16.00 & Sun 14.00-16.00. (closed Dec 25, 26; Jan & May BH's)
Charge: 40p (ch & OAP's 20p)
Collection of late prehistoric antiquities from Glastonbury Lake Village and items of local historic interest
🅿

WATCHET MUSEUM
Map 1 Ba
Watchet (0984) 31824
Market Street, Watchet
Open: Easter; Spring BH-Sept, daily 10.30-12.30 & 14.30-16.30 (July & Aug 19.00-21.00)
Charge: 10p (ch 5p)
Contains local history from prehistoric times to the present day
No dogs
🅿 🅛 ⛬

WELLINGTON MUSEUM
Map 2 Ac
35 Fore Street, Wellington
Open: Easter-end Sept, Mon-Sat 10.30-16.30
Free
Situated in a 17th century posting house the museum depicts the history of the town from the Duke of Wellington to modern times
🅿 🅛 ⛬

WELLS MUSEUM
Map 3 Aa
Wells (0749) 73477
Cathedral Green, Wells
Open: April-Sept, w/days 11.00-17.00; Oct-March 14.00-16.00; June-Sept, Sun 14.30-17.30
Charge: 30p (ch 10p)
Museum illustrates the history and natural history of the caves in the central Mendip area. Exhibits includes coins, prehistoric cave finds, fossils and minerals
🅿 🅛 ⛬

WOODSPRING MUSEUM
Weston-super-Mare (0934) 21028
Burlington Street, Weston-super-Mare
Open: Mar-Oct, Mon-Sat 10.00-17.00; Nov-Feb, Mon-Sat 10.00-13.00 &14.00-17.00
Free
Museum is housed in old workshops of the Edwardian Gaslight Company. Around the central courtyard are displays of the Victorian Seaside Holiday, and old chemists shop, a dairy and a gallery of wildlife in the district. Other exhibits include Mendip minerals and mining, transport from the penny farthing to the Western Autogyro, cameras and the Dentist in the 1900's. Changing exhibitions held in art gallery
No dogs
🅿 🅛 🖵 ⛬

National park

EXMOOR NATIONAL PARK
Designated in 1954, Exmoor is the smallest of the national parks

It is a landscape of superb contrasts with a magnificent coastline of hog back cliffs, wild heather moorland and deep wooded combes

It is administered by the Exmoor National Park Committee of the Somerset County Council. They are responsible for controlling development, with attention to both local life and industry, and to preserving the landscape and wildlife of Exmoor

WOOKEY HOLE CAVES MUSEUM
Small museum containing coins, pottery and tools of the late Celtic and Roman British periods
See Unusual Outings: Wookey Hole Caves

WORLD OF MODELS
One of the world's finest collections of models relating to transport, displayed in furnished setting
See Historic Homes: Oakhill Manor

WYNDHAM MUSEUM
Marston Magna (0935) 75171
Hendford Manor Hall, Hendford, Yeovil
Open: all year, Mon-Sat, 9.30- 13.00 & 14.00-17.00 (closed Thurs)
Free
Contains local history and archaeology and specialised collections of costumes and firearms
🄿

Like all National Parks most of the land is privately owned and as a visitor your rights are few. However by custom and tradition, the walker and the rider will experience little or no restrictions on the open moor if they observe the simple rules of the **Country Code**

For the walking, angling and horse riding enthusiast, Exmoor Park Authority produce a number of leaflets which list various waymarked trails, areas where angling is permitted and riding establishments

EXMOOR NATIONAL PARK CENTRE
Dulverton (0398) 23665
Exmoor House, Dulverton, Somerset
Open: all year, daily
The centre has a wide range of maps, photographs, information leaflets and literature. Experienced staff are on hand to help visitors and callers with their enquiries

Listed below are other Information Centre which are run by the Exmoor National Park Authority. They are open daily from Easter-Sept

BRENDON
Brendon (059 87) 321
County Gate, on A39 between Porlock & Lynmouth

COMBE MARTIN
Combe Martin (0271 88) 3319
Cross St, Combe Martin, North Devon

DUNSTER
Dunster (0643 82) 835
Dunster Steep Car Park, Dunster, Somerset

LYNMOUTH
Lynton (059 85) 2509
Parish Hall, Watersmeet Rd, Lynmouth, North Devon

Nature Reserves

These protected areas allow plants, trees and wildlife to thrive in their natural habitat. Nature reserves are particularly important for the study of ecology and for the conservation of indigenous plants and wildlife. Too many human visitors would destroy the environment and disturb the wildlife so access to many reserves is restricted.   The reserves listed below are accessible to the public. Do not leave the footpaths or in any way disturb the environment

   If you would like to know more about nature reserves or if you require a permit to visit those that are restricted, contact the following organisations which are responsible for the Somerset & Avon reserves

Organisations

NATURE CONSERVANCY COUNCIL (NCC)
SW Regional Officer
Roughmoor, Bishops Hull, Taunton, Somerset TA1 5AA
The governing body for promoting nature conservation in Great Britain. To this end it selects, establishes and manages a series of National Nature Reserves and gives advice about nature conservation. All their work is based on detailed ecological reasearch and survey

AVON WILDLIFE TRUST
Bristol (0272) 743396
209 Redland Road, Bristol, BS6 6YU

SOMERSET TRUST FOR NATURE CONSERVATION
Kingston St Mary
Fyne Court, Broomfield, Bridgwater TA5 2EQ

Reserves

AVON GORGE NATIONAL NATURE RESERVE
Map 4 Ab
3m W Bristol city centre off A369
Warden: Mr R.V. Russell, 1 Rangers Cottage, Valley Road, Leigh Wood, Bristol
Access: unrestricted
The gorge has long been a classic site for the study of rocks of Carboniferous Age, rich in fossils. Since 16th century it has also become a botanical mecca acquiring international fame for its rare plants. Within the reserve lies the Iron Age Hill Fort of Stokleigh Camp
Leaflet available
NCC

BLACK ROCK NATURE RESERVE
Map 2 Ba
3m NE Cheddar off B3135
Access: unrestricted
181 acres of mixed woodland, scrub and downland
STNC

BRIDGWATER BAY NATIONAL NATURE RESERVE
Map 2 Aa
5m NW Bridgwater off unclassified Cannington-Stockland Bristol road
Access: Apr-end Oct, Permit required
Established in 1954 to conserve the bird life of the tidal mud flats and salt marshes. Excellent for waders and

winter wildfowl, including white-
fronted geese and unique moulting
Shelduck which flock to the site in
mid-summer
NCC

EBBOR GORGE NATIONAL
NATURE RESERVE
Map 3 Aa
2m N Wells E of A371
Warden: Mr T.L. Hodgson, 47 Ash
lane, Wells
Access: unrestricted
Natural fissure which includes a high
canopy woodland of Ash, Wych Elm,
Beech and Penultimate Oak.
Geological features include crags of
carboniferous limestone and fine
scree formations
Information centre with displays
illustrating geology and some of the
wildlife to be seen on the reserve
Two nature trails
No dogs
NCC �P 🏕

FYNE COURT
Map 2 Ab
Kingston St Mary (08235) 526
Broomfield, 5m N Taunton off
unclassified Taunton-Enmore road
Access: unrestricted
24 acres of woodland and ponds
Various nature trails and leaflets
available
Information centre with permanent
exhibitions illustrating wildlife of the
Quantocks
STNC �P 🦌 ▭

HURSCOMBE VALLEY NATURE
RESERVE
Map 1 Bb
8m S Dunster E of B3190
46 acres of woodland, scrubland and
grassland around Wimbleball Lake
Self-guided nature trail and leaflet
available
STNC

LEIGH WOODS NATIONAL
NATURE RESERVE
See Woodlands

LONG WOOD
See Woodlands

OTTERHEAD LAKES
Map 2 Ac
7m S Taunton W of B3170
Access: 20 acres woodland, marsh
and scrubland
Nature trails
STNC �P

Other Historic Buildings

ASSEMBLY ROOMS
Bennett St, Bath
Designed in 1769 by John Wood the
Younger with magnificent rooms
including 100ft long ballroom with
Corinthian columns and 5 chandelirs.
Bombed in 1942 it was rebuilt in
1956-61 and fully restored in 1979.
Now houses the Museum of Costume
and the Fashion Research Centre **See
Museums**

ABBOT'S FISH HOUSE
Map 2 Ba
Meare, 6m NW Glastonbury off
B3151
Open: any reasonable time
Free
Restored 14th- century building once
used to salt and store fish caught in
the nearby Abbot's fishpool, which
was drained in the 18th century. The
building has recently been re-roofed
DofE

CABOT TOWER
Bristol (0272) 26031
Open: all year, daily 8.00-dusk
Charge: 10p
Tower with spectacular views over
Bristol, built by citizens of Bristol in
1897 to mark the 400th anniversary
of John Cabot's discovery of North
America
🅿

COUNCIL HOUSE
Bristol (0272) 26031
College Green, Bristol
Open: all year, w/days by
arrangement only
Free
HQ of municipal administration.
Organised tours by arrangement with
City Information Office

GLASTONBURY ABBEY BARN &
FARMHOUSE
Late 14th- century barn of
Glastonbury Abbey is one of the finest
in the country; massive interior
timbers and richly decorated gable
ends and porches. Now contains
relics of farming in bygone days **See
Museums:** Somerset Rural Life
Museum

GUILDHALL
Bath (0225) 61111
High St, Bath
Open: all year, Mon-Thurs 8.30-
17.00; Fri 8.30-16.30
Free
One of the finest examples of neo-
classical architecture in Bath; 18th-
century banqueting room with
magnificent chandeliers and portraits
🅿

KING JOHN'S HUNTING LODGE
Market Place, Axbridge, 10m SE
Weston-super-Mare on A371:
Restored early Tudor house now
housing museum
See Museums

OLD DOVECOAT
Dunster, 1m SE Minehead on A396
Open: Easter-mid Oct, daily 10.00-
dusk
Free
Built in 12th century as part of the
Priory, it still has its rare revolving
ladder for reaching the nesting boxes

THE TRIBUNAL
High St, Glastonbury
Open: Standard DofE times
Charge: 40p (ch & OAP's 20p)
15th-century court house of Abbey
officials. Well preserved with
decorative details from three centuries
it now houses finds from late
prehistoric Lake village. **See
Museums**
DofE 🅿

THOMAS CHATTERTON'S HOUSE
Bristol (0272) 299771
Redcliffe Way, Bristol
Open: by arrangement only
Free
Only house of its type to survive in
Bristol. Built by Thomas Malpas for
use of schoolmaster of Redcliffe
School in 1749. Thomas Chatterton
the boy poet was born here.

YARN MARKET
High Street, Dunster, 1m SE
Minehead on A396
Open: any time
Octagonal building erected by the
Lutterells of Dunster Castle in 1609
and restored in 1647; it was used for
selling locally woven cloth

Orienteering

Orienteering is competitive navigation
on foot. With the aid of a map and

Orienteering

compass, competitors find their way as accurately and skilfully as possible between given points

Courses vary in length from about 2km for children and beginners, to over 12km for experienced adults. There is usually a variety of courses to choose from, including a non-competitive Wayfarers course. These permanent courses are designed especially for the casual orienteerer

Events are usually held in woods, forests, on heath and moorland, whose paths, streams and valleys provide the most diverse navigation problems

The only equipment needed for orienteering is outdoor clothes, a red biro, a whistle, a polythene bag to use as a map case and a compass. The event entry fee is usually about 50p–£1.00 (juniors 25p-50p)

The British Orienteering Federation is the central body for orienteering in England. A full event calendar with telephone numbers for enquiries is obtainable from them on request. All members receive a copy of 'The Orienteer', a bi-monthly magazine containing a full fixture of BOF registered events

After two or three events, if you decide you like orienteering it is best to join your local club

Organisations

BRITISH ORIENTEERING FEDERATION
National Office
Matlock (0629) 734042
'Riversdale', Dale Rd North, Darley Dale, Matlock, Derbyshire DE4 2JB

SOUTH WEST ORIENTEERING ASSOCIATION
Regional Secretary
Bristol (0272) 673160
Mr Peter Downe
28 Rangers Walk, Hanham, Bristol

local clubs

SHERBORNE FORESTERS
Secretary: G. Vince
Little Paddock, Charlton Mackrell; Somerton

QUANTOCK ORIENTEERS
Secretary: I Shakell
30 St Johns Road, Yeovil

AVON SCHOOLS ORIENTEERING ASSOCIATION
Secretary: D. Howell
Sidcot School, Winscombe, Avon BS25

KINGSWOOD SCHOOL ORIENTEERING ASSOCIATION
Secretary: R.J. Lewis
Kingswood School, Bath, BA15 RG

MILLFIELD O.C.
C/- T.E Evans
Midway Compton, Dundon, Somerton, Somerset TA11

Permanent Orienteering Courses

FOREST OF DEAN
Enquiries: Bristol (0272) 713471
Maps available from Christchurch Campsite, Coleford

ASHTON COURT
Bristol
Enquiries: Ashton Court Estate Parks Department, Bristol (0272) 664169
Maps from Golf Kiosk

WORLEBURY WOODS
Enquiries: Quantock Orienteers, Weston (0934) 31701
Maps from Tourist Information Office at Weston-super-Mare

STAPLE HILL FOREST
Enquiries: Bob Lloyd, Quantock
Orienteers, Taunton (0823) 73251
Maps from Elf Service Station, East
reach, Taunton

Picnic Sites

The following sites have been
specially created for picnics and
usually have picnic tables. They are
open at all times and are free unless
otherwise stated

**BRENT KNOLL TRANSIT PICNIC
SITE**
Map 2 Ba
On the North & Southbound
carriageways of M5, 2m N junction
22, 5m S junction 21
A.A. transit picnic site with lavatories
and a public telephone
🅿 � ☕

CASTLE NEROCHE PICNIC PLACE
Map 2 Ac
3m W Broadway on byroad W of
A303
Popular site on site of former
earthworks and near ruin of 11th-
century castle. Fine views of Taunton
Vale, Bristol Channel and Mendips
Castle Neroche Forest walks start
here
See also Woodlands: Castle
Neroche Forest
FC

CHARGOT PICNIC PLACE
Map 1 Ab
4m W Raleigh's Cross on unclassified
Wheddon Cross road

Small roadside picnic place on the
edge of a spruce wood 1,100 ft
above sea level. Excellent views north
towards Croydon Hill
FC

CHEW VALLEY LAKE PICNIC SITE
Map 4 Ab
8m S Bristol on NE side of Chew
Valley Lake. Signposted in advance
and at entrance
4 acre picnic site set in landscaped
grassy mounds, shrubs and trees
beside the Lake
Lavatories
♿ ☕

CLATWORTHY RESERVOIR
Map 1 Bb
8m S Watchet S of B3190
Attractive setting in the Brendon Hills
Nature trail and excellent views
Lavatories

**COUNTY GATE TRANSIT PICNIC
PLACE**
Map 1 Aa
7m W Porlock off A39. Signposted in
advance and at entrance
Natural wooded site in Exmoor
National Park. Views over Exmoor,
Doone Valley and Bristol Channel

CROYDON HILL PICNIC PLACE
Map 1 Ab
3m S Dunster off A396
One acre site partly open and partly in
the glades among tall pines and
Douglas firs
FC

HAWKRIDGE RESERVOIR
Map 2 Ab
7m N Taunton
Attractive picnic site set in foothills of
Quantocks

KENNISHAM PICNIC PLACE
Map 1 Bb
5m W Raleigh's Cross on unclassified
Wheddon Cross road

Small roadside picnic place at the
edge of Brendon Forest
FC

PITTCOMBE HEAD PICNIC SITE
Map 1 Aa
3m W Porlock in Exmoor National
Park. Signposted at entrance
2 acre picnic site situated in
woodlands. Good access point for
Exmoor walks

PRIORS PARK PICNIC PLACE
Map 2 Ac
6m S Taunton on B3170
Set among oak, larch and beech
FC

RAMSCOMBE PICNIC PLACE
Map 2 Ab
2m S Nether Stowey on unclassified
Nether Stowey-Crowcombe road
Streamside picnic site in valley
surrounded by mature douglas firs
and other conifers
Forest trail starts nearby
Lavatories
FC

SUTTON BINGHAM RESERVOIR
Map 3 Ac
2m S Yeovil off A37
Picnic site and viewing area
overlooking reservoir
lavatories

TOG HILL PICNIC SITE
Map 4 Bb
8m E Bristol, 1/2m E junction with
A46. Signposted in advance
Elevated grassy site with grass, trees,
shrubs and spectacular views

WIMBLEBALL RESERVOIR
Map 1 Bb
9m S Minehead off B3190
Picnic site set beside new reservoir in
Exmoor National Park
Hurscombe nature trail starts nearby
Information kiosk and lavatories

Railways

EAST SOMERSET RAILWAY
Cranmore (074988) 417
Cranmore, 3m W Shepton Mallet on
A361
Open: April-Oct, daily 10.00- 17.30;
Nov-Mar, w/ends 10.00-16.00 (last
admission 30mins before closing)
charge: Admission & train fare £1.40
(ch 70p); Admission only 80p (ch &
OAP's 40p) Reductions for groups by
arrangement
Short standard line using 1/2m of
the old Great Western Cheddar Valley
line. A steam hauled train service runs
from West Cranmore Station to
Merryfield Lane, where passengers
may alight and spend some time in
the peace of the Somerset
countryside, returning on a later train.
Also fine replica Victorian engine shed
and workshops housing many
interesting steam locomotives
including David Sheperd's 140 ton
steam giant, 'Black Prince'; signal box
which is now an art gallery selling
David Shepherd's wildlife & railway
prints; wildlife centre with exhibitions
depicting many aspects of wildlife to
be found in the area
P **&** **✕ ⊤⊤**

OAKHILL MANOR MINIATURE RAILWAY
One of Europe's finest miniature
railways and private collection of
transport models in beautiful settings
See Historic Homes: Oakhill Manor

WEST SOMERSET RAILWAY
Minehead (0643) 4996
Minehead
Open: end Mar-end Oct, daily 9.00-
19.00
Charge: return to Bishops Lydeard
£4.00 (ch £2.00). Prices vary
according to length of journey (prices
quoted are 1984, subject to change
1985)
Longest private railway , covering 20
miles between Minehead and
Bishop's Lydeard and stopping at
various stations en route. Passengers
can break their journey whenever they
wish. Diesel and steam locomotives
including an impressive Great
Western 2-6-2 Prairie tank and the
'Flockton Flyer', a GWR 0- 6-0
pannier tank

Riding

This list includes stables offering
riding instruction and hacking (country
rides). Most lessons are in classes or
groups but private tuition is often
available. Hacking is not usually
allowed unaccompanied unless the
ability of the rider is known. Stables
which provide livery or stud services
are not included. Exact locations of
stables are not given since it is always
advisable to telephone in advance

ABBOTS LEA SCHOOL OF RIDING
Bitton (027 588) 3125
Northfield House, Court Farm Road,
Willsbridge
Open: all year, daily
Lessons: £5.00 hour (ch £4.50)
Hacking: £10.00 day
16 mounts

delightful country rides, riding for the
disabled
BHS, POBS, ABRS approved

ADSBOROUGH HOUSE STABLES
Taunton (0823) 412204
Adsborough House, Adsborough
Open: all year, daily
Lessons: group £3.50 hour;
individual £6.00 hour
Hack: £3.00 hour; £11.00 half day

BINGHAM PONY STUD
Templecombe (0963) 70374
Rodgrove House Farm, Wincanton
Open: all year, daily
Hack: £6.00 hour
20 mounts
BHS approved

BURROWHAYES FARM
Porlock (0643) 862463
West Luccombe, Porlock
Open: April-Oct, daily
Hack: £3.00 hour
18 mounts
Rides from Horner valley over
Exmoor. Access to bridleways

CIRCLE 'D' RIDING CENTRE
Axbridge (0934) 732577
Manor Farm, Cross, Axbridge
Open: all year, daily
Trekking/Hacking: 1£4.00 hour
Rides on the Mendips. Access to
bridleways. Hunting available
POB approved

CLOUD FARM
Brendon (05987) 213
Oare, 7m SW Lynton
Open: Whitsun-end Oct, daily
Trekking/Hacking: £3.00 hour,
£9.00 half day, £15.00 full day
15 mounts
Riding on Exmoor including Doone
Valley. Access to bridleways
POBS approved

CURLAND EQUESTRIAN ENTERPRISES
Buckland St Mary (046034) 234
Crosses Farm Stud, Curland, Taunton
Open: all year, daily
Lessons: group £4 hour; individual £9 hour
Hack: £3.50 hour
18 mounts
Road work, also tracks and forestry
Commission land
BHS approved

DEEPLEIGH FARMHOUSE HOTEL RIDING STABLES
Wiveliscombe (0984) 23379
Langley Marsh, Wiveliscombe
Open: all year, daily
Lessons/Hack: £3.50 hour
12 mounts
Riding holidays and rides in varied farmland, forest and moor
BHS; POB approved

EBBORLANDS FARM RIDING CENTRE
Wells (0749) 72550
Wookey Hole
Lessons/Hack: £4 hour (ch £3.50)
20 mounts
Riding on Mendips and Somerset levels. Instructional holidays
BHS approved

EXMOOR AND METROPOLE STABLES
Minehead (0643) 2779
58 Alcombe Rd, Minehead
Lessons: £5.50 hour
Trekking/Hack: £10 half day; £18 full day
Riding on Exmoor, including Doone Valley

GORDANO VALLEY RIDING STABLES
Portishead (0272) 843473
Moor Lane, Clapton-in-Gordano
Open: all year, daily
Lessons: £4.95 hour (ch £3.95)
Hack: £5.35 one and half hours
20 mounts
Riding on Cadbury Camp and in Gordano Valley. Indoor school.
Disabled riders welcomed
BHS approved

GRAZEMOOR FARM
Upton Noble (074985) 204
Witham Friary, 6m S Frome
Open: all year, daily (closed BH's)
Trekking/Hack: £3.00 one and half hours
22 mounts
Riding on undulating farmland.
Disabled riders welcome
BHS approved

GREENHAM EQUESTRIAN CENTRE
Greenham (0823) 672304
Ridge Farm, Greenham
Open: April-Sept, daily
Lessons/Hack: £3.50 hourly
15 mounts
Specialises in side-saddle riding.
Disabled riders welcome

HOLLOW ROCKS RIDING ESTABLISHMENT
Winscombe (093 484) 2284
Lippiatt lane, Shipham, E Weston-super- Mare
Open: all year, daily
Lessons: Private only £4 half hour (ch £3.50)
Hack: £5 (ch £4.50)
14 mounts
Private tuition a speciality, residential riding holidays, hunting available in season
BHSAI approved

HIGHER ELLICOMBE STABLES
Minehead (0643) 3009
Higher Ellicombe, S Minehead
Open: all year, daily
Lessons/Hack: £3 hour
10 mounts
Beginners, children and disabled riders welcomed
BHS approved

HORNER FARM STABLES
Porlock (0643) 862456
Horner, Minehead
Open: Easter-end Oct, daily
Hack: £3 hour
16 mounts
Riding in Horner Oak Woods and
Selworthy Beacon. Specialises in
unescorted riding

HUSK FARM RIDING STABLES
Hendale (0823) 442791
Creech St Michael, E of Taunton
Open: all year, daily
Lessons: £2 hour
Hack: £10 day
21 mounts
Rides on farmland and moorland

HUNTSCOTT HOUSE STABLES
Timberscombe (064 384) 272
Huntscott House, Huntscott, Wootten
Courtenay, Minehead
Open: all year, daily
Hack: £3.75 hour; £15 day
Novices welcomed, all riders escorted
BHS approved

J. VOWLES TREKS
Weston-super-Mare (0934) 22395
Open: all year, daily
Lessons/Hack: £3.50 hour (ch £3)
15 mounts
Riding in Weston Woods and Brean
Sands during the off-season

KNAPLOCK RIDING STABLES
Winsford (064385) 271
Knaplock Farm, Tarr Steps, Dulverton
Open: all year, daily
Lessons/Hack: £3.50 hour
25 mounts
Riding on Exmoor countryside
including moors and wooded valleys

KNOWLE RIDING CENTRE
Timberscombe (064 384) 342
Timberscombe, Minehead
Open: all year, daily
Lessons: £6 hour
Trekking: £8 half day
60 mounts

Wide range of rides and riding
holidays for beginners and
experienced riders; hunting w/ends in
winter
BHS; ABRS; POB approved

LONG LANE FARM RIDING STABLES
Bourton (0747) 840283
Pen Selwood, Wincanton
Open: all year, daily
Lessons: £5.50 hour (ch £4)
Hack: from £3 hour
10-12 mounts
Riding on downland and in woodland,
residential holidays including stable
management
POBS approved

LOWER BURCOTT RIDING SCHOOL
Wells (0749) 73145
Lower Burcott, Wells
Open: all year, daily
Lessons/Hack: £3.50 hour (ch £3)
26-30 mounts (including ponies)
Riding on quiet country lanes,
Instruction on all-weather arena,
jumping, 2 outdoor arenas, cross-
country; disabled riders welcomed
BHS approved

MENDIP EQUESTRIAN CENTRE
Churchill (0934) 852335
Lyncombe Lodge Farm, Sandford, E
Weston- super-Mare
Open: all year, daily
Lessons: group £5 hour; private £6
hour
Hack: £4 hour; £12.50 day
30-40 mounts
BHS approved

MILL HOUSE EQUESTRIAN CENTRE
Bradford (082 346) 322
Bradford-on-Tone
Open: all year, Sundays only
Lessons: £3.50 hour
10 mounts (small ponies)

Riding

OAKHILL FARM RIDING STABLES
Hatch Beauchamp (0823) 480781
Lillesdon, Taunton
Open: all year, daily
Lesson/Hack: £2.00 hour
6 mounts (ponies)
Children welcome
BHS approved

QUANTOCK RIDING CENTRE
Holford (027 874) 374
Beech Hanger Farm, Kile, Bridgwater
Open: all year, daily
Lessons: £4.50 hourly
Hack: £4 hour
Trekking: £10.50 half day; £7.50 day
40 mounts
Caters for all ages and all standards; wide variety of rides in attractive scenery of Quantocks; riding holidays and hunting available
BHS; ERH & TA; POB approved

ROSE TREE FARM
Burnham-on-Sea (0278) 789714
Berrow, Burnham-on-Sea
Open: all year, daily
Lessons/Hack: £3.50 hour
Riding in small groups on country lanes and sand dunes

ROY'S RIDING SCHOOL
Burrowbridge (082 369) 507
7 Curland Lane, Stoke St Gregory, Taunton
Open: all year, daily
Lessons: £1.50 hour
Hack: £3 hour
Trekking: £10 half day
12 mounts
Disabled riders welcomed

SCOTTS RIDING STABLES
Nether Stowey (0278) 732422
St Mary's Street, Nether Stowey
Open: all year, daily
Hack: £4 hour
6 mounts
Riding holidays and hunting available

WALFORD RIDING STABLES
West Monkton (0823) 412676
Walford Gardens Farm, Walford Cross, West Monkton
Open: all year, daily
Lessons: group £3.50 hour; private £6 hour
13 mounts
BHS approved

WHITE CAT STABLES
Bristol (0272) 564370
Howsmoor Lane, Mangotsfield, Bristol
Open: all year, Tues-Thurs
Lessons: £3.60 hour (ch £3.30)
Indoor riding only (stable grounds)
BHS; POBS; ABRS approved

WITHYPOOL RIDING CENTRE
Exford (064 383) 586
Withypool
Open: all year, daily
Lessons: Group £7 hour
6 mounts
Riding on Exmoor
BHS approved

WORLEBURY RIDING SCHOOL
Weston-super-Mare
14 Worlebury Hill Road, Weston-super- Mare
Open: all year, daily
Lessons: group from £6.00 hour; private £7.00 hour
Hack: £5.00 hour (ch £4.00)
Trekking: £10.00 hour (ch £8.00)
39 mounts
Riding in Weston Woods, country lanes, beach rides, bridleways; indoor school; show jumping paddock; dressage
All standards and ages accepted.
Disabled riders welcome
BHS approved

Roman sites

Sailing

KINGS WESTON ROMAN VILLA
Map 4 Ab
Long Cross, Lawrence Weston, 4m
NW Bristol city centre off A403
Open: all year, Sat-Wed 8.30- 17.00.
Key to be collected from Blaise Castle
House Museum
Free
Remains of small, late Roman country
house, includes mosaics and a display
of Romano-British building techniques

ROMAN BATHS
Bath (0225) 61111 ext 327
Abbey Churchyard, Bath
Open: April-Oct, daily 9.00-18.00;
Nov-March, Mon-Sat 9.00-17.00 &
Sun 11.00-17.00
Charge: 1.40 (ch 80p)
Remains of Aquae Sulis, the largest
Roman baths complex in Britain and
the only one with hot water springs.
Also museum containing important
archaeological finds from the City.
Excavations of Roman Temple
Precinct under Pump Room also open
to view
No dogs
🅿 🚻 ♿ ⛽ ✕

SEA MILL'S ROMAN BUILDINGS
**Sea Mills, 3m NW Bristol city
centre off A403**
Open: any reasonable time
Free
Outlines of rooms and courtyards

ROYAL YACHTING ASSOCIATION
Southwest Region
Secretary: A H B Symons Esq
45 Oakfield Rd, Clifton, Bristol
Avon, BS8 2BA

Sailing Clubs

AVON SAILING CLUB
Treasurer: R F Jones Esq
196 Ledbury Rd, Tupsley, Hereford

AXE YACHT CLUB
Secretary: G Davis Esq
Redshard House, Langford, Bristol

BATH UNIVERSITY SAILING CLUB
Secretary: Miss S House
Students Union, Bath University, Bath

BRISTOL AVON SAILING CLUB
Secretary: Miss M S Pearce
36 Badminton Rd, Downend, Bristol

BRISTOL CHANNEL YACHT CONFERENCE
Secretary: D W Jennings Esq
Jacobs Well, Featherbed Lane,
Oldbury- on-Severn, Bristol

BRISTOL CORINTHIAN YACHT CLUB
Secretary: Mrs J Dick
32 Frobisher Avenue, Portishead,
Bristol

BURNHAM-ON-SEA YACHT CLUB
Secretary: Mrs S M Radford
27 Links Gardens, Burnham-on-Sea

CABOT CRUISING CLUB
Secretary: P Cotton Esq
c/o John Sebastian, Bathurst Basin,
Bristol

CHEW VALLEY LAKE SAILING CLUB
Secretary: Mrs M Face
49 Caernarvon Rd, Keynsham, Bristol

CLEVEDON SAILING CLUB
Secretary: E J A Cooke Esq
The Alcoves, The Beach, Clevedon

COMBWICH CRUISING CLUB
Secretary: E Dickinskon
6 Barrow Drive, Taunton

HAWKRIDGE SAILING CLUB
Secretary: G B Thompson
Quarry Breach, Over Stowey,
Bridgwater

HINKLEY POINT SAILING CLUB
Secretary: P P Nurse Esq
5 Belevdere Close, Cannington,
Bridgwater

KINGS COLLEGE TAUNTON SAILING CLUB
Secretary: J M Crabtree Esq
Kings College, Taunton

MINEHEAD SAILING CLUB
Secretary: M Yendole Esq
Pella, Hillview Rd, Minehead

PEGASUS SAILING CLUB
Secretary: B Mulroy Esq
81 Charlton Mead Drive, Westbury-on-Trym, Bristol

PORTISHEAD CRUISING CLUB
The Secretary
Pump Square, Pill, Bristol

PORT OF BRISTOL AUTHORITY SAILING CLUB
Secretary
2 Old Dock Cottages, Cumberland Basin, Bristol

SALTFORD AMATEUR REGATTA & SPORTS CLUB
Secretary: A Whitlock Esq
Alamar, 27 Bristol Hill, Bristlington, Bristol

SHEARWATER SAILING CLUB
Secretary: Mrs D Halls
1 Lynwood Close, Frome

SHIREHAMPTON SAILING CLUB
Secretary: Mrs M A Yeeles
8 St Andrews Rd, Avonmouth, Bristol

SUTTON BINGHAM SAILING CLUB
Secretary: R S Jarvis Esq
51 St Marys Crescent, Yeovil

THORNBURY SAILING CLUB
Secretary: J D K Baillie Esq
Cedars, Hazel Lane, Rudgeway, Bristol

UNIVERSITY OF BRISTOL SAILING CLUB
Secretary
Queens Rd, Clifton, Bristol

WESTON BAY YACHT CLUB
Secretary: D Churchill Esq
The Causeway, Weston-super-Mare

WEYMOUTH WATER SKI CLUB
Secretary: M Waterman Esq
3 Alistair Drive, Yeovil

WIMBLEBALL SAILING CLUB
Secretary: J O Smith Esq
10 Seymour St, Wellington

Sports Centres

These centres offer a wide range of activities. Full timetables and charges are available from each centre. Membership fees given are for a year. Charges given are a selection. Where necessary, changing rooms and showers are provided. Opening times are given for the centre, not for any specific activities. Many of the activities will be organised by clubs. Full details from each centre. Centres often provide detailed brochures

BACKWELL LEISURE CENTRE
Map 4 Ab
Flax Bourton (027583) 3726
Farleigh Rd, Backwell, 8m SW Bristol city centre off A370
Open: all year, w/days 9.00-22.00; w/ends 9.00-19.00
Facilities: various including swimming, badminton, tennis
Charges: swimming 90p, badminton & squash £2.50 hour
Courses: swimming lessons, junior sports club
🅿 ♿ ⌣

BALTIC WHARF WATER LEISURE CENTRE
Bristol (0272) 297608
Under-fall yard, Cumberland Rd, Bristol
Open: all year, daily 8.00-dusk
Facilities: dinghy sailing, windsurfing, waterskiing
Charges: Dinghy sailing £25 day, w/ends £40
Courses: available in all aspects of water sport
🅿 ⌣ ⚲

BATH SPORTS & LEISURE CENTRE
Bath (0225) 62563
North Parade Rd, Bath
Open: all year, daily 8.00-22.30 (BH's 10.00-17.00)
Facilities: various including badminton, squash, table tennis, archery, golf, weights, swimming pool, football, tennis, hockey
Charges: swimming 85p (ch 45p)
Courses: various including martial arts, golf, archery, keep-fit, disabled swimming
🅿 🔧 ⌣ ⚲

BUCKLERS MEAD SPORTS CENTRE
Yeovil (0935) 24454
St Johns Rd, Yeovil
Open: all year, daily
Facilities: various including Badminton, 5-A-Side football, sports hall, volleyball, basketball, tennis, gym
Charges: badminton £2.10 hour; tennis £1.50 hour; 5 A-Side-football £4
Courses: karate, judo, aerobics, childrens school holiday courses
🅿 🔧 ⌣

CHURCHILL SPORTS CENTRE
Map 4 Ab
Churchill (0934) 852303
Churchill, 4m N Cheddar off A38
Open: all year, w/days 16.30-22.00; w/ends 9.00-22.00
Facilities: various including swimming, squash, tennis, hockey, rugby, soccer
Charges: swimming 90p (ch 50p), squash £2.50 hour
Courses: swimming lessons, junior sports club
🅿 ⌣ ♿

DOWNEND SPORTS CENTRE
Bristol (0272) 560688
Downend School, Westerleigh Rd, Downend
Open: all year, w/days 18.30-22.30; Sat 13.30-22.30; Sun 10.00- 17.00
Facilities: squash, tennis, basketball, volleyball, 5-A-Side football, hockey, rock climbing, judo, trampoline, table tennis, cricket
Charges: squash 40mins 95p (£1.20 non- members); tennis, basketball, hockey, etc £11 per court per hour; judo £2.75 per mat per hour; table tennis £1.00 per table per hour
Courses: junior badminton & tennis in winter months
🅿

Sports Centres

EASTON SPORTS CENTRE
Bristol (0272) 558840
Thrissel St, Easton, Bristol
Open: all year, daily 9.00-23.00
Facilities: various including sports hall, badminton, roller skating, volleyball, squash, table tennis, weights room
Charges: badminton £2.30 hour, squash £2.20 hour, table tennis £1.20 hour
Courses: squash, badminton, keep-fit, yoga, martial arts
🅿 ♀

FROME SPORTS CENTRE
Frome (0373) 65446
Bath Rd, Frome
Open: all year, daily 17.00- 22.00
Facilities: various including bowling, squash, sports hall, badminton, multi-gym, trampoline, keep-fit, swimming pool
Charges: swimming 85p (ch & OAP's 35p), squash £2.15 per 40mins, badminton £2.20 hour
Courses: swimming lessons
🅿 ⊐ ♀

KEYNSHAM LEISURE CENTRE
Map 4 Bb
Keynsham (02756) 612745
Temple St, Keynsham, Bristol
Open: all year, daily 7.00-23.00
Facilities: various including swimming pool, sports hall, badminton, cricket, table tennis, volleyball, squash, weights room
Charges: badminton from £2.10, Squash from £2.05
Courses: various including keep- fit, martial arts, disabled sports
🅿 ⊐ ♿ ♀

KINGSDOWN SPORTS CENTRE
Bristol (0272) 426582
Portland St, Kingsdown
Open: all year, daily 9.00-23.00
Facilities: various including squash, badminton, weights, table tennis
Charges: squash, badminton, weights, table tennis. solarium

Courses: yoga, self defense, trampoline, gym
🅿 ⊐ ♀

ROBIN COUSINS SPORTS CENTRE
Map 4 Ab
Bristol (0272) 823514
West Town Rd, Avonmouth, 5m NW Bristol city centre on A4
Open: all year, daily 9.00-23.00
Facilities: various including sports hall, badminton, squash, roller skating, football, karate
Charges: Squash 75p (45mins); Aerobics £1.00 hour; roller skating £1 (1 1/2 hours)
Courses: various including break dancing, keep-fit, aerobics, badminton, squash
🅿

SOUTHWOLD SPORTS CENTRE
Map 4 Ba
Chipping Sodbury (0454) 310111
Station Rd, Yate, Chipping Sodbury
Open: all year, daily 8.30-23.00
Facilities: various including swimming, squash, badminton, multi-gym, archery
Charges: swimming 70p (ch & OAP's 45p), squash £2.10, badminton £2.20
Courses: various including keep- fit, yoga, archery, snooker
🅿 ♿ ⊐ ♀

SOUTH WANSDYKE SPORTS CENTRE
:**Map 4 Bb**
Midsomer Norton (0761) 415522
Rackvernal Rd, Midsomer Norton, Wansdyke
Open: all year, daily
Facilities: swimming, squash, sports hall, weights, solarium
Charges: swim 65p (ch 42p); squash £2.15 hour (peak), £1.95 (off-peak)
Courses: gymnastics, karate, trampoline, disabled swimming
🅿 ♿

SYDENHAM SPORTS CENTRE
Bridgwater (0278) 560870
Parkway, Bridgwater
Open: all year, daily
Facilities: squash, badminton, 5- a-
side football, hockey, volleyball,
cricket, tennis
Charges: entry fee 20p (ch 5p);
squash £1.80 hour; badminton
£1.60 hour
Courses: various including keep- fit,
trampoline
Membership: £8.40 per annum
P ♀

THORNBURY SPORTS CENTRE
Map 4 Ba
Thornbury (0454) 418222
Alveston Hill, Thornbury, 10m N
Bristol off A38
Open: all year, daily 8.30-23.00
Facilities: swimming, sauna, cricket,
gym, archery, badminton, 5-a- side
football, volleyball, squash, snooker,
bowls
Charges: swim 70p (ch 45p);
squash £2.10 hour; badminton
£2.20 hour
Courses: various including
trampoline, keep-fit, aerobics, disabled
swimming
P & ⚲ ♀

WELLINGTON SPORTS CENTRE
Map 2 Ac
Wellington (082 347) 3010
Corams Lane, Wellington, 5m SW
Taunton off A38
Open: all year, daily, 9.00- 21.00
Facilities: badminton, squash,
swimming, sauna, solarium, table
tennis, sports hall, ski slope
Charges: entry fee 20p (ch & OAP's
15p); swimming 50p (ch 25p)
Courses: various including martial
arts and aerobics
Membership: £6 per annum (ch &
OAP's £3); family £12
P ⚲

WHITCHURCH SPORTS CENTRE
Map 4 Bb
Bristol (0272) 833911
Banfield, Whitchurch, 4m S Bristol off
off A37
Open: all year, daily 10.00- 23.00
Facilities: various including sports
hall, badminton, squash, indoor
bowling, weights, athletics track
Charges: recreation sports 75p (ch
35p); squash £2.20 hour (peak
times) £2.00 hour (off peak)
Courses: various including pop
mobility, keep-fit, trampoline, gym,
yoga, judo
P & ⚲ ♀

Swimming Pools

Bristol

BARTON HILL POOL
Bristol (0272) 557020
Queen Anne Rd, Bristol
Open: all year, Tues-Sun
Charge: 70p (ch OAP'S & UB40
25p)
Main pool 25 x 16yds
P

BISHOPSWORTH POOL
Bristol (0272) 640258
Bishopsworth Rd, Bristol
Open: all year, daily
Charge: 70p (ch 25p; OAP's &
UB40 25p)
Main pool 25m x10m
Swimming lessons and aerobics
available
P & ⚲

Swimming Pools

BRISTOL NORTH POOL
Bristol (0272) 43548
Gloucester Rd, Bristol
Open: all year, daily (closed BH's)
Charge: 70p (ch 25p)
Main pool 25m x 10m
Swimming lessons, aerobics and club activities
P ⌓

BRISTOL SOUTH POOL
Bristol (0272) 663131
Gloucester Rd, Bristol
Open: all year, daily (closed BH's)
Charges: 70p (ch 25p; OAP's & UB40 20p)
Main pool 30m x 10m
P ⌓

BROADWEIR POOL
Bristol (0272) 24602
Strand St, Bristol
Open: all year, daily
Charge: 70p (ch 25p)
P

JUBILEE POOL
Bristol (0272) 777900
Jubilee Rd, Bristol
Open: all year, daily
Charge: 70p (ch 25p)
Main pool 25m x 10m

SOUNDWELL BATHS
Bristol (0272) 567090
Soundwell Rd, Staple Hill, Bristol
Open: all year, daily
Charge: 70p (ch 25p)
Main pool 33m x 14m
Spectator facilities, ladies keep-fit classes
P ⌓

Burnham-on-Sea

BURNHAM-ON-SEA SWIMMING POOL
Burnham-on-Sea (0278) 785909
Berrow Rd, Burnham-on-Sea
Open: all year, daily

Main pool 25m x 9m
Spectator facilities, solarium & sun beds
P ⌓

Street

STRODE SWIMMING POOL
Street (0458) 43918
Strode Rd, Street
Open: all year, daily
Charge: 85p (ch 35p)
Main pool 33.3m x 12.5m
Spectator facilities, sauna
P & ⌓

Taunton

TAUNTON SWIMMING POOL
Taunton (0823) 84108
Station Rd, Taunton
Open: all year, daily 9.00-21.30
Charge: 80p (ch & OAP's 55p)
Main pool 33.3m; 1m springboard
Spectator facilities
P ⌓ &

Weston-super-Mare

KNIGHTSTONE POOL
Weston-super-Mare (0934) 29011
The Promenade, Weston-super-Mare
Open: all year, daily
Charge: 90p (ch 50p)
Main pool 33.3m x 25m; small teaching pool
Spectator facilities
P ⌓ &

Tourist Information Offices

Tourist Information Offices can be helpful whether you are a visitor to Somerset & Avon or a resident. They have a wealth of information on local attractions, places to stay and eat, activities, history and much more. For example if you have trouble in contacting any of the places listed in this directory contact the local information office for help. If you want to find out what you can do in your area contact your local information office and always make a point of contacting the information office at any place you are intending to visit

They can usually provide leaflets on hotels and restaurants, town plans and brochures about attractions in the area

WEST COUNTRY TOURIST BOARD
Exeter (0392) 76351
Trinity Court, 37 Southernhay East
EX1 1QN
This is the co-ordinating office for all tourist information in the West Country and it covers Devon, Cornwall, Dorset, Somerset & Avon

BATH
Bath (0225) 62831
Abbey Churchyard, Bath

BRENT KNOLL
Edingworth (093472) 466
Situated on M5 (southbound, between junction 21 & 22)
Open summer months only

BRISTOL
Bristol (0272) 293891
Colston House, Colston St, Bristol

BURNHAM-ON-SEA
Burnham-on-Sea (0278) 78752
Berrow Road, Burnham-on-Sea

CHEDDAR
Cheddar (0934) 742769
The Library, Union St, Cheddar

FROME
Frome (0373) 67271
Cattle Market, Frome

GLASTONBURY
Glastonbury (0458) 32954
Marchants Buildings, Northload St, Glastonbury

ILMINSTER
Ilminster (04605) 5294
Shrubbery Hotel (car park), Station Rd, Ilminster
Open summer months only

MINEHEAD
Minehead (0643) 2624
Market House, Minehead

TAUNTON
Taunton (0823) 74785
Central Library, Corporation St, Taunton

WATCHET
Watchet (0984) 31824
2 Market St, Watchet
Open summer months only

WELLINGTON
Wellington (082 347) 4747
Wellington Museum, 35 Fore St, Wellington

WELLS
Wells (0749) 72552
Town hall, Market Place, Wells

WESTON-SUPER-MARE
Weston-super-Mare (0934) 26838
Beach Lawns, Weston-super-Mare

WINCANTON
Wincanton (0963) 32173
The Library, 7 Carrington Way,
Wincanton

YEOVIL
Yeovil (0935) 22884
Johnson Hall, Hendford, Yeovil

YEOVILTON
Ilchester (0935) 840565
Fleet Air Arm Museum, Yeovilton

Unusual Outings

ALLEMOOR PUMPING STATION
See Museums

CHEDDAR CAVES
Map 2 Ba
Cheddar (0934) 742343
7m NW Wells on A371
Open: Easter-end Oct, daily 10.00-
18.00; Oct-Easter, daily 11.00-17.00
(closed Dec 25)
Charge: combined attractions ticket
£2.50 (ch, OAP's £1.30); reductions
for groups by arrangements
Probably the finest example of show
caves in Britain. Well lit and easily
accesible the caves contain
magnificent stalactite and stalagmite
formations. Attractions include
Gough's Cave, Cox's Cave, Fantasy
Grotto, Museum and Jacob's Ladder
🅿 ♨🍴

CLAVERTON PUMPING STATION
Map 4 Bb
Bristol (0272) 712939
Claverton, 2m E Bath on Bath-
Claverton Rd

Open: late April-late Oct, Sunday
10.30-14.00; In Steam holiday w/
ends Sun & Mon; last w/end of each
month: Sun 10.30-14.00, Mon
12.30-18.00
Charge: 25p (ch 10p); In Steam 70p
(ch 35p)
Water wheel powered pump designed
by egineer of Kennet & Avon Canal
and built in 1813 has been restored
to raise water from River Avon into
the canal which links the Rivers
Kennet and Avon

**CRICKET ST THOMAS WILDLIFE
PARK**
Map 2 Bc
Winsham (046030) 396
Cricket St Thomas, 2m E Chard off
A30
Open: all year, daily 10.00-18.00 or
dusk if earlier
Charge: £2.50 (ch £1.50);
Reductions for groups 20 by
arrangement (all charges subject to
change 1985)
Historic and beautiful park of
outstanding natural beauty. Lakeside
and woodland walks provide excellent
vantage points from which to observe
the large collection of free-roaming
animals and birds. Gracious lawns and
gardens; fascinating tropical aviary;
penguin pool; heavy horse centre;
farm and countryside museum;
elephants & sealions; adventure
playground with giant fort
🅿 ♨ ♿ 🍴✕

MODEL VILLAGE
Royal Parade, Weston-super-Mare
Open: all year, daily 10.00- 20.00
Charge: 35p (ch & OAP's 20p)
Miniature market town with castle,
manor mills, church, school, shops
etc. Also childrens rides

S.S. GREAT BRITAIN
Bristol (0272) 20680
Maritime Heritage Centre, Great
Western Dock, Gas Ferry Rd, Bristol

Open: all year, daily 10.00-17.00
(Apr-Oct 10.00-18.00)
Charge: £1.00 (ch & OAP's 50p);
Reductions for groups by
arrangement
The first ocean-going propeller-driven
iron ship, designed by Isambard
Kingdom Brunel and launched 1844.
Salvaged from Falkland Islands in
1970 she is now undergoing
extensive preservation and restoration
in the dock where she was originally
built
🅿 ⚓ ✕

WESTONZOYLAND PUMPING STATION
Map 2 Bb
West Monkton (0823) 412713
Milverton, 4m E Bridgwater off A372
Open: Apr-Oct, 1st Sun of every
month; Easter, Spring & Aug BH's;
other times by arrangement
Charge: 75p (ch 25p, OAP's 50p)
Steam pumping station dating from
1830, steam engine from 1861. Also
exhibition of diesel pumping station
🅿 ⚓ 🖥

WOOKEY HOLE CAVES
Wells (0749) 72243
Wookey Holes, 2m W Wells off
B3139
Open: Apr-Sept, daily 9.30-17.30;
Oct-March, daily 10.30-16.30: P
Charge: £2.65 (ch £1.75, OAP's
£2.15); reductions for groups 20
Famous caves which have stalactites,
stalagmites, frozen falls, translucent
pools and cliff faces of different
coloured rock. Of the six caves open
to the public the largest measures
135ft across and 12ft high and
contains the Witch of Wookey; a giant
stalagmite. The Papermill where paper
has been made since 17th-century
also contains the unique Lady
Bangors Fairground Collection, a small
museum and Madame Tussaud's
Storeroom
No dogs
🅿 ⚓ 🚻 🍴

Walking

Somerset and Avon consists of
gently undulating countryside with
some sharper gradients in the Avon
Valley and the Mendip and Quantock
Hills. It is mainly agricultural, with a
wealth of quiet villages and attractive
buildings. Apart from the few densely
populated areas, it is an area of hills,
woods, streams, farms and rural
villages and therefore offers excellent
opportunities for either the serious
walker or those interested in a short
stroll in attractive countryside

There are many walking groups in
the county and a great deal has been
achieved through their efforts in
keeping the paths open and
reclaiming public rights of way

For the serious walker there are
many long walks to be taken but
those interested in a casual stroll are
also well catered for. To begin this
this section here are some
suggestions for shorter walks along
marked trails and walks set out in
leaflets. Details can be found in other
sections of the Leisure A-Z.

MARKED TRAILS
Many organisations have marked
walks and produce leaflets to
accompany walks which explain the
landsape and describe the plant life
and wildlife encountered. These walks
are often through Forestry
Commission woodland, country parks,
farms, nature reserves, locations
offering good views and areas of
outstanding natural beauty. Many start
from picnic sites or car parks. For
further information **See Woodlands,
Country Parks, Picnic Sites, Nature
Reserves and Farm sections**
Tourist Information centres also have
prepared leaflets detailing walks of
varying lengths in the area

Walking

Organisations

RAMBLERS' ASSOCIATION

Southern Area
1-5 Wandsworth Road, London SW8
2LJ

The Ramblers' Association campaigns for public access to all rural areas. Its members keep paths clear and fight any development which hinders access to public footpaths. They also waymark paths to make them easier to follow and work to protect the landscape

The RA also organises excursions and group walks, including trips to different areas of the country. There are hundreds of RA groups throughout Britain, keeping a close watch on footpaths and ensuring they are well maintained, as well as enjoying walking together. Even those who prefer to walk alone may consider joining the RA since it is responsible for enabling lone walkers to have unhindered access to the countryside.

If you come across a public footpath which is closed, is not accessible or is in any way impassable you should contact either Avon or Somerset area RA (see below) and report this.

The RA also publishes many leaflets on all aspects of its work as well as a Bed & Breakfast Guide for walkers and a regular journal (free to members)

Membership: £6; couple £7.50; retired couple £3.75; ch18, students, OAP's £3; life membership £210. Members receive free copy of Bed & Breakfast Guide (yearly), free copy of 'Rucksack' (3 per year), local area news, access to Ordanance Survey 1:50,000 map library; special offers and reductions on publications and from shops.

RAMBLERS ASSOCIATION BRISTOL AVON AREA

Ms S Popham
56 Falcon Drive, Stoke Dean
Patchway, Bristol BS12 5RB

RAMBLERS ASSOCIATION SOMERSET AREA

Secretary: : Mrs P. Lord
2 Torre Court, The Avenue
Yeovil, Somerset BA21 4BN

Long Distance Pathways

SOMERSET & NORTH DEVON COASTAL PATH

Beginning at Minehead, this section provides an easy start to South West Penninsular Coast Path. The scenery is magnificent, as the route passes through Exmoor National Park and the North Devon Area of Outstanding Natural Beauty

Route: 82 miles from Minehead Quay, Somerset to Marsland Mouth, North Devon, following the coastline as closely as possible. Leaflets are produced by the Countryside Commission, John Dower House, Crescent Place, Cheltenham, Glos. GL50 3RA

Highlights: Selworthy Beacon; Culborne Church, which claims to be the smallest in England; Valley of Rocks; Clovelly, Devon

THE AVON WALKWAY

Not strictly a long distance pathway but a good stretch of recreational pathway created by the Avon County council. Leaflet available from County Public Relations and Publicity Department, P.O. Box 11, Avon House, The Haymarket, Bristol BS99 7DE

Route: 13 miles beginning at Pill and following the River Avon through the Avon Gorge and the centre of Bristol, along the Avon Valley via Bath to Dundas Aqueduct on the Kennet and Avon Canal

WEST MENDIP WAY

Opened in 1979 to commemorate Queen Elizabeth II's Jubilee Year, The West Mendip Way links a series of footpaths and existing rights of way from Wells to Weston-super-Mare. Waymarking throughout the route is by fingerless oak posts: yellow arrows indicate use of public footpath, blue a bridleway, and connecting links utilising sections of public carriageway are identified by red arrows. Leaflet is available from Somerset & Avon District Councils (10p)

Route: 30 miles beginning at the Norman Church, Uphill quarry, Weston-super-Mare and continuing along the Mendip Hills to Wells.

Highlights: Cheddar Gorge; Ebbor Gorge; Wookey Hole Caves; Wells Cathedral; Bishops Palace, Wells.

Walking Groups

BRISTOL GROUP
Miss J Holley
13 Oakwood Road, Henleaze
Bristol BS9 4NP

NORTON/RADSTOCK GROUP
Mrs M. Thomas
12 Milton Rd, Westfield, Radstock
Bath BA3 3XH

SOUTHWOLD (YATE) GROUP
Mr F R Hollister
27 Sunningdale, Yate
Bristol, BS17 4HD

MENDIP GROUP
Secretary: Mr L D Nicholls
Wells (0749) 870260
11 High Green, Easton, Wells

WEST SOMERSET GROUP
Secretary: Mr C Bedwell
Minehead (0643) 2061
'Lindisfarne', 2 The Terrace
Bircham Rd, Minehead

SEDGEMOOR GROUP
Secretary: Mr G Jones
Burnham (0278) 782771
18 The Grove, Burnham-on-Sea

SOUTH SOMERSET GROUP
Secretary: Mrs P J Lord
Yeovil (0935) 74011
2 Torre Court, The Avenue
Yeovil BA21 4BN

WEST SOMERSET RAMBLING CLUB
Chairman: Mr K Young
Blagdon Hill (082342) 435
Old Smithy, Sellicks Green, Taunton

Women's Institute

The Women's Institute is a completely independent voluntary organisation, with a total membership of about 400,000 women in England, Wales, The Channel Islands and the Isle of Man

The broad purpose of the WI is to give countrywomen the opportunity of working together to improve the quality of life in rural areas; and to provide a wide variety of educational and leisure activities. New members are always welcome. WI's usually meet once a month in a hall, parish room or perhaps a school

If you want to find out more about the WI in your area contact the NFWI or one of the local secretaries

NATIONAL FEDERATION OF WOMEN'S INSTITUTE
Membership Secretary
01-730 7212
39 Eccleston Street, London SW1W 9NT

AVON FEDERATION OF WOMEN'S INSTITUTE
Secretary: Mrs Bibbams
Bristol (0275) 64782
WI House, 11 Station St, Keysham
Bristol BF18 2TBH

SOMERSET FEDERATION OF WOMEN'S INSTITUTE
Taunton (0823) 84261
Secretary: Mrs E Emund
Wilton Lodge, 11 Trull Rd
Taunton TA1 4PT

Woodlands

This section includes forests and woods. Most of them are owned and managed by the Forestry Commission (FC). Woodlands mentioned are open at all times and access is free unless otherwise stated

LEIGH WOODS
Map 4 Ab
Avon Gorge, 2m W Bristol city centre off B3129
159 acres of mixed conifer and broadleaf woods planted in both limestone and heath soils
Variety of short forest trails; nature reserve
Lavatories
NT FC🅿

LONG WOOD
Map 2 Ba
2m E Cheddar off B3135
42 acres of woodland designated Site of Special Scientific Interest
Nature trail
STNC

NEROCHE FOREST
Map 2 Ac
Castle Neroche 5m NW Chard off unclassified Chard-Widcome Rd
Mixed broadleaf and conifer woodland. Forest walks (3m & 2m) start at picnic place. Guide available
FC🅿🏕

QUANTOCK FOREST
Map 2 Ab
Nether Stowey, 9m NW Taunton on A39, signposted from village
Mixed woodland with remanants of old oak coppice and birch
Quantock Forest trail starts near picnic place. Guide available
Lavatories
🅿🏕

Zoos

ANIMAL WILDLIFE CENTRE
Map 2 Ac
Hatch Beauchamp (0823) 480156
Little Creech, West Hatch, 4m SE Taunton W of A358
Open: all year, daily 9.00-16.30 (closed Dec 25)
Free
Rehabilitation centre for birds, particularly oiled seabirds. The centre offers sanctuary for injured birds and then sets them free when they are healed
🅿🐾

BRISTOL ZOO
Bristol (0272) 738951
Clifton Down, Bristol
Open: all year, Mon-Sat 9.00-dusk;
Sun 10.00-dusk (closed Dec 25)
Charge: £2.50 (ch £1.20)
Set in 12 acres of beautiful gardens
with more than 400 species of
mammal including elephants, tigers,
colourful birds, fascinating collection
reptiles, monkey complex and
nocturnal house
No dogs
🅿 🐾 ♿ ⊒✕ 🍴

CHEDDAR TROPICAL HOUSE
Map 2 Ba
Cheddar (0934) 742688
The Cliff, Cheddar
Open: April-end Oct, daily 10.30-
dusk
Charge: 60p (ch 40p)
Exhibition of many exotic creatures
including tarantulas, scorpions, giant
snails and tropical butterflies
🅿 🐾

**CRICKET ST THOMAS WILDLIFE
PARK**
See Unusual Outings

– About the Author –

Former managing director of the old Regent Film
Corporation and Seven Seas Films Ltd, Jack Rayfield was
a founder member of the Lord's Taverners charitable
organisation and still sits on the board.

He retired to Somerset in 1974 and became founder
editor of Somerset & West, Somerset & Avon Monthly,
Dorset Life etc., as well as co-editor of the Royal Bath &
West & Southern Counties Society Journal.

Despite his love of touring throughout Europe he is
happiest in his rural Somerset home where he devotes
much of his time to researching and writing about
his surroundings.

Acknowledgments

The author and publishers would like to thank the following
individuals and organisations for their help and co-operation in
providing information for this book:

Avon County Council Planning Department; City of Bristol
Information Centre; Department of the Environment;
Forestry Commission; Nature Conservancy Council; National
Gardens Scheme; National Trust; Royal National Lifeboat
Institute; Royal Society for the Protection of Birds; Somerset
and Avon Ramblers Association; Somerset Tourist Office;
Somerset Trust for Nature Conservation; South West Sports
Council; Mr R.T. Webb, Chairman British Sports Association
for the Disabled, Somerset; Wessex Tourist Office; West
Country Tourist Board.

Particular thanks go to the historian Dr Robert Dunning for
his invaluable advice.

Thanks also go the the many individuals who provided
information through tourist information offices and through
other societies and organisations too numerous to mention.

Notes

Notes

Notes

Notes

Notes

Notes